Pricing the Priceless

The Walras-Pareto Lectures, at the École des Hautes Études Commerciales, Université de Lausanne

Mathias Dewatripont and Jean Tirole, *The Prudential Regulation of Banks*, 1994

David M. Newbery, *Privatization, Restructuring, and Regulation of Network Utilities*, 2000

Stephen L. Parente and Edward C. Prescott, *Barriers to Riches*, 2000

Joseph P. Newhouse, *Pricing the Priceless: A Health Care Conundrum*, 2002

Pricing the Priceless

A Health Care Conundrum

Joseph P. Newhouse

The MIT Press
Cambridge, Massachusetts
London, England

This book was set in Palatino on 3B2 by Asco Typesetters, Hong Kong, and was printed and bound in the United States of America.

Library of Congress Cataloging-in-Publication Data

Newhouse, Joseph P.
  Pricing the priceless : a health care conundrum / Joseph P. Newhouse.
    p.   cm. — (Walras-Pareto lectures)
  Includes bibliographical references and index.
  ISBN 0-262-14079-9 (hc. : alk. paper)
  1. Medical care—United States. 2. Medical economics—United States. 3. Insurance, Health—United States. I. Title. II. Walras-Pareto lectures (Unnumbered)
  RA395.A3 N483   2002
  338.4′33621′0973—dc21   2002024407

Contents

Preface and
Acknowledgments

Reflecting the nature of the Walras-Pareto lecture series, this book is directed to the general economist without much background in health economics, as well as to noneconomists interested in health policy who have some economics background. Much of the book will be familiar ground for specialists in health economics. Nonetheless, the lectures contain material that has not appeared before in the general literature, so I hope specialists in health economics can also profit from reading the book. Because I wanted to book to be accessible to those with an interest in health policy whose economics or mathematics may be rusty, I have sometimes added explanations or shown more detail in derivations than would be necessary for many professional economists. I hope the latter will read right through these without feeling that I am talking down to them.

I am indebted to many people who have helped me with the preparation of this manuscript, especially to Tom McGuire whose close reading found several errors and stimulated my thinking on many points. I know, however, that he does not agree with all of the views I put forth here. The contributions of several other colleagues are clear in the citations, especially those of John Chapman, David Cutler, Karen Eggleston, Richard Frank, and Emmett Keeler. Victor Fuchs suggested the main title. Tony Culyer, Alan Garber, and Alberto Holly provided me with space and support at York, Stanford, and Lausanne, respectively, during a sabbatical leave from Harvard that allowed me to finish a first draft of the book, albeit much later than I had hoped. The audience at the University of Lausanne asked many helpful questions when the lectures upon which this book is based were delivered. David Newhouse helped me puzzle through a few points. Jack Ashby, Tim Greene, Scott Harrison, Kevin Hayes, Sally Kaplan, Jesse Kerns, Julian Pettengill,

Ray Wedgeworth, and Dan Zabinski of the Medicare Payment Advisory Commission staff all helped in tracking down facts on Medicare. Patricia Seliger Keenan provided able research assistance, and Kathleen Caruso's editing improved the clarity of the manuscript.

I would like to thank the Commonwealth Fund, the Alfred P. Sloan Foundation, and the Hans Sigrist Foundation for support in completing this work. Above all, I am grateful to Alberto Holly who invited me to give these lectures in the first place and was a splendid host during my two all too brief sojourns in Lausanne, and to my wife Margaret, who has been a source of support for more years than I care to contemplate.

Introduction

Why Should One Care?

This book is about pricing in the health insurance and medical care industry—or industries. Whether health insurance and medical care are one industry or two is an important issue that I address shortly, but before investing the time in reading further, the reader deserves a discussion of why one should care about such a seemingly arcane subject as pricing in these industries. There are at least six reasons.

First, as I show, one cannot presume that standard economic textbook models of pricing apply in the medical industry; indeed, administratively set prices are common throughout the world. Nonetheless, in medical care, as elsewhere in the economy, pricing affects resource allocation and therefore economic efficiency. Although there may be some instances in which price does not matter, they are exceptional; there is compelling evidence, some of which I present in what follows, that both patients and providers respond to changes in price. Among other implications, this undermines the notion of a clinically or technologically determined unique method for treating ill health.

Second, unlike most other industries, the *basis* of pricing is unsettled in medical care. Indeed, this subject forms the core of the book. In some instances a medical provider such as a physician may accept a fixed sum in return for providing all "necessary" services within a specified time period such as a year; the British general practitioner is an example.[1] In other cases a provider may accept a fixed amount for providing necessary services to treat a given illness or disease, but only the services for that disease. The American Medicare program, for example, pays hospitals a lump sum per admission, and the amount of the lump sum depends on the disease that principally caused the patient's admission. In still other cases, the provider may accept a fixed fee for each specific service. For example, the American or Canadian physician could be paid a given fee for a brief office visit and a much larger fee for performing a cardiac catheterization, a diagnostic procedure to determine the degree of any obstruction of the coronary arteries. Alternatively, a medical provider may be reimbursed on the basis of cost; the American Medicare program, for example, along with many American Blue Cross insurance plans, reimbursed hospitals on the basis of cost before 1983. And there are, of course, various combinations of payment schedules with which payers, whether public or private, contract with medical providers.

Just as does the *level* of price, the various *bases* of price also affect resource allocation and economic efficiency. For example, a predetermined fee set by the insurer gives the provider an incentive to produce whatever service the fee covers at minimum cost, in contrast to cost reimbursement. Producing any given service at minimum cost, of course, is not the necessarily same as treating the illness at minimum cost—much less the same as preventing the illness in the first place. In general, the more inclusive the basis for payment—for example, a single payment for the entire hospital admission rather than a fixed payment per day in the hospital—the greater the incentive for minimum cost production in treating the illness.

As I show, however, the multiplicity of bases of pricing is not an accident. The advantage of more inclusive bases of payment may be offset by incentives for providers to select good risks and to stint or skimp on the delivery of services. In other words, choices about pricing will generally involve trade-offs, and the medical care sector typically operates in the world of the second or even third best.

Third, although it may offer lessons for other industries such as defense, medical care is an important part of the economy in its own right. As is well known, medical care is a large and growing component of most countries' economies. Although the United States is an outlier in the share of its GDP that it devotes to medical care— between 13 and 14 percent in recent years—virtually all developed countries spend from 7 to 10 percent of their GDP on medical care (Anderson and Poullier 1999). Most observers expect this percentage to increase over time, as it has over the past half century, though not necessarily in each year. In short, the size and likely continued growth of the medical care sector in developed economies justifies an effort to understand its complicated institutions, and in particular the pricing of medical services. When the popular press resounds with allegations of overly rapid expenditure growth, an economist's first instincts should be to look at how prices are determined.

Fourth, in many countries the organization or structure of the medical care industry has recently changed or, more accurately, is in the process of changing. The change has probably been most pronounced in the United States, but change of various forms has occurred in many other countries as well, such as the United Kingdom, Germany, the Netherlands, Switzerland, and Israel. These changes have in turn led to changes in pricing and contracting within the medical care industry, which should, as they play out, offer important natural experiments in furthering the economic understanding of how the participants in this industry behave.

Fifth, in every developed country medical care constitutes a substantial share of the public budget. Anyone concerned with budgeting for the public sector must therefore be concerned about how to purchase or produce health care services. Because public revenues are raised through taxation, and because higher taxes imply greater inefficiencies, the growing demands on the public treasury are of concern beyond the medical care industry.

Finally, although I focus on its relationship to economic efficiency, there are many other reasons to care about pricing. How much people pay and which people pay for medical care, both at the time of use and through taxes and premiums, affects notions of equity, a fair distribution of burden, and a just society. Pricing and payment also affect the political economy of health care. Although neither equity nor political economy is my principal focus, I touch on both in what follows.

Information and Institutions in Health and Medical Care

Clearly pricing is a central topic in the economics of health and medical care. Before turning to that narrower subject, however, I sketch for economists without much background in health care how medical care markets differ from the standard assumptions that economists make about markets. It is remarkable to observe that with the exception of adverse selection, these differences are all described in Kenneth Arrow's seminal article on health economics (Arrow 1963). In particular, Arrow emphasized that many of the important institutions of the medical marketplace are a social response to the lack of full information in the market.

First, consumers do not know if or when they will fall ill, but they do know that if they become ill, most of them will want medical treatment, some of which may be very expensive relative to income. Indeed, the ongoing expense of some chronic diseases—for example, renal dialysis (treatment for kidney failure)—can exceed the income of most households, although the infrequency of the disease means that insuring against it does not require a large fraction of income. Thus, the uncertainty about whether or to what extent one might want costly medical treatment in the future, along with risk aversion, implies a demand for health insurance to finance such care; that is, a demand to shift income from healthy to sick states.

Second, in many cases consumers are poorly informed about how or what medical services may benefit them should they become ill, which implies an agency relationship, typically with a physician. The agency relationship in turn means the terms of the contract under which the physician works are important. One expression of agency is embodied in the medical profession's code of ethics, which has existed for centuries—at least since ancient Greece. The code's purpose has been to offer the patient protection against the physician's exploiting his or her superior knowledge, and there can be little doubt that it helps serve this purpose. At the same time, in some instances physicians have used the code of ethics to enrich themselves.[2] Another expression of agency is the prevalence in most countries of governmental institutions and in some countries of nonprofit institutions rather than private, for-profit institutions for delivering medical services. Public-sector production is especially prominent in mental health services, where agency issues may be most difficult (Frank and McGuire 2000).

Third, even if consumers know what medical services may benefit them given their condition, they may be ill informed about the quality of the services that they actually receive, or they may be unable to observe that quality. In some cases they may be receiving the services under a general anesthetic! After the fact, of course, the consumer can observe his or her state of health, but may be poorly placed to distinguish whether any adverse outcome is attributable to suboptimal medical treatment or to the underlying disease process.

The inability to observe certain dimensions of quality creates a demand for both professional and public regulation (licensing or certification) of medical care providers such as hospitals and physicians. As a result, in all developed countries entry into the medical profession is not free. In the United States and several other countries physicians may also be held liable for monetary damages if they fail to deliver a customary standard of care. Under American law determining liability for physicians differs from determining liability for manufacturers of defective products in that the law looks to the medical profession itself to define the standards to which a medical provider is to be held.

Finally, in medical care insurance there exists the presumption of asymmetric information between the insurer and insured about the insured's likely demand, creating adverse selection and in some instances market failure in the health insurance market (Akerlof 1970; Rothschild and Stiglitz 1976).[3] Such failures are especially prominent in the individual and small group insurance market, which is why in all developed countries health insurance is either social insurance or else predominantly group insurance provided through entities such as employers or employer associations.

Such failures are also a likely reason for the enactment of the American Medicare insurance program for those over the age of 65. At the time of Medicare's enactment in 1965, most persons' eligibility for employer-provided health insurance ended with retirement, forcing the elderly who wanted health insurance—and the variance of spending among the elderly is substantially greater than among the nonelderly—into the individual insurance market, which did not function well. By contrast, employer-provided insurance tends to function reasonably well among those under 65 because employees are groups not primarily formed for purposes of obtaining health insurance. As a result, selection problems are not as severe in the group health insurance market as in the individual market. As firm size becomes smaller, however, selection in the employer market can become a problem; at the extreme, the market for health insurance among the self-employed is an individual insurance market.

Even from just this brief description, it is clear that Arrow was correct in concluding that many of the institutions of the health care economy can be viewed as a response to information problems. Because different societies have taken different approaches to resolving these information problems, the institutions of medical care delivery and health insurance differ substantially among the major countries of the world. Some countries, such as Great Britain, have national health services (i.e., public financing and public production), while others, such as Canada, have universal or near universal social insurance schemes (i.e., public financing and private production), and a few, including the United States, substantially rely upon private institutions for both insurance and the production of services; some of those American institutions are for-profit.[4]

In addition to differences in financing, countries also differ in the organization for the delivery of physician services. For example, most European countries have one or more physicians treating a patient for inpatient care but another physician treating the patient outside the hospital, whereas in North America it is common for the same physician to treat the patient in both settings.[5]

This book will mostly abstract from these institutional differences among countries. That does not mean the differences are unimportant; indeed, accounting for them is essential when applying the theories and models that follow to a particular context. But those theories and models are typically sufficiently general that they will apply to many institutional contexts. The reader will find, however that the illustrative examples I use come overwhelmingly from the United States. I apologize to my non-American readers if the American focus causes them problems. Not only is my own experience much greater with the American system, but the relatively greater availability of data about the American system has meant that the empirical studies in the literature come predominantly from the United States. Nonetheless, the same issues are found to a greater or lesser degree in every medical care financing and delivery system. The non-American reader may sometimes have to work a bit to relate the examples to the institutions of his or her country, but I believe this will almost always be possible.

In discussing the pricing of medical services, one can adopt either a normative view—this is what a decision maker interested in economic efficiency would do—or a political economic view—this is why a decision maker has opted for the observed choices and in particular these are the private interests to which he or she is responding. Both views are represented in the chapters that follow, although the emphasis is more on the former than the latter.

1　Fee-for-Service Medicine and Its Discontents

In this chapter I address the pathologies of administratively set fee-for-service medical prices. I then contrast those pathologies with the pathologies of more market-oriented methods in much of the remainder of the book. (Economists sometimes say that everything is relative. "More market-oriented methods" is definitely meant as a relative statement.) Before coming to the pathologies of fee-for-service prices, however, I need to lay some background.

American physicians and hospitals, like those in many other countries, were traditionally paid a fee for each service rendered to a patient. A service in this context was typically narrowly defined—for example, a brief office visit, or the interpretation of an electrocardiogram, or a simple blood test. In a world with little or no insurance it may have been reasonable for economists to make standard competitive market assumptions about how fees or prices for such services were set. After all, at least for physicians' services, there are typically many sellers in most urban locations, and there are many buyers as well. But if standard competitive models applied to medical care pricing, there would be no need for this book. One can question the realism or usefulness of an assumption of competitive pricing even in a world with no insurance, but that is not the world in which we live, and I therefore do not propose to discuss such a world here.[1]

Rather, given the widespread insurance or public delivery that exists in every developed economy, the market for the purpose of price determination works through prices set by insurers or the government.[2] For some analytical purposes it is reasonable to abstract from how price is set,[3] but the questions of resource allocation to and within the medical care economy, which are central to both the economics of medical care and to health policy, require that one address that issue. That is the task of this book.

Are Insurance and Competitive Pricing Compatible?

Under some circumstances the presence of widespread insurance might be compatible with competitive pricing, but those circumstances typically do not obtain in medical care. First, insurers might contract to pay consumers a lump-sum payment, conditional on a certain state of the world.[4] In practice the most plausible form of such insurance would be to condition the fixed amount on the patient's disease or diagnosis. It would make little sense, for example, to give a person with kidney failure in need of dialysis or a transplant operation the same sum as a person with a streptococcal throat infection who simply needed an inexpensive antibiotic. Taking account of search costs, the consumer who received the lump sum could presumably then shop for the provider that offered the best combination of quality and price in treating that disease, just as if shopping for food with a voucher for food. The consumer would be motivated to do so for the usual reason—he or she would keep any savings in price.

In fact, insurance, at least in the United States, functions in exactly this way for some goods such as auto repair. An appraiser observes that the automobile's fender, say, is damaged and pays the consumer a lump sum for the fender's repair. The consumer may then shop among alternative suppliers for a favorable price. Sometimes the insurer may give the consumer a list of auto repair businesses that have agreed to repair the fender for the amount of the lump sum, analogous to a network of providers in health insurance who agree to accept the insurer's payment as payment in full. In the case of auto insurance the consumer typically receives the lump sum whether or not the fender is repaired and may in fact choose not to repair it and use the funds for other purposes, though one might then wonder why the consumer has paid a loading fee to purchase the insurance.[5]

The payment of a lump sum is generally not observed for medical care because of the difficulty of determining the lump sum. A physician's services typically consist of both diagnosis and treatment. At the diagnosis stage considerable expense may be incurred just to establish what precisely ails the patient. Generally it would not be satisfactory to establish a lump sum before any diagnostic measures have been undertaken, because how to proceed will often depend upon further information, as results from laboratory tests or radiologic images of various sorts become available. Even at the treatment stage establishing a lump sum is problematic, since the illness may respond in various ways to treatment or the disease itself may worsen or improve independent of treatment, both of which may dictate changes in an initial treatment plan. After initial chemotherapy or radiation treatment, for example, a cancer patient may or may not have a remission. Any consumer paid a lump sum that was to cover the entire treatment of an established diagnosis could thus be left bearing considerable risk. Although one occasionally observes insurance policies that pay a lump sum conditional on a specific diagnosis, they are rare.[6]

The difficulty of setting an appropriate lump-sum payment in advance of treatment exemplifies the information problems in medical care. These information problems shape many of the supply-side pricing institutions I consider in this book.

Second, competitive pricing models might also apply if insurers themselves took bids from providers and channeled consumers to the providers they deemed had provided the most favorable bid, including the quality of the services, as with the list of firms that will repair the automobile fender for the lump sum the insurer allows. This arrangement was not the traditional American arrangement, perhaps because different consumers value different physicians or other providers differently, and it was costly to write a contract that covered only the consumer's preferred physician(s), or because the consumer may not know what physicians he or she would prefer in future states of the world. In other words, consumers were willing to pay something for a free choice of physician—or more precisely were willing to pay for a policy that left them paying the same or nearly the same amount at the point of service irrespective of their choice of physician. A different argument is that organized medicine conspired or lobbied to keep policies without free choice off the market (Goldberg and Greenberg 1978). In any event, free choice of physician was how American insurance policies were structured for many years, and in many other countries consumers still pay the same amount irrespective of their choice of physicians (e.g., Canada). Traditional American insurance also constrained the physician not to bill the patient additional amounts over and above what the insurer paid.[7]

Free choice of physician means the services of almost all physicians must be covered by any insurer who wishes to compete in the insurance market. In turn this means that in any negotiation over price between a physician and an insurer physicians have substantial bargaining power; in practice, the traditional American insurer named a fee in a take-it-or-leave-it contract that ensured the participation of most physicians. Physicians, seeing the advantages of such arrangements, sometimes successfully pressed for legislation that required insurers to contract with all physicians who would accept a given price ("any willing provider"). Even without legislation widespread consumer purchase of such insurance plans exerted pressure on any remaining physicians to contract with the insurer, even if, as was often the case, the insurer did not allow physicians to bill the patient for any amount the physician could not claim from the insurer. In other countries—for example, Germany and Canada—a physician association negotiates a fee schedule with private or public insurers on behalf of virtually all physicians, and physicians are not allowed to bill patients for additional amounts. As in the traditional American system, the presumption is that the patient should have choice among all physicians, which precludes the insurer from just sending patients to physicians with low bids. In more recent years, however, the rise of managed care in the United States has somewhat constrained patients' freedom of choice through the use of provider networks and drug formularies, as I come to in chapter 2.

Third, price competition among traditional American insurers took place only over a minor portion of the insurance premium, the loading or retention kept by the insurer. The expenditures incurred in the medical care system were largely taken as a given by all insurers. The net result was that private insurers acted as both price and quantity takers in the market for medical services.

Why the United States saw little or no price competition over medical services for several decades is puzzling. The proximate explanation is that a passive, self-insured employer generally paid the premium for the insurance policy on behalf of the employee, or paid a large percentage of it, but that explanation, of course, begs the question of why the employer was passive. Employers could potentially have bargained directly with providers for lower fees, but they faced large transactions costs to do so and until relatively recently, they did not do so.[8] Moreover, as long as employers sought to provide their employees with an insurance policy that covered all or almost all providers, they had little bargaining power.

In the case of the large public Medicare program, the government acted in a similar passive fashion for nearly two decades after the enactment of the program in 1965; as described in what follows, it set fees such that almost all physicians would willingly see Medicare patients, and it simply paid for whatever services those physicians ordered on behalf of their patients; in other words, it made no effort to ration covered services.[9] From the point of view of the physician, ordering a service was equivalent to writing a check on the Treasury.

In other words, the prevailing American model from the 1940s into the 1980s in both private and public insurance was that of indemnity insurance—indemnify the insured after the fact for financial losses suffered. Insurance companies and employers behaved as if medical treatment and the resulting bills were an act of God—like an earthquake or a tornado—and independent of the price paid to the physician for the care. It was as if insurers assumed that physicians treated patients according to a template they learned in medical school and postgraduate training, a template that was invariant to reimbursement. As I show, the evidence does not support this assumption.[10] Economists may think this assumption quaint, but many physicians and others still speak in a language of delivering the services that the patient needs, which appears to leave little role for price.[11] Indeed, virtually all American insurance contracts are written so as to cover services that are "medically necessary."

The failure of insurers to compete on the amounts they paid for medical care services meant there was little or no price competition in the provider market. In particular, the individual provider had little, if any incentive to cut price because the demand facing him or her would be little changed if the fee charged were lower. That was because the price to the insured patient, or the demand price, typically changed only modestly, if at all, when the provider changed the price charged the insurer, or the supply price. Thus, the standard market mechanisms for eliminating rents—or prices above average cost—were weak in the market for medical services, and did not operate at all in the limiting case of insurance that reimbursed patients in full at the margin (Newhouse 1981). The rise of managed care in the United States and the consequent development of provider networks—meaning the ability of the insurer to write a contract that reimbursed patients at a less favorable rate unless they used specific providers—increased the elasticity of demand providers faced and hence reduced rents, as I come to in chapter 2.

Given free choice of physician, fees were set in an administrative transaction between the insurer and the provider. In the United States insurers often named a price that was above the reservation price of most physicians and so ensured their participation. Indeed, the Medicare program, the largest insurance program in the world after its establishment in 1966, building on language developed in the private insurance industry, agreed to pay "customary, prevailing, and reasonable" fees to physicians. Such fees came to be defined operationally by an elaborate set of rules—rules that grew steadily more elaborate over time as is typical of administered price systems. In describing these rules, the word *rococo* comes to mind.

One can presume that the resulting American fees included rents, however, because the passivity of the employer offered little incentive for the insurer to bargain for prices near competitive rates and because of the provider's participation constraint; that is, in the long run payment of less than cost would result in exit from the industry, whereas the industry has in fact been growing substantially.[12]

By contrast, in Canada and Germany, governments have tried to lower fees. Although this can be seen as reducing rents, it might also be seen as holding up physicians who have made investments in their education, because the physician who has invested in training will usually have a distinctly inferior alternative to medicine after the training. Hence, he or she is likely to continue to practice even if fees are lowered. Over time, of course, entry could well be affected if fees are kept below competitive rates. My personal experience with the political economy of the American Medicare program, however, suggests that tax financing is no guarantee of the absence of rents. In that program lobbying by providers for higher rates and other forms of rent seeking are ubiquitous.

Many years ago Vincent Taylor and I proposed what we termed Variable Cost Insurance, a mechanism we thought would bring greater price competition to the provider market (Newhouse and Taylor 1970, 1971a,b). The essence of our idea was that providers should quote a unit price; consumers would then choose a provider and their insurance premium would vary according to the unit price of the provider chosen. Although this idea was something of a precursor to the type of preferred provider and point-of-service arrangements one sees today in the United States, as proposed it had two difficulties:[13]

1. Providers varied substantially in their style of care or volume of services they provided to similar patients.[14] Thus, the cost or "loss" incurred by the insurer if the patient sought care from a certain provider was not necessarily well correlated with the unit price charged by that provider. Directly relating the premium to the named price, therefore, did not internalize the proper incentives.

2. Although most consumers could name a primary care or first contact physician, they could not necessarily name what other physicians they might want to use in various states of the world. For example, if they were diagnosed with heart disease, they might want to consult, or their physician might want to refer them to, a cardiologist, but perhaps only if the heart disease were sufficiently severe; if they then needed surgery, they would want a cardiac surgeon and an anesthesiologist, and so forth. Moreover, they would need not only to name the specialist physicians they would want in each of a vast number of possible states of the world, but also whom they would want to see in some future states of the world, which implied they would have to anticipate how the relevant medical technology might evolve.[15]

Proceeding further along the lines Taylor and I had proposed would have to await future changes in the financing and organization of medical services that would allow payer-driven competition, to use the phrase of Dranove, Shanley, and White (1993).

Rents and Administered Prices

With this as background, I am now ready to turn to the problems caused by administratively set prices. Most of the subsequent chapters take up problems of more competitive or market-oriented arrangements. One of the virtues of such arrangements is their lesser reliance on administratively set prices. In terming that a virtue, however, I am assuming that rents would be less if traditional market-oriented arrangements were more prominent in price setting.[16] Because administered prices are so prevalent, however, it is difficult to provide evidence on that key assumption. In any event, it is important to be clear about the problems of administratively set prices when appraising alternative institutions for determining medical prices.

Table 1.1
Discounted Value of Income and Rate of Return, by Specialty, 1985

Specialty	Present Value (1985 $)	Rate of Return (%)
Pediatrics	1,068,000	−3.9
General and family practice	1,075,000	−3.8
Psychiatry	1,149,000	0.8
General internal medicine	1,229,000	3.4
Medical subspecialties	1,634,000	10.4
General surgery	1,635,000	10.6
Surgical subspecialties	1,864,000	14.1
Radiology	1,888,000	14.4
Anesthesiology	1,944,000	17.9

Source: William Marder, Philip R. Kletke, and Anne B. Silberger, "Physician Supply and Utilization by Specialty" (Chicago: American Medical Association Center for Health Policy Research, 1988), 82.

A principal defect of administered pricing is the presence of rents. Because of the insurers' need to meet the reservation prices of providers as well as the weak incentives of insurers to keep provider fees down, it is plausible that traditional American fees contained substantial rents. But two pieces of evidence support the notion of rents.

Earnings by Specialty

Many years ago Milton Friedman and Simon Kuznets (1945) sought to document rents by contrasting the rate of return to physician training with that of dentist training. Later evidence in that spirit is shown in table 1.1, which gives the present discounted value of lifetime earnings using a 5 percent discount rate, as well as the implied rates of return for various specialties in 1985.[17] Clearly there is a substantial difference among the specialties.

An economist who knew nothing about medical care and who was asked to interpret these differences would probably first ask about nonpecuniary differences among the specialties. Is it the case, for example, that surgeons and anesthesiologists have more onerous working conditions than pediatricians or psychiatrists? In that case the differentials shown in table 1.1 might simply be equalizing differentials. Although one might make such an argument, it seems a bit strained.[18] For example, internal medicine subspecialists (e.g., cardiologists, pulmonologists) make almost a third more than general internists, yet their working conditions seem rather similar.[19]

A more plausible explanation than equalizing differentials lies in the insurance arrangements.[20] For many years indemnity insurance in the United States was much more extensive for inpatient services, whereas outpatient services were much less well covered. The rationale was that outpatient services were relatively inexpensive and hence it was not worth the consumer's paying a loading charge to insure them. Thus, if insurers tended to pay fees that included rents and if entry were controlled, those specialists whose work was predominantly hospital based, such as surgeons and anesthesiologists, would tend to earn substantially more per hour or per year than specialists whose work was primarily outpatient based, such as pediatricians.[21] Indeed, pediatrics was often referred to by its practitioners as a "cash and carry" business, because most of the practice was in the office as opposed to the hospital, and there was rather little insurance for services in the office. In sum, although there could be some element of equalizing differentials in the data in table 1.1, the greater incomes for hospital-based specialists are certainly consistent with the role of insurance in inducing rents.[22]

Sticky Prices

A second piece of evidence supporting the notion of rents is the pricing of new procedures, of which the past half century has seen an abundance. When procedures are first introduced, productivity tends to be low, but over time learning-by-doing can greatly improve productivity. Administered prices, however, are notoriously sticky. Thus, a fee, which may be set appropriately for a new procedure, may after several years of being unchanged be substantially above a competitive price because of increased productivity.[23] For example, cardiovascular surgeons and invasive cardiologists earn much more than the average physician. In 1992 cardiovascular surgeons averaged $575,000 and invasive cardiologists $364,000, whereas the average physician earned $182,000 (Center for Research in Ambulatory Health Care Administration 1993; U.S. Bureau of the Census 1999, 134).[24] In both cardiac specialties much of the work is from procedures where productivity has greatly increased, but the administered prices have not much fallen.[25] All this led to a widespread view by the late 1970s that American physician fees for many procedures were overpriced, whereas fees for evaluation and management (intellectual) services were underpriced, a phenomenon the Resource Based Relative Value Scale (RBRVS), which I come to in what follows, was intended to correct (Hsiao, Braun, Dunn et al. 1988).

Rents in fees have at least two and possibly three negative effects on economic efficiency. First, the rents along with imperfect information create incentives for supplier-induced demand or overservicing (Pauly 1980; McGuire and Pauly 1991).[26] Second, both the rents and any associated supplier-induced demand raise financing requirements—so that premiums or taxes are higher than they otherwise need to be. The greater requirements for financing imply greater deadweight loss, meaning the inefficiency from additional taxes if a tax-based system is used or from the inefficiencies in the labor market if an employment-based premium system is used.[27] Third, and perhaps even more important but also much more speculative, the rents could lead to an excessive rate of technical change (Weisbrod 1991).[28]

One proposed remedy that potentially addresses rents in administered prices is a large deductible.[29] Although usually advocated for purposes of reducing moral hazard, large deductibles could also potentially reduce rents by inducing those consumers who do not expect to satisfy the deductible to shop more carefully for lower prices as in a standard market.[30] (Moral hazard in health care refers to services whose private value exceeds their cost to the consumer but not their total resource cost.)

But the evidence on the efficacy of this approach, which the literature terms demand-side cost sharing, is mixed. The RAND Health Insurance Experiment demonstrated that a large deductible does reduce the use of medical services by about 30 percent relative to no cost sharing. Moreover, for the average person the reduction in demand or use appears to cause little or no adverse consequences (Newhouse and the Insurance Experiment Group 1993). Thus, a large deductible does seem to reduce moral hazard, as its proponents claim.[31]

But such a deductible carries with it a number of drawbacks. First, it clearly increases the financial risk borne by the consumer (Zeckhauser 1970). This seems particularly important in the case of the chronically ill, whose spending may approach or exceed the deductible in each accounting period (typically each year). Indeed, with an appreciable deductible that must be met each year there is a form of market failure; a person cannot insure against the financial risk of becoming chronically ill. I present some simulation results showing the effect of deductibles on risk in chapter 6.

More important for my purpose in this book, a large deductible does not address the bulk of the problem of rents in administratively determined prices, because, at the size of a deductible that appears reasonable in terms of risk aversion, the share of spending by individuals over the deductible is large, implying that much care at the margin would still be heavily subsidized. In the RAND experiment, for example, some families were randomized to a plan with a $1,000 family deductible in late 1970s dollars; this deductible was reduced for the poor.[32] In this plan 95 percent of the spending was by families that exceeded the deductible.[33] Even in a plan with 25 percent coinsurance, where it took three to four times as much gross spending to exceed the deductible, 85 percent of the spending was by families that exceeded the deductible.[34] Although Milton Friedman (1991) has proposed much larger annual deductibles that approximate median family income, his proposal seems both impractical and undesirable in terms of the risk families would bear. Even in the individual insurance market, one simply does not observe the purchase of such policies on any substantial scale.[35]

Third, the evidence from the RAND experiment was that prices paid to physicians per unit of service were approximately independent of the degree of cost sharing across plans despite considerable variation in price within specialties and sites (Marquis 1985).[36] Thus, consumers in the high cost-sharing plans either did not shop on the basis of price or were ineffectual at finding lower-priced providers. In sum, demand-side cost sharing appears to have a role to play in reducing moral hazard, especially the initiation of episodes of treatment, but it is not sufficient to achieve first best in the medical sector.

I spend relatively little time on demand-side cost sharing in this book.[37] Instead, I focus on supply prices, or the prices that providers receive. This is not to denigrate demand-side cost sharing, which I think has a role to play in medical care financing, but its function is well understood, at least conceptually, by both health economists and general economists alike. On the other hand, outside a coterie of health economists, supply-side cost sharing is less well understood. The more integrated health care delivery systems now emerging in the United States frequently employ some modest demand-side cost sharing, as one might expect if managed care cannot easily "manage" the initiation of episodes.[38] But aside from its function to steer consumers toward certain ("in network") providers or drugs, it is generally not a large feature of such systems. I therefore mostly abstract from demand-side cost sharing.

Rents in Supply Prices and Their Effects

Rents offer physicians an incentive to deliver more services than an informed consumer might wish (Pauly 1980). The empirical literature on supplier-induced demand, which seeks to establish the degree to which this incentive is acted upon, is lengthy and in my judgment tortured. For my purposes here, I only want to establish that physicians—and presumably other providers as well, many of which are for-profit—do respond to supply prices.

A common genre of study of physician response to supply prices looks at physician behavior in response to variation in fees. One well-known study of this type found that after changes in Medicare fees, both up and down, in Colorado in the 1970s, physicians responded as if their supply curve were backward-bending; that is, in areas in which fees were reduced, the quantity of services increased (Rice 1983). This was interpreted as demand creation in order to maintain incomes. Zuckerman, Norton, and Verrilli (1998), using more recent Medicare data on how physicians responded to changes in fees, confirmed this result. A relatively recent study used cross-sectional variation in relative Medicaid fees for a Cesarean section to ascertain the supply response; in contrast with the Medicare studies, the observed response was normal, meaning that the higher the relative fee, the greater the number of Cesarean sections that were observed (Gruber, Kim, and Mayzlin 1999).[39]

Other studies have observed the behavior of physicians paid by fee-for-service and by other methods. Two of these are particularly notable. Shifting Danish physicians from full capitation (no revenue at the margin for additional services) to partial fee-for-service resulted in more services per visit, fewer hospitalizations, and fewer referrals (Krasnik, Groenewegen, Peterson et al. 1990). Another study observed the behavior of pediatric residents who had been randomized to be paid either by fee-for-service or by salary. Those in the fee-for-service arm of the trial behaved differently; their patients missed fewer recommended visits and exhibited greater continuity of care (Hickson, Altmeier, and Perrin 1987). These two studies are particularly relevant to the discussion of stinting in chapter 3, where some additional studies of physician behavior are discussed.

Static and Dynamic Efficiency

Although I focus in this book on static inefficiency, or inefficiency at a point in time given medical technology, the sustained increase in medical care costs in almost every developed country means the amount of any welfare loss in the cost increase may be even more important than the inefficiency at a point in time (Weisbrod 1991; Newhouse 1992). Consider a developer of a new medical device, drug, or procedure. If the new product is used predominantly by consumers who are covered by insurance for their marginal dollar (e.g., over any deductible), then the usual market test for innovation is distorted. The informed, fully insured (at the margin) consumer will demand all services that offer any positive expected health benefit, irrespective of their cost. Depending on the supply price, that consumer's physician may well want to deliver all those services. How much inefficiency in the introduction of new products and procedures results, however, is problematic. Although I am skeptical that the welfare loss is as large as often portrayed and therefore skeptical of the claim that cost containment is urgent, I have left the critical topic of dynamic inefficiency mainly outside the scope of this book.[40]

In addition to the possible degree of welfare loss from the rapid rate of technological change in medical care, there is the issue of how new products and procedures will be priced. I have already mentioned the static inefficiency that results from the sticky rents in administered price systems for procedures or products where productivity improves. But new products in a world of administered prices raise another source of possible inefficiency. In a standard market the developer of a new product simply prices the product and puts it on the market. With an administered price system, however, the developer must persuade whatever agency is administering prices to allow a price sufficient to recoup the investment. In one well-known example, the case of cochlear implants to improve hearing, the price Medicare allowed was insufficient, and the product encountered problems in coming to market (Kane and Manoukian 1989).[41] Such an outcome may, of course, have been efficient in this particular case. I return to the issue of regulatory lag in pricing later in this chapter.

The Medicare Program as a Case Study of the Discontents in Administered Fee-for-Service Prices

In addition to rents, several other pathologies are associated with administered prices. I illustrate the nature of these pathologies by focusing on the fee-setting institutions of the traditional U.S. Medicare program. For the most part in this discussion, I ignore the existence of other payers. I do so principally for simplicity but also because for many years, though no longer, American private payers operated in a fashion similar to Medicare. Moreover, although the details of several pathologies are specific to Medicare, the generic problems with which Medicare grapples are common to the payment systems of most developed countries and to American private payers.

I have chosen to focus on Medicare for three reasons. First, in sheer size it is the largest health insurance program in the world. In 1999 it spent $209 billion (2.3% of U.S. GDP) and accounted for around 12 percent of the federal budget.[42] By 2010, on the eve of the postwar baby boom cohort's becoming eligible for Medicare, the Congressional Budget Office (CBO) projects that Medicare will spend 2.9 percent of GDP and perhaps 5 to 6 percent by 2030, though the latter figure is obviously highly uncertain.[43]

Second, some of the Medicare program's best known payment methods, such as paying hospitals an amount per admission on the basis of Diagnosis Related Groups (DRGs), are used by other American insurers and in other countries. Third, I know the Medicare program well, partly from having served on the Medicare Payment Advisory Commission (MedPAC), which recommends payment changes in Medicare to Congress, as well as its predecessor commissions.[44]

The Medicare program is the nearly universal public insurance program for those Americans over 65 years of age, and 85 percent of its monies go to health care for the elderly. The remaining 15 percent pay for the care of certain disabled persons (those who had worked and paid payroll taxes) and those with end stage renal disease (kidney failure). All insurance plans have idiosyncratic features, and as a result the reader, especially the non-American reader, will learn more about Medicare than he or she probably wishes to know. I take this liberty with the reader largely from my desire to be concrete.

The Medicare program now consists of two types of health plans. First there is the traditional program, patterned after traditional American indemnity insurance, which enables beneficiaries to obtain covered services from almost any physician and hospital to the extent that their physicians deem necessary. Second, there are so-called Medicare + Choice plans, which for my purposes I take to be Health Maintenance Organizations (HMOs).[45] In this chapter I focus more on the traditional program because of its use of fee-for-service pricing, but the HMO part of the program also exhibits some pathologies of administered pricing, as I come to at the end of this chapter. I emphasize issues in the traditional program because it is by far the largest part of Medicare, accounting for 86 percent of the beneficiaries in 2001 and approximately that share of the dollars.

Implemented in July 1966, Medicare spending grew at an annual *real* rate of 7.3 percent between 1970 and 1999, an even more rapid rate than all of the American health care sector, which itself grew at a real rate of 5.3 percent.[46] In July 2000 the CBO projected that Medicare would grow at about a 3.7 percent real rate in the decade to 2010.[47] Even this rate, which seems optimistic given the historical experience, is well above the growth rates of both the entire economy and federal tax revenues, which typically grow at about the same rate as the economy, or 1.5–3.5 percent over longer periods of time.[48]

The future direction and financing of Medicare was a major issue in the 1996 presidential campaign. As a result of that campaign and in response to the projections of future financing difficulties, Congress in 1997 implemented a series of reimbursement reductions and other reforms that reduced the projected rate of growth in spending substantially. Indeed, in the 1997–1999 period Medicare spending actually declined 0.7 percent per year, although no serious observer thinks such a decline can be maintained. Because it is such a large and complex program that affects so many individuals, Medicare will surely remain high on the American political agenda for the forseeable future.[49]

Because traditional Medicare was patterned after the private indemnity insurance of the 1960s and because such insurance was designed to cover the cost of acute medical services, Medicare excludes the cost of chronic, long-term care. Moreover, at that time private insurance typically did not cover outpatient prescription drugs, and Medicare excludes them from coverage as well. In the meantime most private insurance has expanded to include drug coverage, and Medicare coverage for drugs is now under active discussion.[50] Partly as a result of these exclusions, traditional Medicare coverage is now not very generous when compared with employment-based insurance for those under 65; consequently,

many beneficiaries buy individual supplementary insurance, or so-
called Medigap policies. Others have such policies provided as a
fringe benefit by former employers. Here, however, I want to focus
on traditional Medicare's methods for paying providers—in particular, its methods for paying for hospital and physician services, as
well as post-acute or post-hospital services such as skilled nursing
facilities and home health agencies.[51] Medigap policies are much less
important for supply prices, because Medigap simply tends to fill in
the prescribed consumer cost-sharing amounts in the underlying
program.

Hospital Pricing in Medicare

When it was first established in 1966, Medicare patterned not only its
coverage but also its reimbursement methods after private insurance.[52] In the case of hospitals, that meant it paid each hospital a
share of the hospital's total allowable costs, where the share was
proportionate to Medicare's share of patient-days at the hospital.[53]
Under this pricing system hospital costs increased rapidly, rising in
real terms by about 10 percent per year from 1970 to 1980.[54] As
a result, starting in October 1983 the cost reimbursement system
was replaced over a five-year period with the Prospective Payment
System (PPS), which reimbursed a fixed amount per case (i.e., per
admission).[55] The motive for introducing the PPS was explicitly to
increase hospitals' incentives to produce care efficiently. The Report
of the Department of Health and Human Services to Congress recommending the system minced no words on this point: "No payment system contains as many intractable undesirable incentives
as does the present cost based system" (Department of Health and
Human Services 1983, 33).

By fixing a price in advance for a hospital admission, the government was setting unit prices for hospital services, thereby hoping to
gain control over total spending. In doing so it had to define what
the hospital service was to which the price that it fixed applied.

A Brief Description of the PPS and DRGs

The cornerstone of the PPS was the DRG classification system. In this
system, those admitted to a hospital are classified by their principal
diagnosis, the diagnosis most responsible for the admission (e.g., a

heart attack), as well as by any major procedures that are performed (e.g., a coronary artery bypass graft operation). Because there are thousands of both diagnoses and procedures, the DRGs are aggregations ("Groups") of the diagnoses and procedures. Altogether there are around 500 groups. In carrying out the aggregation of underlying diagnostic and procedure codes, clinically related problems are kept together; thus, an admission for cancer is not placed in the same DRG as one for coronary heart disease. Subject to this constraint of "clinical coherence," admissions that are of approximately similar cost are grouped together. More specifically, the algorithm that aggregates diagnosis and procedure codes into groups minimizes the variance of within-group cost subject to the constraint of keeping clinically related problems together and a constraint that there be approximately 500 groups.

Given the approximately 500 groups into which all hospital admissions are classified, the next step is to attach relative prices or weights to the groups. Originally this was done on the basis of the average accounting cost of cases in the group, but in 1986 the average of the list price ("charges") was substituted for average accounting costs. Medicare also specifies a conversion factor, or the number of dollars it will pay for a DRG with a weight of 1.0. The size of the conversion factor was initially set on a budget neutral basis; it has subsequently been updated annually by Congress, based upon recommendations from the Secretary of Health and Human Services and the Medicare Payment Advisory Commission.[56] A full technical description of the initial system can be found in Pettengill and Vertrees 1982; see also McClellan 1997 for a description of the system. The changes in the system since 1984 can be found in various issues of the *Federal Register*, although the major outlines of the system have remained intact.

To illustrate, DRG 90 is simple pneumonia and pleurisy without complications, and in 1997 it had a weight of 0.6978. DRG 122 is acute myocardial infarction ("heart attack") without complications and discharged alive; in 1997 it had a weight of 1.1617.[57] Although the two previous examples of DRGs reflect only the patient's diagnosis, other DRGs are based on certain procedures that may be performed during the admission. A patient with an uncomplicated acute myocardial infarction, for example, who had a bypass graft operation with a cardiac catheterization, would not be classified in DRG 122 but rather in DRG 106, coronary bypass graft operation

(1997 weight 5.5564). One who had angioplasty performed rather than a bypass graft would be classified in DRG 112, percutaneous cardiovascular procedures (1997 weight 2.0946). Finally, if a patient has secondary diagnoses (also termed comorbidities or complicating conditions) that are related to the principal diagnosis, the patient is generally classified in a different DRG, reflecting the additional costs of treating such patients. For example, a patient with pneumonia and complicating conditions would not be classified in DRG 90 but rather in DRG 89 (1997 weight 1.1156) and a patient with an acute myocardial infarction with complications would not be classified in DRG 122 but rather DRG 121 (1997 weight 1.6482).

In sum, all Medicare patients in general acute care hospitals are assigned a weight, and in most cases reimbursement to the hospital is proportional to that weight. The average weight across all patients at a given hospital is termed the hospital's Case Mix Index. Thus, hospitals treating patients with more costly diagnoses are paid more. There is nontrivial variation across hospitals in the Case Mix Index; 80 percent of hospitals in 1998 had case mix indices between 1.0 and 1.7. In addition to the Case Mix Index, payments to hospitals are adjusted for the level of wages in the hospital's geographic area.[58] In 1998 80 percent of the hospitals had wage indices between 0.75 and 1.15.

Outlier Payments

For patients with exceptionally costly stays, an additional payment is made equal to 80 percent of the accounting costs above some threshold or deductible. The threshold is set so as to be a given dollar amount above each DRG's mean payment rate.[59] By law 5 percent of total payments are reserved for outlier payments; the outlier threshold is then set such that outlier payments will be 5 percent of the total.

Initially the outlier system defined two types of outliers, one for exceptionally costly patients and one for patients with exceptionally long lengths of stay, even if they were not exceptionally costly. Subsequent economic analysis led to several changes, including abolishing the length-of-stay ("day") outliers and basing payments solely on the costliness of the case (Keeler, Carter, and Trude 1988). The analysis that led to these changes cast the outlier program as insurance at the case level, with a premium equal to 5 percent of total payments, a deductible equal to the difference between the outlier threshold and the mean payment in the DRG, and a coinsurance rate equal to the difference between marginal cost and 80 percent of average (accounting) cost.[60] From the point of view of minimizing risk it was clearly better to insure against high costs from whatever cause than long lengths of stay. In addition to eliminating long lengths of stay as a basis for outlier payments, the changes standardized the deductible across different DRGs (it had been highly variable) and decreased the coinsurance rate from 40 to 20 percent by increasing reimbursement from 60 to 80 percent of the cost over the threshold. The decrease in coinsurance was an effort to approximate better marginal cost.

The Teaching Adjustment

Two other adjustments are made to a hospital's payments, one for hospitals with teaching programs and one for hospitals serving large proportions of poor patients. I describe only the first here.[61] Hospitals with teaching programs, meaning those with interns and residents, receive two types of supplemental payments from the Medicare program, indirect and direct medical education payments. In the original work underlying the PPS, the following regression, estimated using 1979 data from 5,071 hospitals, was used to set the indirect medical education payment amount (Pettengill and Vertrees 1982):

$$\ln(\text{mean operating cost/case}) = \alpha + \beta_1 \ln(1 + (\text{interns} + \text{residents})/\text{bed})$$
$$+ \beta_2 \ln(\text{wage index}) + \beta_3 \ln(\text{case mix index}) + \beta_4 \ln(\text{bed size})$$
$$+ \beta_5 (\text{Dummy variable for metropolitan area} > 1{,}000{,}000)$$
$$+ \beta_6 (\text{Dummy variable for metropolitan area between 250{,}000}$$
$$\text{and } 1{,}000{,}000) + \beta_7 (\text{Dummy variable for metropolitan area}$$
$$\text{smaller than 250{,}000).}[62]$$

In calculating this regression, all the coefficients except β_7 were highly significant.[63] In particular, β_1 was estimated to be 0.569 with a standard error of 0.042. Thus, there could be little doubt that the intensity of the teaching program, as measured by the house staff-to-bed ratio, was correlated with a hospital's per case cost. Before the system was actually implemented in fiscal year 1984, this equation was reestimated using 1981 data, and the estimated value for β_1 was 0.5795, very close to the 0.569 value with 1979 data.

The additional costs per case at teaching hospitals could stem from many factors. At the time they were often explained as the inefficiency of patient care delivered by residents, who were learning how to treat patients. A common story was that residents would over-order tests. This reason for the additional costs, however, does not stand up well to economic analysis, as I explain subsequently.

Based on the estimated coefficient of 0.5795, the Department of Health and Human Services initially proposed to pay hospitals 5.795 percent more per case for each 0.1 increment in their intern-and-resident-to-bed ratio. These additional payments would be budget neutral; thus, nonteaching hospitals would have their rates reduced to finance them. The remainder of the payment formula, however, did not mimic the regression equation. Most important for these purposes, the payment formula took no account of bed size.[64] That is, two hospitals that were otherwise similar but differed in bed size were each paid the same rate. Omitting bed size from the formula stemmed from the prevailing view that the United States already had too many beds, and so additional beds should not be subsidized. (In light of the subsequent fall in hospital admission rates and lengths of stay, this judgment was surely correct.[65]) The Department of Health and Human Services, however, did not re-estimate the regression equation omitting the beds variable to obtain a new estimate of β_1. Any such reestimation would have produced a larger value for β_1, because hospitals with many residents tend to be large (Anderson and Lave 1986). In short, the effect of the department's proposal was to pay the average teaching hospital less than its incremental costs.

The teaching hospitals protested this proposed payment to Congress, which was eager to implement the entire PPS as soon as possible and did not wish to be held up over this issue. As a result, rather than reanalyze the issue, Congress simply doubled the 5.795 percent value to 11.59 percent, taking the additional monies from payments to nonteaching hospitals (i.e., the doubling was budget neutral). Subsequently, the Congress has decreased this percentage value, although as of 2001 it has not come down to the so-called empirical level (i.e., the estimates in later years corresponding to the original 5.795% figure), showing the political difficulty of modifying a formula that simply redistributes money.[66]

Additionally, the Medicare program had from its inception in 1966 paid a share of the so-called direct costs of graduate medical education, where share was defined by the Medicare share of patient days. Most of these direct costs were the salaries of interns and residents, but they also included some faculty salary costs and some overhead costs. These costs were not included in the regression defining indirect costs just described (i.e., they were not part of the dependent variable), although economic theory would suggest that they should have been, because residents bear the cost of general training (Newhouse and Wilensky 2001). Hence, these costs were more properly attributed to patient care, which was the purpose of the indirect adjustment. Put another way, the additional costs at teaching hospitals did not reflect training costs, because those would have been netted out of the salaries paid the residents. Hence, the additional costs the teaching hospitals wrote down on their cost reports reflected something other than teaching.[67]

Excluded Hospitals and Units

Because the initial DRG system did not provide sufficient homogeneity for patients in certain specialty hospitals, patients in those hospitals were excluded from the PPS system. The most prominent types of excluded hospitals were psychiatric and rehabilitation hospitals, as well as psychiatric and rehabilitation units of general acute care hospitals.[68]

Post-Acute Providers

A series of other providers may care for patients after their discharge from the acute care hospital. Such providers include Skilled Nursing Facilities, rehabilitation hospitals or units within hospitals, and home health care agencies. In the mid-1980s, when the PPS was implemented, these providers were relatively small, accounting for only 3 percent of the program's costs. Because there was no analog to the PPS for them at that time, they, as well as hospital outpatient departments, remained largely under cost-based reimbursement, subject to limits or ceilings on reimbursable costs. Costs, however, grew at very high rates after 1988 for reasons I explore in the next section. Since 1997, however, the Health Care Financing Administration (as of 2001 the HCFA was renamed the Centers for Medicare and

Medicaid Services or CMS) has begun transitions to prospective payment systems for the various post-acute care providers.

The PPS and the Pathologies of Administered Pricing

Seventeen years of experience with the PPS now exist, and it appears to be a permanent feature of the Medicare payment landscape. Indeed, the Balanced Budget Act of 1997, a major piece of legislation on Medicare, called for the extension of the principle of prospective payment to many providers not previously covered by it—most notably, hospital outpatient departments, excluded hospitals and units (such as rehabilitation), home health agencies, and skilled nursing facilities—and these additional prospective payment systems are now being implemented. Certainly at a political level, therefore, the PPS is regarded as a successful innovation and much preferable to the cost-based system it replaced. The approbation is partly because the PPS gives Congress more budgetary control over the Medicare program and partly because the fall in hospital-days after the implementation of PPS was interpreted as an increase in the efficiency of the hospital sector.

Some evidence consistent with a decrease in cost and an increase in efficiency is shown in table 1.2; the first two years of the program saw a dramatic fall in patient-days, a drop of 15 percent from 1983 to 1984, and another 12 percent from 1984 to 1985, resulting in a combined 25 percent fall in patient-days.[69] Rogers, Draper, Kahn et al. (1990), in evaluating this change, found only modest adverse health effects, so that the cost savings from the reduction in days was mostly a gain in efficiency.[70] Moreover, independent evidence existed that in the early 1980s the medical services delivered on about a third of patient-days could have been carried out outside the hospital without adverse consequences (Newhouse and the Insurance Experiment Group 1993, chap. 5), suggesting a substantial scope for improved efficiency.[71] The magnitude of the changes in patient-days in the 1983–1985 period shows that how providers are paid can have large consequences for costs and efficiency.

Given the gain in efficiency that it seemingly brought about, it may appear churlish to critique the PPS, but in fact the PPS exhibits many of the pathologies of administered pricing; furthermore, several of these pathologies extend to other Medicare-administered pricing schemes and will be exacerbated by the extension of the principle of prospective payment to other services.

Table 1.2
Substitution of Post-Acute Care for Medicare Inpatient Hospital-Days

Year[a]	Inpatient days per 1,000 beneficiaries	Length of stay (days)	Skilled nursing facility days per 1,000 beneficiaries	Home health visits per 1,000 beneficiaries	Rehabilitation admissions per 1,000 beneficiaries
1981	3,827	10.4			
1982	3,889	10.2			
1983	3,786	9.8			
1984	3,217	8.9			
1985	2,823	8.6			
1986	2,784	8.7	268	1,106	2.8
1987	2,815	8.9	229	1,104	3.3
1988	2,804	8.9	334	1,104	3.7
1989	2,721	8.9	889	1,350	4.0
1990	2,749	8.8	749	2,052	5.1
1991	2,728	8.6	669	2,880	6.0
1992	2,642	8.4	812	3,763	6.6
1993	2,474	8.0	948	4,661	7.2
1994	2,436	7.5	1,006	6,020	7.8
1995	2,317	7.0	1,053	7,125	8.8
1996	2,056	6.5	1,053	7,546	
1997	1,979	6.2	1,519	7,519	
1998	1,895	6.1	1,527	4,590	
Average annual growth rate	−4.1%	−3.1%	15.6%	12.6%[b]	12.1%

Sources: Inpatient Days through 1993, *Health Care Financing Review,* "Statistical Supplement, 1996," Table 23. Inpatient Days, 1994 and 1995, *Statistical Abstract of the United States, 1997,* 115–116. 1996–1998 inpatient days from ⟨http://www.hcfa.gov/stats/stats.htm⟩. Length of stay through 1996: *Health Care Financing Review: Medicare and Medicaid Statistical Supplement, 1998,* 206; 1997–1999 calculated from Medicare Payment Advisory Commission, "Report to the Congress," March 2001, Table B.1. Other values calculated from Prospective Payment Assessment Commission, "Medicare and the American Health Care System," June 1997, chapter 4. SNF values for 1997 and 1998 and home health value for 1997 are unpublished data from the Health Care Financing Administration. 1996–1998 data for rehabilitation admissions are not available.
[a] Calendar year for hospital-days through 1993; fiscal year for other values. 1994 value from *Statistical Abstract* because 1994 value in Statistical Supplement excludes managed care enrollees and so is biased upward.
[b] Value through 1997 is 20.5 percent. The sharp decline in visits in 1998 reflects some undetermined mix of greater anti-fraud enforcement efforts and changes in payment that were effective in October 1997.

Average, Not Marginal Cost

The intent of the PPS is to pay average cost, not marginal cost, almost certainly because average cost is easier to calculate. Because the general view, supported by some empirical evidence, is that the marginal cost of hospital services is less than the average cost, paying average cost could induce additional hospitalization and is not efficient.[72]

Moreover, even the calculation of average cost is distorted in two ways. First, the average costs that are used are accounting costs, and the allocation of joint costs between the inpatient unit, to which the PPS applies, and other units of the hospital, such as the outpatient department, is arbitrary. Second, initially only operating costs were paid prospectively; capital costs were passed through so that hospitals had an incentive to substitute capital for operating inputs. Much like the Averch-Johnson (1962) effect in utility regulation, therefore, hospitals responded by increasing their capital intensity, from about 6 percent of total costs to 9 percent.[73] In 1991 the Congress mandated a ten-year transition to inclusion of capital payments in the PPS, which has now been completed. The length of the transition indicates the degree to which losing hospitals needed to be protected (or were successful in demanding that the political process protect them). Inclusion of capital costs in the administratively set price, however, further emphasizes that accounting costs will differ from economic costs because of the considerable degree of arbitrariness in accounting for capital costs, for example, depreciation life.

Economies of Scale

A further problem arises because small hospitals, which tend to dominate in rural areas, have higher-than-average costs. Their higher costs arise in part from stochastic demand; standard queuing theory models show that occupancy rates will be higher at larger hospitals, other things equal, as in fact they are empirically. Higher average costs can also arise from various indivisibilities. The PPS, however, does not adjust for the higher costs; implicitly it is attempting to force hospitals to an efficient scale and scope.

Doing so, however, fails to consider both the travel costs that might be imposed on rural residents from closing small hospitals, as well as the political economy of reducing federal payments to a given community. As a result, there are numerous exceptions to the PPS for small rural hospitals.[74] These exceptions, which apply to over 20 percent of all American hospitals (though a much smaller percentage of the beds), dilute the power of the PPS for those hospitals. In other words, substantial elements of cost reimbursement exist for those hospitals.

Within DRG Heterogeneity

Many of the DRGs, especially the medical DRGs as opposed to the surgical DRGs, have substantial within-DRG variance. Coefficients of variation over 1.0 are common. There is thus scope for selection of profitable cases, although rather little has been detected.[75]

The within-group heterogeneity in cost is, of course, affected by the total number of DRGs; hence, that the number of DRGs was administratively set to around 500 was an important choice.[76] The limitation to 500 categories was justified on the grounds of administrative simplicity and understandability. The mapping from ICD-9 codes to the 500 categories, however, is done by computer, using a program known as the "Grouper," so the incremental gain in simplicity and understandability from limiting to 500 groups is far from clear. Nonetheless, the number of categories has only expanded by around 5 percent over the first fifteen years of the program.

Little analysis has been done on the optimal number of groups. The fundamental constraint on disaggregation is the accuracy and stability of the weight that is used, because the weight is estimated from the costs or charges for the cases in the DRG.[77] Indeed, some of the 500 DRG categories are aggregated for the purpose of assigning a weight, because the number of cases within the DRGs are deemed too few to develop reliable weights.[78] Thus, there are only about 350 unique weights in the current PPS.

The Medicare Payment Advisory Commission, in its March 2000 report to the Congress, analyzed the expansion of the number of categories to around 1,420 and documented that there is a nontrivial gain in payment accuracy from doing so (Medicare Payment Advisory Commission 2000a). The value 1,420 was chosen because there is an existing system that uses approximately that number of groups whose effects could be analyzed without having to develop an entirely new classification system.

Although a system with more groups would be more accurate at the level of the individual case, the chances that it would ever be introduced are uncertain, because it redistributes monies away from small rural hospitals, which tend to serve the lower-cost cases within DRGs. Congressmen from rural districts, not surprisingly, wish to see federal tax monies continue to flow to their districts, and so such redistribution will be unwelcome. In effect, expanding the number of DRGs would reduce the "export" earnings from Medicare services delivered in the district. (Since the rest of the country pays for those services through taxes, they are analogous to exports.) If the system with more groups were to be introduced, it would almost certainly have to be with a long transition or provisions to hold losing hospitals harmless for a time, just as was the case with introducing capital costs into the lump-sum payment. This is another example of the political difficulties of redistributing money in an established program.

Technological Change and Regulatory Lag

Determining a reasonably precise figure for average cost, let alone marginal cost, is not straightforward because of the rapidity with which modes of treatment for a given diagnosis change. For the most part Medicare cannot observe the prices of a competitive market, because the private market itself is distorted by extensive insurance coverage. Moreover, the private market price appears to reflect the actions of Medicare. Since the inception of the PPS in 1984 there is a negative correlation of -0.84 ($R^2 = 0.70$) between annual Medicare payment/accounting cost margins and private payment/accounting cost margins (figure 1.1). This is consistent with a game in which Medicare moves first and then hospitals contract with private payers given the Medicare price.[79] Private-payer contracts will reflect the constraint that hospitals must recover their joint costs such as the salary of the CEO.

Furthermore, the size of any update may determine the amount of technological advance that will be put in place. Congress took note of the cost of technological change in the legislation that established the PPS. By statute the executive branch and the Prospective Payment Assessment Commission (now the Medicare Payment Advisory Commission) were to recommend annual update amounts to the Congress based on the following factors: "changes in the hospital market basket [an input price index unadjusted for quality change in inputs], hospital productivity, technological and scientific advances,

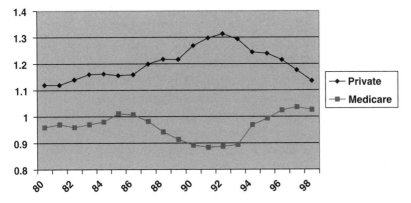

Figure 1.1
Ratio of Medicare and Private Payer Reimbursement to Accounting Cost. The R^2 for all years is 0.47. For the years of the Prospective Payment System, 1984 and later, it is 0.70. (*Source*: Prospective Payment Assessment Commission, "Medicare and the American Health Care System: Report to the Congress," June 1996, 21, and June 1997, 23. Medicare Payment Advisory Commission, "Report to the Congress: Selected Medicare Issues," June 2000 (Table C-12)).

the quality of health care provided in hospitals (including the quality and skill level of professional nursing required to maintain quality care) and [the] long-term cost effectiveness in the provision of inpatient hospital services."[80] Although this list was appropriate conceptually, in practice the only factor that can be measured in reasonably straightforward fashion is the input price index (ignoring the caveat about input quality change). The measurement of productivity, quality, and cost effectiveness founders on the difficulty of assessing the quality of care, and the measurement of technological and scientific advance begs the question of which advances one might wish to pay for.[81]

Regulatory lag may slow technological advance below its optimal level. First, the supplier of the new good or service may need to persuade the insurer that the product should be covered. Assuming it is covered, in the case of a new hospital supply, the initial DRG payment will not incorporate the cost of the good, but if it diffuses anyway, the DRGs in which it is used will increase in relative weight. In the case of physician services or outpatient supplies, which are paid for in a more disaggregated fashion than the DRG payment, payment will require issuing a new billing code, which may result in delay. For further discussion of lags in Medicare's coverage of new products, see Newhouse 2002.

Unbundling

A hospital that is paid a case rate has an incentive to break out
services from the bundle for which the fixed rate is paid if it can bill
additional amounts for the services it breaks out and thereby increase reimbursement. Because additional revenue was available for
post-acute care use, hospitals acted upon this incentive by shifting
care from the inpatient unit to the post-acute setting. As a result,
although the initial effect of the PPS in 1984 and 1985 was simply a
decrease in patient-days with little change in post-acute care use,
between 1988 and 1996 there was a further 16 percent reduction in
inpatient days and a large increase in so-called post-acute care days
(Skilled Nursing Facility or SNF, home health, rehabilitation hospitals and units), as well as hospital outpatient care (tables 1.2 and
1.3).[82]

Table 1.3
Medicare Program Spending for Outpatient Facility Services, 1983–1997

Year	Outpatient department payments (billions of 1996 dollars)
1983	$4.8
1984	5.4
1985	6.2
1986	7.1
1987	8.2
1988	9.0
1989	9.3
1990	10.0
1991	11.0
1992	12.1
1993	13.2
1994	14.6
1995	15.8
1996	16.6
1997	16.9
1998	18.1

Source: Medicare Payment Advisory Commission, "Report to the Congress," March
1999, Table 6.1, and "Report to the Congress," June 2000, 36. GDP deflator used to
convert to 1996 dollars. Data exclude payments to physicians and ambulatory surgery
centers.

Many SNFs, as well as rehabilitation units, are physically located in a hospital; thus, the patient using post-acute services may simply be discharged from a general medical and surgical floor and wheeled on a gurney to another floor of the hospital building. The hospital, of course, collects not only the DRG payment for inpatient services but also the additional revenue for the post-acute services. Importantly, the PPS system for several years did not adjust the DRG rate for this unbundling. Between 1998 and 2002 the hospital update framework used by the Medicare Payment Advisory Commission included a "site-of-service" adjustment, the intent of which was to adjust (or "rebase") for the unbundling, but as of 2001 the Medicare Payment Advisory Commission estimated that only about two-thirds of the unbundling was adjusted for.[83] Moreover, the initial windfall gains from the unbundling have remained with the hospital industry.

The Balanced Budget Act of 1997 sought to discourage unbundling by modifying hospital payment in ten DRGs that made frequent use of post-acute care (e.g., stroke, hip fracture). Specifically, if a patient was in one of ten DRGs, used post-acute care, and stayed in the hospital less than the geometric mean stay for the DRG, the hospital was paid a per diem rather than a per case payment for the hospital stay.[84] This effectively changed the incentive at the margin to keep the patient in the hospital and made payment more neutral between a marginal day in the hospital and a marginal day of post-acute services. Another way to put this is that for some patients, payment policy became lower powered (Laffont and Tirole 1993).

Treatment of New Entrants

All administered price systems face the problem of how to treat new entrants, and the remarkable growth of post-acute care after 1988 was facilitated by generous reimbursement of new entrants. New entrants were reimbursed their costs for at least their first two years, subject to rather generous limits, and some of them were allowed to keep a portion of any subsequent cost reductions, further increasing the incentive for high initial costs.[85] Because output at these new facilities often grew over time, any economies of scale added to their profit, as did learning-by-doing.

The generous treatment of new entrants led to a dramatic increase in the number of facilities. For example, between 1990 and 1996 the number of skilled nursing facilities increased 7 percent annually and the number of home health agencies increased 9 percent annually (Prospective Payment Assessment Commission 1997a, 105). The Balanced Budget Act of 1997 considerably tightened the reimbursement for new entrants into post acute care, but the horse was long since out of the barn (Medicare Payment Advisory Commission 1998).

Many of the new entrants, especially entrants into the home health industry, were for-profit firms. By 1998 58 percent of the agencies were for-profit firms, whereas prior to 1981 such firms were not permitted to be Medicare home health providers; at that time most home health care agencies were visiting nurse associations (VNAs).[86] It was easier, of course, for for-profit firms to raise the capital to exploit the profitable opportunities for new entrants that Medicare offered.[87]

Interactions among Different Payment Systems for Sites that Are Substitutes

For many years only inpatient hospital care was reimbursed on a prospective system; post-acute care providers were paid largely on the basis of cost, as were hospital outpatient departments. Thus, in principle profitability was unaffected by where post-acute care was received. Now, however, not only post-acute providers but also hospital outpatient departments are being moved to prospective payment systems. This raises the distinct possibility that patients will be cared for in the site that yields the maximum profit, although that may be neither the most appropriate site clinically nor the most convenient for the patient.

Consider, for example, a stroke patient who needs speech therapy. The therapy could be delivered in the acute care hospital's rehabilitation unit or in a freestanding rehabilitation hospital, in the SNF (either the hospital's or a freestanding SNF), in the outpatient department, or at home. But with each of these facilities paid at a different fixed rate for the same procedure, the amount of reimbursement from giving the therapy in a different place could differ substantially. The differing rates arise for two reasons. First, rates reflect the average cost of the cases treated in the different facilities, and the case mix of the providers differs—home care patients, for example, tend to be in the best health. It is unlikely that the case mix systems that are being implemented can fully adjust for the differences across sites.[88] Second, accounting costs of the facilities differ because some of them are part of hospitals, and the PPS has given hospitals an incentive to shift as much joint cost as possible to these facilities and away from inpatient care in order to take advantage of cost reimbursement for these facilities.[89]

These problems could be addressed by paying a lump sum for the entire hospital episode including the post-acute care, a so-called bundled payment. Although paying a lump sum raises concerns about possible stinting (i.e., such a system may be too high powered), the prospective payment systems for post-acute care that are being developed make lump-sum payments to the specific post-acute providers; hence, the incentive to stint would not be any greater under this system than under the system being put in place. The incentive to stint could be mitigated by basing a portion of the payment on the number of services delivered, an issue I take up with respect to health plan payment in chapters 5 and 6. Existing post-acute providers, however, are strongly opposed to bundling, fearing that rents they now receive may be eliminated if hospitals could contract for services.[90] Their opposition has succeeded in blocking this reform.

A similar, but more intractable problem arises with payment of hospital outpatient departments in part because there are several relevant margins; outpatient department care may substitute for inpatient care, for care in the physician's office, or for care in an ambulatory surgery center.[91] For example, reimbursement for many outpatient procedures can differ substantially, depending on the site. Three examples are given in table 1.4. Medicare is currently changing its methods for reimbursing hospital outpatient departments; there is little reason, however, to believe that the new system will be more neutral across sites than the old.

Distortion of the Market for Interns and Residents

The teaching adjustment appears to have led to a major expansion of the number of house staff, as accords with a simple model of a subsidy in a competitive market. Before examining that model, I note that the labor market for residents approximates a competitive market. On the buying side there are around 1500 teaching hospitals throughout the country, with perhaps 100 to 200 being "major" teaching hospitals. On the selling side there are over 20,000 first-year

Table 1.4
Reimbursement Rates for the Same Outpatient Procedure in Different Sites, 1998

CPT (Procedure)	Office practice expense	Ambulatory surgery center	Hospital outpatient department
56350 (Hysteroscopy)	$95	$481	$675
58120 (D&C)	115	458	720
58340 (Catheterization and introduction of saline solution for hysterosonography)	356	n/a	155

Sources: Federal Register, June 5, 1998, June 12, 1998, September 8, 1998.

residents at any point in time. Collusion on either side of the market would therefore appear difficult.[92]

Figure 1.2 shows that the teaching adjustment has worked more or less as one would have expected a subsidy in a competitive market to work. Given the approximately fixed number of U.S. medical school graduates (around 16,000 per year), hospitals have increased the number of residents by hiring graduates of medical schools outside the United States and by lengthening the training period. The number of residents is up about 30 percent since 1985 (table 1.5).[93] The figure has been stable since 1993, suggesting that by that time a new equilibrium had been reached.

Rent Seeking

Any administered price system is vulnerable to rent seeking. With Medicare taking around an eighth of the federal budget, the amount of redistribution in even seemingly small changes in reimbursement can be substantial. Hence, a strong incentive exists for provider groups to attempt to influence policy, and virtually every provider group engages in some sort of lobbying effort on its behalf. This is not surprising, but it means that more efficient reimbursement systems may not be feasible because of distributional considerations. Several examples of the political difficulty of changing the system, such as increasing the number of DRGs, have already been mentioned, and there are many other examples.

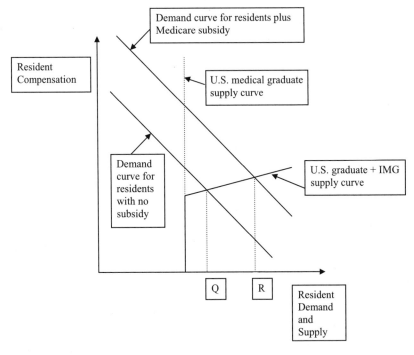

Figure 1.2
Demand and supply of residents, with and without the Medicare subsidy. With the subsidy equilibrium quantity increases from Q to R, IMG = International Medical Graduate.

How High-Powered Is the PPS?

I end this section on hospital pricing by commenting on the popular impression that payment under the PPS is independent of a provider's actions. In other words, much writing treats the PPS as if it were a high-powered payment system that, except for the outlier payments, pays a lump sum per case that is independent of provider actions. Moreover, because the outlier payments are only 5 percent of the total dollars, their influence is often thought to be modest. Mark McClellan (1997), however, has shown that this impression is misguided for two principal reasons.

First, in over 40 percent of the DRGs, payment is related not only to diagnosis but also to the performance of specific procedures. Most of these are related to the performance of surgical procedures. Virtually all the DRGs that have been added since the beginning of the PPS are treatment rather than diagnosis related. Thus, by performing

Table 1.5
Numbers of House Staff, by Year

	Number of residents		Percent international graduates	
Year[a]	First year	Total	First year	Total
1980	18,702	61,465	21	20
1985	19,168	75,518	14	17
1990	18,322	82,902	19	18
1991	19,497	86,217	24	20
1992	19,794	89,368	25	20
1993	21,849	97,370	27	23
1994	21,949	97,832	27	24
1995	21,372	98,035	26	25
1996	21,394	98,076	25	25
1997	21,808	98,143	24	26
1998	21,732	97,383	24	26
1999	22,320	97,989	26	26

Source: 1980–1992, Physician Payment Review Commission, "Annual Report, 1997," 352. 1993–1998, Rebecca S. Miller, Marvin R. Dunn, and Thomas Richter, "Graduate Medical Education, 1998–1999," *Journal of the American Medical Association*, September 1, 1999, 282(9): 856. 1999, Sarah E. Brotherton, Frank A. Simon, and Sandra C. Tomany, "U.S. Graduate Medical Education, 1999–2000," *Journal of the American Medical Association*, September 6, 2000, 284(9): 1122, Figure 1. The figures on first-year residents in the first source and second source for 1993–1995 are discrepant; the second source has been used. (The figures on total residents are the same.)
[a] Year is the academic year beginning in year shown; for example, 1996 is academic year 96–97.

the procedure the hospital incurs higher costs but also receives higher reimbursement. For example, a patient who has suffered a heart attack and is not catheterized and does not have a bypass operation or angioplasty will be classified in DRG 121, 122, or 123, whereas a patient who has one of those procedures will be classified in a (much) higher-weighted DRG, as noted previously.

McClellan (1993) shows that such treatment-based DRGs might be optimal under reasonable assumptions about demand and production technology. In particular, if hospitals have some market power and can impose capacity constraints, making DRGs purely diagnosis based can lead to underinvestment in treatment intensity. For example, if care for all heart attacks were reimbursed at the same rate, the hospital may well not make the investment in the specific capital needed to support catheterization units, bypass grafting, and angioplasty, because all of the incremental costs associated with those procedures would reduce its residual dollar for dollar. This result is in the same spirit as a model of Chalkley and Malcolmson's (1998) that I describe in chapter 3. In their model and in the absence of agency, quality will be at the minimal legally permitted level if there is some element of prospectivity in reimbursement (i.e., if reimbursement is not fully cost-based).

Second, the outlier system makes the system lower powered than it otherwise would be, because for outlier cases reimbursement depends upon the quantity of services delivered. And McClellan (1997) showed that the effect of the outlier system on the power of the PPS is substantially larger than might be conveyed by its 5 percent share of payments.

More generally, McClellan tried to measure the extent of cost sharing in the PPS.[94] Using variation in cost and reimbursement across patients in 1990, he found that an additional dollar of reported Medicare costs at an average hospital was associated with 55 cents of additional Medicare reimbursement. This proportion varied substantially with patient demographic characteristics, treatment choices, and diagnoses. McClellan focused on the implications of this dependence for technological change and cost increases, but his presumption is that the degree of cost sharing should vary with elasticities of supply (Ramsey pricing on the supply side) and also with the degree of agency.[95] In particular, to the degree that hospitals are less responsive to reimbursement levels, reimbursement can be a greater function of cost.

Important for my purposes in this book, McClellan found that the information in diagnoses, as aggregated in the DRG system, explained less than 20 percent of the variance in both reimbursement and cost across all cases. In other words, a prospective system based purely on diagnosis does not match cost variation at the patient level very well. (Of course, the amount of observed cost variation could well be less if payment were not a function of procedure.) Indeed, as already noted, this is presumptively why the PPS includes treatment-related reimbursement features; otherwise the system would discourage the provision of potentially beneficial treatments.

By contrast, procedure as embodied in the DRG system explained around 30 percent of the variance in cost across cases in both 1987 and 1990; thus, how the PPS reimburses hospitals for the specific services given to a patient is important. This 30 percent of explained variance was almost entirely attributable to surgical admissions;

reimbursement for medical admissions was nearly invariant to what is done in the hospital.

Although only accounting for five percent of the total dollars, outlier payments explained 30 percent of the variance in reimbursement in 1987 and fully 46 percent in 1990. The noteworthy amount of variance explained by outlier payments implies that there is substantial variation in reimbursement across patients that neither diagnosis nor major procedure can explain, a theme to which I return in the discussion of partial capitation in chapters 5 and 6.

That the PPS is not independent of the actions of a provider should not necessarily be treated as a distortion, an essential consideration for subsequent chapters. Although the lack of independence could well lead to higher a higher cost of production for treating certain illnesses, full supply-side cost sharing, meaning in this context placing all the risk of a higher cost admission on the hospital, is likely not optimal, as I attempt to show in subsequent chapters. I am, however, getting somewhat ahead of the story.

Physician Pricing in Medicare

Medicare uses a different administered pricing method for physician services, and so the resulting pathologies differ from those for hospital services. Unlike the PPS, which classifies hospital treatment into one of 500 groups, there are over 7,000 different codes for physician services, each of which has its own price. In other words, payment for physician services has a much more disaggregated basis of pricing than does payment for hospital services.

For the first twenty-six years of the Medicare program, the prices Medicare actually paid for each physician code were based on "usual, customary, and reasonable" fees, the definition of which was sufficiently complicated that it is not worth describing here. Suffice it to say that the scheme was initially based upon existing fees, with complex rules for updating the fees. Like many administered price schemes, the method grew more complex and more unwieldy over time. Largely in response to the view that the relative prices of procedures (e.g., surgery) were too high relative to so-called evaluation and management services (e.g., taking a patient history), the RBRVS was launched in the 1980s to create a new set of relative prices.

The scale relied upon physician ratings of relative "work" within specialty; for example, a sample of general surgeons was asked to

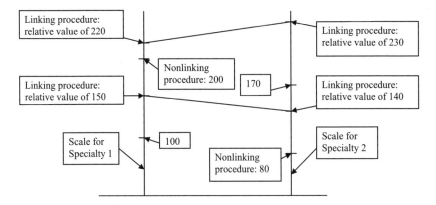

Figure 1.3
A schematic of relative prices in the RBRVS. The nearly horizontal lines connect values for two linking procedures and minimize the sum of squared errors for prices of specialty 2, given that specialty 1 has prices of 150 and 220 for the linking procedures: $(150 - 140)^2 + (220 - 230)^2 = 200$. The other tick marks show relative prices of non-linking procedures.

rate the relative work in repairing an inguinal hernia relative to an appendectomy and a cholecystectomy. Payment for each procedure was then to be proportional to work. Empirically, physicians had a substantial degree of consensus on relative prices or weights for procedures within their own specialty.[96]

In order to set relative prices across specialties, an effort was made to find "linking" procedures that two or more specialties commonly perform (e.g., both neurosurgeons and orthopedic surgeons perform laminectomy) or procedures that a panel composed of physicians from many specialties regarded as equivalent work. Relative prices for such linking procedures were then set so as to minimize the sum of squared errors for the linking procedure prices. Figure 1.3 illustrates the procedure by showing relative values for a small number of hypothetical procedures, including two linking procedures. For more detail on the construction of the RBRVS see Hsiao, Braun, Dunn et al. 1988; Hsiao, Yntema, Braun et al. 1988; Becker, Dunn, and Hsiao 1988, and Braun, Yntema, Dunn et al. 1988.

What Is the Optimal Fee?

Setting aside for now issues of unobserved or noncontractible physician effort to minimize the cost of achieving a given outcome, an

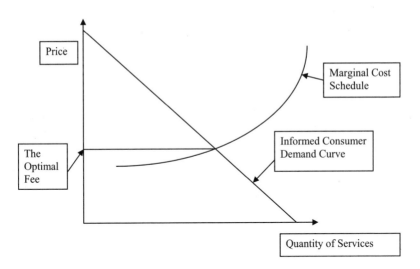

Figure 1.4
The optimal fee.

issue to which I return in chapters 3 and 5, a basis for determining the optimal fee for a single physician service was set out by Mark Pauly (1980) and is shown schematically in figure 1.4. The model depicted shows the demand curve of an informed consumer and a physician-level marginal cost curve; the model assumes a competitive supply side.[97] Suppose the physician has some discretion over the level of demand for the service and responds to the level of fees in the intensity of treatment he or she recommends to the patient. The physician is assumed not to want to induce demand for services that are of little or no value to the patient, but will do so if the reward, or the excess of fee above marginal cost, for doing so is sufficiently high.[98] The key point is that where the marginal cost curve cuts the informed consumer's demand curve, the physician has neither an incentive to deliver excess services nor an incentive to stint (underserve).

How Well Does the RBRVS Match the Optimal Fee?

Although the developers of the RBRVS intended that it match the outcome of a competitive market (Hsiao, Braun, Dunn et al. 1988), which would be the optimal fee shown in figure 1.4, in practice it cannot do this for many reasons.

The Conversion Factor and Updating

At most the RBRVS only yields appropriate relative fees. Congress then sets a conversion factor that translates the relative value into a dollar value. In doing so, it has to take account of the recommendations of the Secretary of the Department of Health and Human Services and the Medicare Payment Advisory Commission.[99] When the transition to this new set of relative prices began in 1992, the initial conversion factor was set so as to be budget neutral. Because of the high likelihood of rents in the prior system, however, the resulting fees were almost surely above competitive levels. In other words, budget neutrality implied that any prior rents were simply redistributed across services.

In principle, any initial rents could have been squeezed out of the prices over time by adjusting the rate of increase of the conversion factor downward. Subsequent updates to the conversion factor, however, were set on a formulaic basis. The initial system was termed the Volume Performance Standard (VPS) system, and the current system is termed the Sustainable Growth Rate (SGR) system. The essence of both these systems is to make the conversion factor an inverse function of the total number of units of service, so that total spending will equal a budgeted figure.[100] That is, if the quantity of services rises above what was planned or desired, the price paid per service will be reduced, so as to keep total spending constant.

Congress's dominant motive for adopting this method was to impose budgetary control on Medicare spending for physician services, which had grown in real terms by 8.8 percent per year from 1970 to 1990; by contrast, the real growth in the economy was 3.2 percent per year and in federal tax revenue was 3.0 percent per year.[101] Initially Medicare financing for physician services was financed equally between federal general revenues (mainly personal and corporate income taxes) and elderly premium payments.[102] But the 8.8 percent real annual increase in spending was not only greater than the growth in tax revenue; it was also much greater than the growth rate of the elderly's income. In a contest between the elderly and (the mainly nonelderly) taxpayers, the elderly won; Congress acted to shield the elderly from the increase by steadily lowering the share of physician spending to be financed by elderly premium payments from 50 to 25 percent of the total. Thus, the financing of this increased spending on physician services fell increasingly upon federal general revenues, and in fact by the time the RBRVS was adopted, Part B of Medicare, 75 percent of whose dollars covered physician services, had become the largest domestic program financed from general revenue.[103]

When the VPS constraint on total spending was adopted in 1992, however, it was portrayed as giving physicians an incentive to "control" the volume of services, which were generally viewed as excessive because of the rents in the fee-for-service system.[104] A collective incentive to hundreds of thousands of physicians, of course, makes no economic sense because of the free-rider problem; to any individual physician the loss of income from "controlling" his volume of services swamps the increase in his fees from such control, because the fee increase is averaged over hundreds of thousands of physicians. This collective incentive, however, turned out to have a pernicious side effect, another instance of the importance of the political economy of the program. To understand the side effect requires a little background.

Although a principal rationale for the VPS was to control spending, it had a feature that was designed to allow for growth in spending from new capabilities in medicine. A five-year moving average of past quantity increases was computed, and each year this moving average entered the calculation of the target rate of increase. Thus, other things equal, if the five-year moving average had increased 3 percent per year, the target rate of increase was to increase 3 percent per year. The logic was that the additional quantity of services was attributable to new procedures and devices, which should be available to the elderly, and an average growth rate would approximate the monies that should be devoted to financing increased capabilities. In other words, quantity-increasing technical change was assumed to occur at a reasonably constant rate.

After the program was enacted, however, surgeons seized upon the rhetoric that the VPS was a collective incentive to hold down services to argue that surgical services should not be in the same pool as services supplied by internists and others for purposes of computing the rate of increase of fees. Their position was prompted by a more rapid growth in the quantity of nonsurgical than in surgical services.[105] Congress, responding to the surgeons' argument that they should not be responsible for or disadvantaged by other physicians' "profligate" use of services, allowed a separate conversion factor for surgeons effective in 1991.

Recall that the growth rate in fees in any given year is inversely related to the growth in the quantity of services. As a result, the separate surgical conversion factor combined with the slow growth in the quantity of surgical procedures initially gave the surgeons very high increases in fees, approaching 10 percent per year in real dollars for a few years. From the logic of the collective incentive, this was a "reward" for keeping down volume. Because the marginal cost of surgery almost certainly did not rise by anything like 10 percent in real terms, any rents that surgeons were receiving initially increased.[106]

Recall, however, that the expenditure target was a function of a five-year moving average of past quantity or volume increases (the technological change factor). As a result, after a few initial years of large fee increases from the small changes in quantity of services, the years with little change in quantity started to reduce the five-year moving average of quantity increase, which meant the target for the overall increase in spending on surgical services was to fall. Indeed, the fall would have been so large that, had the formula continued, surgeons' fees would have actually decreased in nominal terms. Implicitly the formula was sending a signal that quantity-saving technical change was occurring in surgery. Moreover, Congress, in its frustration over quantity and spending increases among all physicians, had enacted provisions that arbitrarily reduced the spending target below what it otherwise would have been, which added to the potential decrease in the surgeon's fees.[107]

Partly because such a fall could have jeopardized surgeons' willingness to supply services to Medicare beneficiaries, Congress in 1997 abolished the VPS system and replaced it with the SGR system. This new system retains the expenditure target feature of the prior system, but ties the growth of the target to the growth of GDP rather than to the five-year moving average of the growth rate in quantity. Thus, fee increases now depend on the growth in the quantity of services relative to GDP growth. Although the demise of the VPS is partly a case study in the difficulty of managing an administered price system, it also illustrates the point that there is nothing in either the five-year-moving-average method (VPS) or the change-in-GDP method (SGR) for updating the conversion factor to suggest that the resulting dollar fee will equal marginal cost.[108]

Moreover, by 1997 a number of years of differential updates to surgical services and evaluation and management services had occurred, which caused the conversion factors applied to different services to differ by 21 percent. This difference undid the logic of the linking across procedures performed by various specialties described earlier and thus threatened the integrity of the RBRVS. In the 1997 Balanced Budget Act, Congress therefore mandated that there be one conversion factor for all physician services, as in the original system. This was done in a budget-neutral fashion, so fees for surgical procedures did fall.

Average Costs, Not Marginal Costs

Just as with the PPS for hospitals, the physician pricing system intends to estimate average cost rather than marginal cost. But setting physician fees to approximate marginal cost is probably even more important than for hospital services because of the physician's potentially greater ability to induce services.

Because of lumpiness in ancillary personnel hours, capital equipment, and office space, average costs probably do not equal marginal costs for many physician services.[109] If marginal and average cost differ, two problems arise. First suppose that marginal cost is always below average cost because economies of scale are not exhausted over the relevant range and that Medicare is the only payer. Then the RBRVS method must pay an additional amount that exceeds marginal cost in order to keep physicians in business. If this amount is paid as a per unit subsidy (i.e., a simple increase in the fee for each service), an incentive to induce demand will arise. With other payers and Medicare moving first in setting price, the subsidies will come from other payers and in practice are likely to be paid as a per unit subsidy, resulting in the same outcome.

Alternatively, suppose that there is a textbook U-shaped cost curve, or perhaps economies or diseconomies of scope, and that some physicians are not operating at the minimum point where marginal and average costs are equal. Because of spatial differentiation among physicians, among other reasons, such differences could exist in equilibrium in a private market. The RBRVS method ignores these economies or diseconomies and implicitly attempts to force all practices to the least cost scale and scope. As in the case of rural hospitals, in small markets the least cost scale and scope may not be feasible because the market is too small.

Geographic Adjustment

The Medicare program is a national administered price system. Medical care markets, however, are mainly local. Moreover, Medicare as a large but generally not dominant payer must compete with private insurers in attracting physicians to serve its beneficiaries. The fact of competition is dramatically underscored by physician reaction to the Medicaid program, the American program for certain low-income and disabled persons. Many states have set Medicaid fees well below both the private market and Medicare, and, as a result, many physicians will not accept Medicaid patients.[110]

Because Medicare competes in local markets, it would optimally set a price appropriate for each local market. If its fees fall too far below fees paid by private insurers in any given market, the Medicare program could begin to look like the Medicaid program. This is, however, politically unthinkable. Numerically the beneficiaries of the Medicaid program are mainly low-income women and children, many of whom do not or, in the case of the children, cannot vote. Moreover, the elderly beneficiaries of the Medicare program vote at higher rates than any other age group, and for many of them Medicare is a decisive issue in determining their vote. It is similarly an important issue for their adult children (Blendon, Altman, Benson et al. 1995). Thus, the law setting up both the Prospective Payment Assessment and Physician Payment Review Commissions to monitor Medicare gave the commissions a special charge to monitor "access." As a result, the annual reports of the commissions have generally contained a chapter concerning access. Although access has a number of meanings, the principal meaning in this context is that Medicare beneficiaries should have no trouble seeing a physician if they wish to.

The result is that Medicare fees must not fall far below private fees in each market. But the Medicare fees are set centrally. They do have a geographic adjustment factor, which is an index of input prices. Inevitably, however, local markets will have more or less competition. Towns of under 25,000 inhabitants, for example, rarely have more than one hospital, and even considerably larger towns may have only one hospital. Similarly, smaller towns may have only one specialist of a given type. For very specialized services, such as burn services, there may be only one facility for a substantial geographic area. Consequently, private prices in local markets may contain varying degrees of markup over a competitive price, but Medicare has no mechanism to account for this variation. As a result, the difference between Medicare and private prices almost certainly varies from market to market, although the difficulty of obtaining transaction prices for private payers makes it hard to ascertain the degree of variation. To prevent access problems in any market, however, the variation implies that Medicare will pay rents in more competitive markets in order to match rents in private fees in less competitive ones.

Overhead Expense

On average in the United States about half of a (nonsalaried) physician's gross income goes to pay practice expenses and the other half is net or take-home income. Many expenses, such as rent, utilities, and accounting, however, are joint costs across the services or product lines of the physician, and there is no nonarbitrary method of allocating such costs to one of the thousands of disaggregated services for which Medicare is setting prices. Moreover, any such allocation could readily lead to fees above marginal cost for the specific service.

Given the possibility of demand inducement if fees exceed marginal cost, Wedig (1993) and I (Newhouse 1991) have both proposed that Medicare adopt a supply-side variant of Ramsey pricing.[111] Under this proposal Medicare would allocate joint expenses disproportionately to services where inducement is high, or so-called nondiscretionary services. In practice, however, the relative degree of inducement across services is unknown, and with thousands of services will never be known with great precision.

The RBRVS was developed only for the so-called work component of the physician's fee, that is, the nonoverhead half of the fee. There remained the issue of how to incorporate "practice costs," or overhead costs, into the Medicare fee schedule. The Health Care Financing Administration (HCFA) delayed for many years implementing so-called resource-based practice costs.[112] Although the work component of the RBRVS was implemented between 1992 and 1996, implementing resource-based practice costs did not commence until 1999 after Congress mandated it in the 1997 Balanced Budget Act. In the interim the HCFA continued to use the older "usual, customary, and reasonable" portion of the fee schedule for practice cost. The HCFA initially sought to gather empirical evidence on practice costs through a survey of physicians, but its attempt failed for a variety of reasons, including low response. Ultimately the agency relied upon groups of physician-specialists to estimate practice costs that could be directly attributed to procedures. These initial estimates are now being refined by advisory panels of physicians, although the HCFA retains final authority. Practice costs that could not be directly attributed to specific services were ultimately included proportionately, thereby keeping fees above marginal cost for a given service.

Problems of Cross-Specialty Linking

Although members of a given specialty tend to agree among themselves about the appropriate relative fee for the various services they render, there is sharp disagreement across specialties on the relative fees for services that different specialties provide. The disagreement largely reflects the historical income differentials across specialties (table 1.1). Those specialties that primarily provide so-called evaluation and management services (e.g., taking histories, making diagnoses, recommending a course of treatment) argue that they are underpaid relative to those specialties that primarily perform procedures (e.g., surgery, endoscopy, radiologic services, etc.). Not surprisingly, the specialists who perform the procedures and who have substantially higher incomes, do not agree that they are overpaid. As a result, interspecialty fee differentials are particularly contentious.

As described earlier, relative fees across specialties were set using so-called linking procedures, with an algorithm that minimized the sum of squared errors of relative fees (figure 1.3). Such a procedure is appropriate if two conditions are satisfied: the services provided by the two specialties actually are identical (or are deemed equivalent), and all relative fees within each specialty are a function only of a hypothetical true value and random measurement error.

But are services with the same procedure code when performed by different specialties in fact identical? Consider a physician taking the history of a patient who presents to the physician with a fever of undetermined origin. The physician is taking the history in order to determine how to proceed in treating the patient. The diagnostic skill of the physician should vary across specialties, because of variation in the amount of training. For this particular problem an infectious disease specialist would have had the most training and therefore would likely make the correct diagnosis most frequently, perhaps followed by a general internist, a family practitioner, and finally a (now disappearing in the United States) general practitioner. The logic of the RBRVS, however, is that a visit is a visit, regardless of the specialty that supplies it or the medical problem for which it was supplied, and thus Medicare should pay the same amount.[113] "Equal pay for equal work." Although exaggerated to make the point, this is something like saying that because all cars provide transportation, they are all similar.

Furthermore, there are over thirty specialties whose fees must be linked to each other. Some of these specialties, for example, ophthalmology and anesthesiology, mainly provide services that other specialties do not provide.[114] As a result, among the actual linking procedures are several that are judged to be equivalent across specialties. It seems evident that errors can enter at this point, and that therefore the relative values across specialties can be in error.

Estimation Errors

Ignore all the foregoing problems but assume that those responsible for determining the administered price are trying to set a price equal to marginal cost.[115] Doing so will surely be fraught with error. For openers, if the pricing system is very disaggregated, there are thousands of services to price. The data base required for reliable estimation would have to be very large. Moreover, one would need to control for any variation in the quality of service that affected marginal cost, but current measures of quality are almost surely not sufficient for this task and are better in some dimensions than in others.[116] And even if one could satisfy oneself that quality variation were adequately controlled for, ongoing changes in medical technology and learning-by-doing will change production possibilities and costs. As a result, even valid empirical estimates of marginal cost may be out-of-date by the time they are available.

In sum, for many reasons physician fees in practice are not likely to equal the optimal fee described previously but rather contain rents that will induce demand and cause distortions in financing. This is particularly the case in programs such as traditional Medicare that offer "free choice" of physician and hence have little ability to negotiate for lower prices or improved performance by threatening not to contract with a given provider. In the United States traditional private insurance also paid providers on a fee-for-service basis and offered free choice of physician—indeed, Medicare was patterned after private insurance plans of the 1960s, especially Blue Cross and Blue Shield plans. Thus, most of the traditional American system for financing care suffered from the distortions of administered fee-for-service prices. In recent years, however, American private insurers have moved sharply away from the traditional model, as described in chapter 2. I conclude this chapter by describing how Medicare pays health plans and summarizing several ills of administered medical care prices in general and fee-for-service prices in particular.

Health Plan Pricing in Medicare

Although this chapter has principally focused on fee-for-service pricing, I end it with a discussion of how Medicare sets prices to health plans. This will serve as prelude to subsequent chapters.

During its first decade Medicare did not contract with HMOs on a prospective basis, but, beginning with a demonstration at one health plan, it began to do so in 1976 (Eggers 1980). Contracting on a prospective basis did not move past demonstration status, however, until April 1985, nearly two decades into the program.[117] At that time Medicare began to pay any qualified plan a fixed amount per enrollee per month, and all enrollees were allowed to choose the option of a health plan, provided a plan existed in their area whose enrollment was open. For the first several years of contracting, however, enrollment in prospectively paid health plans was small, only about two or three percent of Medicare beneficiaries. The overwhelming number of Medicare beneficiaries remained in the traditional Medicare program. Starting in the 1990s, however, both the number of plans paid prospectively and number of beneficiaries in such plans grew rapidly until 1997, when it has stabilized around a value of about 15 percent (figure 1.5) and has recently begun to decline (not shown).

Several features of Medicare contracting with HMOs deserve comment. The feature that the analytic literature focuses on most intensively is risk adjustment, and I begin there.

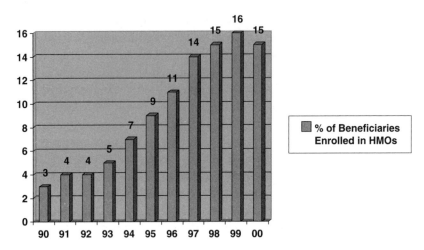

Figure 1.5
Percentage of medicare beneficiaries enrolled in HMOs. (*Source*: Medicare Payment Advisory Commission 1998, p. 5, and unpublished data.)

Risk Adjustment

The prospective amount that Medicare pays plans for each enrollee, termed the Adjusted Average per Capita Cost (AAPCC), varies with the characteristics of the enrollee, just as the PPS varies with the DRG of the patient who is admitted. Before 1998 the AAPCC was computed as follows. First, a national average payment for traditional Medicare was computed, the United States per Capita Cost (USPCC). This was then mapped to the county level by multiplying the ratio of a five-year moving average of traditional Medicare's payments in each county to the same five-year average nationally; the five-year moving average was used to achieve stability, because spending per beneficiary can fluctuate greatly from year to year in small counties.[118] This yielded an estimate of per beneficiary spending in each county, which was reduced by 5 percent as an estimate of HMO savings that might be returned to the government. Finally, demographic adjusters were introduced in the form of a rate table. From 1984 until 1998 the cells of the table pertaining to elderly enrollees were described by age (5 groups), sex (2 groups), Medicaid status (eligible or not), and institutional status (yes or no) for a total of forty groups.[119] The multiplier for each cell was simply per beneficiary spending in that cell relative to the national average. For example, if 65- to 69-year-old noninstitutionalized males who were not eligible for Medicaid spent 90 percent of the national average amount, the multiplier for them was 0.9.

Starting in 2000, Medicare began making a transition to include Principal Inpatient Procedure-Diagnostic Cost Groups (PIP-DCGs) as an additional risk adjuster.[120] PIP-DCGs are a capitation analog to DRGs that incorporate diagnostic information into the payment. For example, all else equal, a man with staphylococcus pneumonia would have higher expected spending during the upcoming year than a man with no chronic disease. Although the old formula would have paid the same amount for the man with pneumonia as for a similar man with no chronic disease, in the new formula the plan will receive more for a man with pneumonia.[121]

When adding PIP-DCGs as a risk adjuster to the demographic variables it used previously, the HCFA lacked reliable outpatient diagnostic data. As a result, only inpatient diagnoses will "count" for reimbursement purposes (hence, the "I" in "PIP"). This nonneutrality between inpatient and outpatient care means there is a potential for substantial moral hazard, namely, patients being admitted to the hospital in order to qualify for additional reimbursement.

To reduce moral hazard, the HCFA took three steps. First, the DCGs are being implemented in a prospective fashion. That means a hospital diagnosis in a given year will not affect plan reimbursement until the following year. Moreover, the increase in reimbursement in the following year will only be the average cost of persons with that diagnosis (or in that DCG) in the following year. As a result, the average cost of the initial hospitalization will not be reimbursed. In other words, a diagnosis in year t will increase reimbursement in year $t + 1$ by an amount that reflects expected spending in year $t + 1$ by those who received a given diagnosis in year t. But the health plan does not receive the increment in year $t + 1$ if the enrollee dies or disenrolls, further reducing the potential gain from hospitalizing a person in year t. Second, certain diagnoses that the HCFA has deemed particularly susceptible to moral hazard, so-called discretionary admissions, will not receive additional payment; they will be assigned to the lowest cost group. Third, diagnoses made during one-day stays will also be assigned to the lowest cost group. These measures probably make the cost of the great majority of admissions greater than the additional revenue the plan would receive from a higher classification. These steps to mitigate moral hazard, however,

Table 1.6
Likelihood of a Claim with the Given Diagnosis in 1995, Conditional on a Claim for that Diagnosis in 1994

Diagnosis	Likelihood (%)
Hypertension	59
COPD	62
Stroke	51
High cost diabetes	58
Dialysis	56
Quadriplegia/paraplegia	52
Coronary artery disease	53
CHF	61
Dementia	59
Rheumatoid arthritis	58

Source: Medicare Payment Advisory Commission 1998, vol. 2, chap. 2.
Note: COPD = Chronic Obstructive Pulmonary Disease; CHF = Congestive Heart Failure.

come at a price; they impair the ability of risk adjustment to reduce selection, a topic I return to in chapter 6.

The unreliability of outpatient diagnoses was shown in a 1998 analysis by the Medicare Payment Advisory Commission (1998). The Commission analyzed outpatient claims from 1994 for selected serious, chronic diagnoses (table 1.6) and determined the probability that there would be an outpatient claim with that diagnosis in the following year. Those who died during 1994 or 1995 were eliminated from the sample. Although a small percentage of the individuals with these diagnoses may have made no visits in the following year, the data in table 1.6 suggest massive undercoding of diagnosis in the outpatient data. This is not surprising because diagnoses made on an outpatient claim do not affect payment.[122] By contrast, inpatient diagnosis coding is reasonably accurate, since it is used to determine the DRG. Moreover, the accuracy of inpatient coding is audited, and coding that results in overpayment is subject to penalties for fraud.[123]

If outpatient diagnosis were to be used as a risk adjuster, therefore, adjustments in payment would have to be made for coding changes. When DRGs were initially implemented in 1984, substantial problems were found with upcoding, or coding the same patient with additional or more serious diagnoses in order to justify additional reimbursement. This was generally not fraudulent; with the introduction of DRGs it paid hospitals to be more careful with diagnosis coding, including hiring a higher level of personnel to do the coding. As a result, Medicare payments in the initial years of the PPS were several percent above what was intended (Carter, Newhouse, and Relles 1990). Such upcoding is a once-and-for-all change and in principle can be subsequently adjusted by reducing updates, although the initial increased Medicare payments were in fact not recouped.[124]

Because the DRG system has been in place for many years, coding of inpatient diagnoses is now reasonably stable. Indeed, the HCFA estimates that in 1997 and 1999 there was no overall change in coding practices and in 1998 there was a modest amount of downcoding, probably because of increased auditing efforts (Medicare Payment Advisory Commission 2000b). Hence, introduction of risk adjustment for health plan payments based on inpatient diagnosis should not change coding practices.[125] But when outpatient diagnostic coding is introduced, potentially large upcoding (relative to the information in the claims that is used to norm the system) may be observed. For this reason it seems prudent to phase in risk adjustment based on outpatient diagnosis. Because only 10 percent of the payment is currently based on diagnosis, it probably pays providers to engage in rather complete coding, but the risk to Medicare from large payouts is reduced by an order of magnitude.

Other Features of Health Plan Payment

Through 2001 Medicare beneficiaries were able to disenroll from their health plan every month, whereas those under 65 in employer-based insurance are generally locked into their choice of plan for the year. The ability to change plans monthly is intended as a Medicare beneficiary protection, but it clearly increases the likelihood of adverse selection because beneficiaries can react quickly to changes in their health status. Starting in 2002 Medicare has moved to a modified annual enrollment period.[126]

Medicare requires that plans cover at least the services that would be covered in traditional Medicare, although plans are allowed to provide additional services. Plans are allowed to use cost sharing, and they are allowed to substitute a premium for cost-sharing amounts, but the actuarial level of the combination of premium and cost sharing cannot be above the actuarial level of the cost sharing in traditional Medicare. In practice, this constraint has rarely been binding.

Although plans may reduce the amount of cost sharing at the point of service (and starting in 2003 they may charge lower Part B premiums), they may not actually pay individuals to enroll. As a result, there is no direct price competition among plans, and more important, there is no price competition with the traditional Medicare program.

Plans are de jure limited in the profit rate they can make. In particular, if the observed profit rate is above an adjusted profit rate that the plan earns on its commercial business, the so-called Adjusted Community Rate (ACR), the excess is to be returned to beneficiaries in the form of additional benefits or returned to the government.[127] Needless to say, any excess is always returned in the form of additional benefits. In most metropolitan areas, however, this constraint on profits is not binding because competition forces plans to pass most rents through to beneficiaries and because the adjustments to the rate used to calculate any excess profit are somewhat arbitrary.[128] That competition forces plans to pass through rents in their payments to consumers is shown by the variation in the value of additional benefits provided by plans according to the level of plan payment. As table 1.7 shows, additional benefits are markedly higher in high-payment areas where rents to plans are likely to be highest.[129]

This large disparity in benefits across areas led to a change in policy in 1997, which might be classified as another example of the pathology of administered pricing. Over a five-year period the AAPCC is moving to a 50-50 blend of the county rate and the national mean; additionally, all counties with an AAPCC below a certain level will receive at least a certain threshold or floor payment, and all areas are guaranteed at least a 2 percent update (3% in 2001). Reimbursement in traditional Medicare, however, is unaffected. As a result, payment within local markets is no longer neutral between health plans and traditional Medicare, except for those plans whose payment is near the national mean. As a result, this policy change will unbalance local markets and give enrollees in high-rate areas an incentive to shift back toward traditional Medicare as their supplementary benefits are cut. I return to the Medicare experience with health plan pricing in chapters 5 and 6.

Table 1.7
Standardized Extra Benefits as a Function of Plan Payment, 1996

Decile	Plan Payment Index	Standardized Extra Benefits
U.S. average	1.0	$77
10	1.29	121
9	1.15	86
8	1.09	80
7	1.06	86
6	1.03	92
5	0.99	78
4	0.94	68
3	0.88	57
2	0.82	53
1	0.75	48

Source: Prospective Payment Assessment Commission, "Medicare and the American Health Care System," June 1997, Table 2.8. Plans are grouped in deciles of equal numbers of plans according to the level of the AAPCC. The value of extra benefits is the actuarial value of any waived premium for noncovered services and reduced cost sharing divided by the hospital wage index for the area.

Some Lessons from the Medicare Experience

The Medicare-administered price methods illustrate several points about administered prices in general and fee-for-service reimbursement methods in particular:

1. If one assumes a single universal insurance plan, a fee-for-service reimbursement system, and free choice of physician, it is extremely difficult, if not impossible, to set up marketlike institutions that yield outcomes approximating the desirable features of usual markets. In general, there will be little or no incentive for patients to find physicians or other providers who offer the same service or same outcome at a lower cost, and providers will face nearly perfectly inelastic demand curves. The insurer must therefore set supply prices administratively.

2. It is extremely difficult in practice for the insurer to approximate optimal supply prices, especially when technology continues to change.

3. Both capitated and fee-for-service administered price systems are likely to include rents. These cause deadweight losses from additional

financing requirements and also offer incentives to use real resources to influence policy to allocate rents in one direction rather than another.

4. Related to the previous point, the political economy of the program tends to promote rents for those providers who are most effective in the political process, which in turn influence their behavior.

5. Fee-for-service pricing requires setting many prices, over 7,000 in the case of physician services alone. Setting administered prices is inevitably fraught with error, and because of lags in adapting to technological change, the extent of the error increases as pricing systems age. The United States has not, for example, "rebased" the PPS after more than fifteen years.[130] Given a fixed level of resources to devote to administering the system, it seems likely that the errors in price setting in a disaggregated fee-for-service system will exceed those in a more aggregated system simply because there are fewer administrative resources to focus on the accuracy of each price.

The errors in fee-for-service pricing lead to the discontents of fee-for-service medicine. Rents offer an inducement to overserve. Having to set many prices administratively inevitably results in distortions among relative prices of different services, which can be especially problematic when those services are substitutes, as in the case of whether a service should be performed on an inpatient or outpatient basis or where a post-acute care service should be delivered.

Partly because of the problem of pricing thousands of disaggregated services without creating incentives to overserve and other distortions, the traditional indemnity commercial insurance market in the United States has shrunk enormously in favor of managed care and capitated payment of health plans. The health plans, in turn, tend to negotiate prices with providers. For the same reason there is a desire on the part of many in Congress to increase the use of capitation and decrease the use of fee-for-service in both the Medicare and Medicaid programs.

Capitation payment to integrated health plans is the subject of much of the remainder of the book, but the fee-for-service reimbursement method is still dominant in traditional Medicare. Furthermore, fee-for-service is used by many managed care plans to pay individual providers, so material in this chapter is relevant even in a world of competing health plans that are paid by capitation.

Despite these drawbacks, many theoretical advantages of disaggregated payment systems exist relative to more aggregated systems such as capitation. In the rest of the book I emphasize two of those advantages in particular. First, capitated and other more aggregated systems are more vulnerable to selection problems because the payment for an episode of illness does not correspond to how sick the patient is. Second, because the product on which payment is based ("necessary care") is harder to define and contract for, payment systems that are more aggregated than fee-for-service are more vulnerable to stinting and unbundling. These drawbacks of capitated methods must be set against the disadvantages of fee-for-service methods. This is the conundrum of the pricing of health care services, which is taken up in detail in chapters 3 through 6.

A Remark on the Use of Salary

Some reformers consider that the use of salaries to pay physicians or other health care personnel is a way around the problems associated with fee-for-service and capitation that this book describes. Because I do not take up problems in administering a salaried system elsewhere in the book and because I do not believe salaried physicians are a solution to the health care conundrum, I make two remarks here.

First, the organization employing salaried physicians or other health professionals must receive its funds through some sort of budget. A capitation payment can be considered a per person budget, so the issues associated with capitation considered in chapters 3–6 are not so dissimilar from those associated with an overall budget. The key is the implicit incentives in the budget-setting process, and how those incentives are transmitted to influence employee performance within the organization. In any event, the basis for salary increases and promotion are surely important incentives at the individual level. Second, a salaried system requires methods to minimize shirking and more generally monitor and reward appropriate behavior. Thus, the information problems discussed in this book apply to salaried systems as well. For more material on incentives within firms, see Prendergast 1999.

2

The Integration of Medical Insurance and Medical Care

As described in chapter 1, American commercial insurers were traditionally passive about reimbursing the cost of medical care services, which were in effect delivered by a separate industry.[1] Moreover, price competition among the commercial insurers took place over loadings, or the relatively small proportion of the premium not paid out in benefits, rather than over the entire premium, which mainly reflected the underlying cost of the medical services. For example, the loadings in large group policies tend to be only on the order of 6 to 10 percent, and in individual policies on the order of 25 to 40 percent. The remainder of the premium represents the cost of medical services being insured against.

Although price competition in the American commercial insurance market has always been robust, even if it was only over loadings, price competition in provider market(s) was traditionally weak.[2] One initial result of managed care, therefore, was to shift some of the rents in the provider market to managed care companies. Perhaps for this reason some physician commentators focus attention on the size of insurance company loadings and other administrative costs as evidence of the inefficiency of the American financing system rather than on the inefficiencies and rents in the delivery system, including rents in physician fees.[3]

In recent years, however, the American health insurance and medical care delivery systems have begun to integrate, and one observes price competition not only over loading charges but also over the cost of the medical services being delivered. The most common form of "integration" is technically not integration at all, but a stable contractual relationship, for example, a physician's contracting to be in a health plan's network of physicians. Nonetheless, for ease of exposition, I refer to these contractual relationships as integration because it is a sharp break from the past. Moreover, there is increasing true vertical integration within the medical care industry—for example, between hospitals, skilled nursing facilities, and home health agencies.

In countries with national health services, such as the United Kingdom, integration of the insurance and delivery functions are necessarily present. Traditionally such systems had no price competition. But as the American system has moved toward integrating insurance and delivery, which has had the effect of increasing price competition, the United Kingdom has also attempted to introduce or increase elements of price competition in its delivery system.[4] Other countries that have attempted to increase price competition include the Netherlands, Israel, and Switzerland, although these countries do not have national health services.[5] In this chapter I briefly sketch some of the recent changes in the American delivery system. This sets the stage for the analytical chapters in the rest of the book.

The Traditional American Industry Structure

Up until the past ten to fifteen years, most Americans with health insurance, or about 85 percent of the population, obtained that coverage through a public or private insurer that had no formal connection with the delivery system.[6] For those with indemnity policies the insurer verified that the insured was eligible for reimbursement (e.g., the premium had been paid) and that the services for which reimbursement was claimed were in fact covered by the policy (e.g., were not "experimental").[7] If those conditions were satisfied, the insurer generally reimbursed after the fact according to the terms of the contract.[8]

Under these arrangements demand was limited by excluding certain services from coverage (e.g., mental health services) and by implementing demand-side cost sharing arrangements such as deductibles and coinsurance for those services that were covered. These arrangements led to the well-known trade-off between risk aversion and moral hazard (Zeckhauser 1970)—namely, the more complete the coverage, the greater the moral hazard, but the less the risk borne by the insured.

Medical care services were delivered by hospitals, physicians, and other providers, who were either firms or self-employed professionals that were independent of the insurer. There were contractual relationships between the Blue Cross and Blue Shield insurance plans and providers (in particular, providers who "participated" in the Blue plans agreed not to balance bill the patient for amounts above the plan fee schedule), but providers had few or no contractual relationships with other (commercial) insurers.[9] Indeed, for ideological reasons some physicians would not even consent to bill the insurer directly, and instead billed the patient, who then submitted the bill to the insurer. The Blue plans set reimbursement at a sufficiently high level that almost all providers participated. As described in chapter 1, the watchword was that the patient should have freedom-of-choice of provider, so all private insurers, as well as Medicare, reimbursed virtually all providers. Moreover, providers and patients both expected that the insurer should simply reimburse whatever services the physician ordered.

Except for the few salaried physicians employed by Health Maintenance Organizations (HMOs), providers were paid largely on a fee-for-service basis.[10] Insurers obviously could not agree to reimburse any fee a physician named, especially in cases in which there was no coinsurance (e.g., because a stop-loss provision in the insurance policy had been exceeded). Hence, insurers developed either fee schedules or maximum fees that they would pay.[11]

An alternative, integrated insurance and services provider had existed in a few local markets for many years, but typically had a market share in those local markets of under 25 percent. In return for a monthly premium, these organizations agreed to provide "all necessary medical services."[12] In the 1970s these organizations were dubbed HMOs, and the federal government enacted legislation to promote their spread.[13] Nonetheless, until the 1980s such organizations had only a small proportion of the population enrolled (table 2.1).

The Rise of Managed Care

Managed care is a term that means different things to different people, but I shall take it to mean *efforts by the insurer directed toward reducing moral hazard or rents in the delivery of medical care services,* either by financial incentives embodied in methods of paying physicians and other providers of medical care, or by direct command-and-control interventions, such as prior authorization for hospitalization, or by choice of networks. Managed care may also

Table 2.1
Health Maintenance Organization (HMO) Enrollment Growth

Year	% of population enrolled in HMOs
1976	2.8
1980	4.0
1985	8.9
1990	13.4
1995	19.4
1998	28.6

Source: U.S. Department of Health and Human Services, *Health United States, 1999*, 304.

improve the quality of care by improving coordination across providers, by offering financial incentives, or by other methods. For a
review of the literature on managed care, see Glied 2000.

The moral hazard that is the target of managed care is shown in
the well-known figure 2.1. Because the consumer is insured, she has
an incentive to demand services whose value is less than the cost to
society (but equal to or greater than the cost to her). If the consumer
is well informed and the physician (or other provider) market is
competitive, the consumer can shop for a physician who will deliver
these services. If the consumer is not well informed, as is often the
case, the physician acts as the patient's agent, and the incentives to
the physician matter more. Indeed, the physician's incentives, and
more generally the incentives of other providers or suppliers, are the
subject of much of the remainder of this book.

In appraising alternative financing arrangements, I sometimes
make positive predictions and sometimes draw normative conclusions, in which case I will use conventional welfare economics. Some
argue, often passionately, that conventional welfare economics does
not apply to medical care.[14] Most parties to this debate, however,
would probably agree that the marginal valuation curve does reflect
the expected benefit as perceived by the patient (indeed, this is how
the curve is defined); the controversy concerns whether the patient's
valuation should carry any normative force and especially whether
price competition is desirable. The subject of the book, however,
largely (though not fully) sidesteps whether the consumer's demand
curve should have normative force. How insurance plans or public
health services should pay providers and how the insurance plans
themselves should be paid are questions that in principle arise irrespective of the degree of price competition.

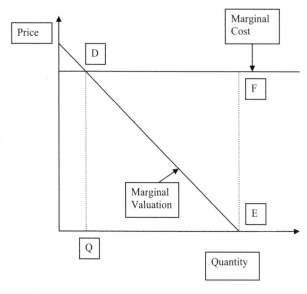

Figure 2.1
Classic moral hazard. Once marginal valuation falls below marginal cost (for quantities greater than Q), there is a welfare loss on each unit equal to the vertical difference between the marginal cost curve and the marginal valuation curve. This ignores externalities, income effects, and risk aversion. See text.

Moreover, moral hazard arises in every health care system. Just as American managed care can be seen as an effort to reduce moral hazard, a national health service can also "manage" care or capacity in an effort to reduce moral hazard. As spending for medical care services has everywhere increased, many observers have felt that there was a disproportionate increase in moral hazard—even if they did not use or even know that term. This may or may not have been true, but there can be little doubt that the rising spending has led many countries to attempt various reforms to combat moral hazard and to increase the value received for the monies spent on health care services.

In the American context a principal reform—many would say the principal reform—has been the rise of managed care. Managed care has also been accompanied by price competition among health plans. Such competition is sometimes referred to as managed competition (Enthoven 1988), although in practice the price competition appears more unmanaged than managed. Managed competition and managed care are sometimes used interchangeably and sometimes confused, but they are not synonyms. Managed care refers to either the command-and-control techniques or the financial incentives given providers, especially physicians, to reduce moral hazard. Managed competition refers to efforts to increase price competition in the markets for health insurance and health care services, which is the principal mechanism through which rents have been reduced.

Although price competition among traditional insurance plans was limited to loading charges, insurers can clearly reduce their costs—and therefore in a competitive insurance market, the premiums they charge consumers—by obtaining lower prices from providers or by intervening directly in the care management process to reduce the quantity of services through such measures as prior or concurrent utilization review. Intervention in the care management process should in principle be limited to those cases in which the insurer believes the benefit to the particular patient does not warrant the expenditure on the service. I take up the issue of intervention more formally in what follows.

The longest established form of managed care in the United States is the HMO. In the classic group or staff model HMO, physicians worked exclusively for the HMO; either they were employees of the HMO (the staff model) or exclusively contracted with the HMO (the group model). Traditionally most physicians in the community had no relationship with the group or staff model HMO, but rather practiced fee-for-service medicine within the context of the dominant indemnity insurance system. HMO enrollees could not receive reimbursement for care received from physicians who were not employed by or did not have contracts with the HMO. Thus, anyone enrolling in an HMO could generally use only a minority of the physicians in the community if the services were to be covered by the HMO insurance plan. In some communities, however, individual practice associations or network HMOs developed; these were associations of most physicians in the community who agreed as a group to accept a capitation payment.[15]

In the past two decades two changes have occurred among HMOs. First, almost all of them have made an effort to contract with more physicians in the local market, especially primary care physicians. In the current jargon, many physicians in the community have become members of the plan's network, meaning that patients have access to those physicians on more favorable terms than before.[16] But the greater choice of physicians than in the old-style HMOs comes at a

Table 2.2
Characteristics of Insurance Policies

| Dimension | Indemnity insurance | Managed care | | | |
		PPO	POS	IPA or network HMO	Group or staff HMO
Qualified providers	Almost all	Almost all (network)	Network; Out of network almost all	Network	Network
Payment of providers	Fee-for-service	Discounted Fee-for-Service	Network: like HMO; Out of network: fee-for-service	Capitation or mixed capitation-FFS	Salary
Demand-side cost sharing	Moderate	Low in network; Moderate otherwise	Low in network; Very high otherwise	Low in network; High out of network	Low in network; High otherwise
Role of insurer	Pay bills	Pay bills; Form network	As in underlying HMO	Pay bills; Form network; Monitor utilization	Provide care
Limits on utilization	Demand-side	Supply-side (price)	Supply-side (in network); Demand-side (nonnetwork)	Supply-side (price, quantity)	Supply-side (price, quantity)

Note: PPO = Preferred Provider Organization; POS = Point-of-Service; IPA = Independent Practice Association; HMO = Health Maintenance Organization.

price. With most physicians contracting with many plans, each plan has a smaller incentive to engage in quality improvement efforts because of the free-rider problem (Beaulieu 1998). Nonetheless, choice of provider is still limited relative to the past; in a 1998 survey only 38 percent of health plans (enrollment-weighted) contracted with more than 75 percent of the primary care physicians in the relevant market (Newhouse, Buchanan, Bailit et al. 2001).

Second, new types of plans have evolved that are less restrictive if a patient seeks care outside the "network" of HMO physicians. Thus, the traditional dichotomy of HMO and indemnity insurance contracts has been replaced by a variety of insurance contracts, which in table 2.2 have been classified into five types of contracts. A Preferred Provider Organization (PPO) is most closely related to indemnity insurance. Typically a consumer who belongs to a PPO can seek care from any physician, but if the consumer seeks care from certain "preferred" providers, the demand-side cost sharing is reduced. In turn, the insurance company will have contracted with the preferred provider for reduced fees and may in addition give the provider a bonus if his quantity of services is less than some prespecified amount.[17] In some instances the insurer may have the right to not authorize services—that is to say, to declare that certain services are not covered. This command-and-control approach to the quantity of services consumed is termed utilization management but is used rather sparingly in PPO arrangements.

Another type of insurance shown in the table is Point-of-Service (POS). Consumers in this plan belong to an HMO, but the HMO will allow some reimbursement if care is sought from non-HMO physicians. The difference in cost sharing for out-of-network use, however, is typically large; for example, there may be a $500 deductible and 20 percent coinsurance for out-of-network use compared with minimal charges of $5 or $10 per visit for in-network use. Moreover, the HMO will generally retain some control over which services are reimbursed under the POS option (services must be "authorized"); that is, most POS options are not simply an indemnity plan overlaid on an HMO. In response to the differential in cost sharing between in- and out-of-network use, over 90 percent of use is typically within the network.[18] A common use of a POS option is to use a particular specialist (or perhaps hospital) who is not in the HMO's network, but who the patient prefers to those in the network.

The increase in the integration of financing and delivery in recent years in the United States has been striking. The number of enrollees in traditional indemnity or nonintegrated insurance arrangements fell almost by a factor of two, from 53 to 28 percent, just between 1993 and 1997 (table 2.3).

In any insurance arrangement, whether integrated or not, the premium must cover the product of the fee times the volume of services plus administrative costs and profit. As a result, all health plans in a competitive market are at an advantage if they can reduce medical costs and if the costs being reduced are either in rents or in services whose cost does not equal their value (i.e., reducing moral hazard).

In subsequent chapters I explore the consequences of the institutions that plans have developed for reducing these costs. I emphasize the pricing features of the contracts between the plan and

Table 2.3
Enrollment in Different Types of Insurance Plans, 1993 and 1997

| | 1993 | | 1997 | |
	Enrollment (millions)	Percent of insured	Enrollment (millions)	Percent of insured
Total*	219.1	100.0	224.9	100.0
FFS	116.8	53.3	63.7	28.3
HMO	39.8	18.2	63.3	28.1
POS-HMO	2.5	1.1	8.7	3.9
PPO	60.0	27.4	89.1	39.6
Employment based	181.1	100.0	188.2	100.0
FFS	83.1	45.9	39.8	21.2
HMO	35.7	19.7	50.7	26.9
POS-HMO	2.3	1.3	8.6	4.6
PPO	60.0	33.1	89.1	47.3

Source: EBRI, 1999, data from EBRI tabulations of March CPS, InterStudy 1993–1998, AAHP 1996.
*Total includes employment based, individual private, Medicare, and Medicaid.

medical providers and between the plan and consumers, partly because the sketchy evidence suggests that pricing features are important and partly because economists have well-developed tools for analyzing the likely effects of pricing features.

The Instruments of Managed Care

Integrated delivery systems in general can in principle both reduce rents in the prices paid to providers for their services and reduce moral hazard. The remainder of this chapter describes the three types of instruments a health plan has available to do so.

First, the plan can *choose providers for its network*; this was the classic strategy of American group or staff model HMOs, which, as explained earlier, either employed or contracted with an exclusive group of physicians to serve only the plan's enrollees (Ma and McGuire 1999). By providing its enrollees' incentives to use the providers in its network, typically not paying anything if enrollees used other providers, the insurance plan gains bargaining power with providers over price and thereby potential reductions in rents.[19] By contrast, in the traditional world of indemnity insurance, in which

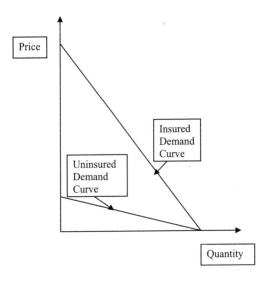

Figure 2.2
The insured demand curve with 20 percent coinsurance has a slope five times as steep as the uninsured demand curve.

patients were to have access to any provider, providers had little incentive to keep their prices down and in the extreme no incentive at all if the plan was paying in full (i.e., if there was no coinsurance).

The simple model in figure 2.2 illustrates this lack of incentive. Suppose each physician faces a market of uninsured consumers, but because of location or other patient preferences will not lose all her patients if she raises her price somewhat. That is, each physician faces a downward-sloping demand curve. The demand curve by definition shows what the patient is willing to pay for an additional service. If all patients now acquire indemnity insurance that pays 80 percent of the cost, a typical figure, the demand curve rotates to have a slope five times as steep as the uninsured demand curve, since each point on the original demand curve is five times as high.[20] Hence, the profit-maximizing price will rise—without limit if there is no coinsurance or a fixed absolute dollar copayment. Even with coinsurance, in some actual cases the provider colluded with the patient to bill a high price and then to either forgive or treat the patient's 20 percent share as uncollectible bad debt, in effect nullifying the intent of the coinsurance. If, however, health plans do not passively reimburse 80 percent of patients' expenditures, no matter how incurred, but are willing to exclude physicians from their network if the physician's unit price or ordering of services is excessive, then the analysis of figure 2.2 is inapplicable.

Second, the plan has some *discretion in the choice of the basis for reimbursing the providers*; if it is a staff model HMO, for example, that employs physicians, it might offer them a salary and various performance bonuses if the physician group keeps utilization below a certain target. In the former unintegrated system, the principal tool for managing moral hazard was demand-side cost sharing. In an integrated system, however, it is possible for the plan to write a contract with the provider that leaves the *provider* partially or even fully at risk for additional utilization. The literature terms this supply-side cost sharing (Ellis and McGuire 1986, 1993), a concept I address more formally in chapter 3.

Supply-side cost sharing has two potential advantages over demand-side cost sharing. First, the trade-off between risk aversion and moral hazard may be more favorable on the supply side. The supplier will generally be able to tolerate more risk than the patient because the financial risk from random variation in the cost of any individual's care can be averaged across all the provider's patients, and the resulting variation in the mean may not be large relative to the total revenues of the practice. Second, and of greater importance in this book's context, providers may be better able to control cost and moral hazard. Particularly for inpatient care, providers are the dominant decision makers.[21]

Nonetheless, demand- and supply-side cost sharing are not perfect substitutes. The RAND Health Insurance Experiment found that demand-side cost sharing primarily affects patients' willingness to initiate treatment or the number of episodes of care (Newhouse and the Insurance Experiment Group 1993, chap. 4). Once under a physician's care, demand-side cost sharing has only a modest effect on the average amount spent to treat a given episode. Although the evidence on the effect of supply-side cost sharing is much sparser, it is plausible that the effects would be the opposite of demand-side cost sharing; one would expect supply-side cost sharing to affect primarily the amount spent on an episode of treatment and not the patient's willingness to seek treatment in the first place.

Demand-side cost sharing can also reinforce supply-side cost sharing. Consider, for example, the recent introduction in the United States of so-called three-tier formularies, which vary the prices of prescription medications to patients.[22] Patients prescribed generic drugs have the lowest copayment; a typical amount would be $5 to $10 for a month's supply. Patients prescribed brand-name drugs that are on the formulary may pay a somewhat higher amount, perhaps $10 to $20. Brand-name drugs not on the formulary may cost $25 or even $50 for a month's supply. At the same time, the physician may have financial incentives that tie physician reimbursement to the cost of the drugs she prescribes. Differential patient payments make the patient more willing to accept the physician's recommendation for a generic drug or a brand-name drug that is on the formulary.

Third, the plan can use *command-and-control methods*, generally referred to as utilization review, to reduce low-valued utilization.[23] It could, for example, say that it would not cover a specific hospital admission because it did not think the patient needed to be hospitalized for that condition. This specificity of coverage was not found with indemnity insurance, with the result that a strikingly high percentage of admissions and an even higher percentage of hospital-days in the RAND experiment, around 20 to 25 percent, were found to be unnecessary conditional on what was done for the patient (Newhouse and the Insurance Experiment Group 1993, chap. 5). Similarly, rates of "inappropriate" procedures in the unmanaged traditional Medicare program have been found to be as high as one-sixth to one-third (Chassin, Kosecoff, Park et al. 1987).[24] Consistent with this finding and with the spread of command-and-control methods in the 1980s (along with greater demand-side cost sharing), discharges from American hospitals fell 12.6 percent from 1980 to 1997 (table 2.4). Because the population grew 17.7 percent over this interval, the fall in discharges per person was over 25 percent. And this was in the face of an aging population.[25]

And there is other evidence that these tools are effective. Part of the sample in the RAND Health Insurance Experiment, described earlier, was randomly assigned to a staff model HMO. Among the group assigned to the HMO, hospitalization rates were 39 percent less than under indemnity insurance (neither group faced any demand-side cost sharing). Outpatient use was about the same in the two groups.[26] Imputing fee-for-service prices to both inpatient and outpatient utilization yielded an estimated 25 percent saving in expenditure. Moreover, as was the case with demand-side cost sharing, these reductions in utilization did not appear to affect the health of the average person (Newhouse and the Insurance Experi-

Table 2.4
Admission Rates and Hospital Days, 1980–1997, All Patients, U.S. Community Hospitals

Year	Beds (thousands)	Admissions (thousands)
1980	988	36,143
1981	1,003	36,438
1982	1,012	36,379
1983	1,018	36,152
1984	1,017	35,155
1985	1,001	33,449
1986	978	32,379
1987	958	31,601
1988	947	31,453
1989	933	31,116
1990	927	31,181
1991	924	31,064
1992	921	31,034
1993	919	30,748
1994	902	30,718
1995	873	30,945
1996	862	31,099
1997	853	31,577

Source: AHA, *Hospital Statistics*, 1999.
Note: Data for U.S. registered community hospitals (nonfederal, short-term general, and other special hospitals).

ment Group 1993, chaps. 8, 9). Additional data from observational studies are reviewed in Miller and Luft (1994, 1997).

Managed care plans may also use techniques that combine aspects of command-and-control methods with financial incentives. A plan may, for example, specify a protocol or guidelines for how a particular disease should be treated and reward physicians who are in greater compliance with its guidelines.

In addition to the potentially better control of moral hazard and reductions in rents, integrating the delivery of services and the insurance functions, whether through an integrated firm or by contract, offers at least two other potential advantages. The first is *possible improvement in quality*. Although there has long been rhetoric in the United States about having access to the best medical care in the world (less is made of the fact that it is also the most expensive, at least by spokespersons for the medical profession), in fact there is evidence of much substandard care. This manifests itself in several ways. First, as just noted, a group under Robert Brook at RAND has documented large absolute amounts of what they term "inappropriate" care in both the United States and elsewhere (Chassin, Kosecoff, Park et al. 1987; Brook and McGlynn 1991; Brook 1993; Leape 1994; Leape, Bates, Cullen et al. 1995). Bates, Leape, Cullen et al. (1998) and Bates (2000) have shown that computerized entry of drugs can reduce in-hospital medication errors by more than 50 percent. Weiler, Hiatt, Newhouse et al. (1991) found in a sample of charts from New York State in 1984 that 4 percent of hospital admissions had an injury caused by medical treatment that resulted in death, disability that lasted beyond the hospital stay, or that prolonged the stay.[27] A quarter of these injuries were judged negligent, meaning they resulted from substandard care. One can, of course, ask what the optimal amount of injury prevention is or whether the marginal benefit of further reduction would fall short of the marginal cost. This was not addressed in the Weiler, Hiatt, Newhouse et al. study, but the absolute amount of injury and the consequences flowing from it make it plausible that the benefits of quality improvement outweigh its costs.

Indeed, it was easy in the fragmented system to blame an error on the individual physician or nurse without asking what mechanism might have prevented the error in the first place or how its consequences might have been ameliorated. For example, prior to the 1980s oxygen flow to anesthetized patients was sometimes impaired, often with disastrous consequences. The anesthesiologist might rationalize this as an occasional lapse of concentration, much as a driver might rationalize carelessness in failing to look carefully when backing out of a parking place. But a systemic study of injuries under anesthesia suggested that impaired flows of oxygen could be virtually eliminated if the flow was monitored mechanically and a bell rang when the flow fell.[28] An integrated system facilitates this type of study, whereas the earlier, fragmented system did not.

Lack of coordination among providers has also traditionally impaired quality, and in principle an integrated system could also help here. The treatment of complex illnesses often requires the services of many types of specialists; these specialists sometimes were ignorant of what drugs or other treatments one another might be ordering; for example, one specialist might order a drug that would adversely interact with a different drug that another specialist had ordered. Or the results of tests that one physician ran might not be immediately available to a second physician, so the second physician repeated the test. Or if a patient were discharged from one facility and admitted to another, for example from a hospital to a nursing home, providers at the receiving facility might not know what treatment plan those at the discharging facility had in mind. If a patient were discharged to home, monitoring was frequently poor. In principle, an integrated delivery system should facilitate information flow among various providers.

The market, of course, had developed mechanisms for addressing the issues of quality, especially reputation effects and agency. Reputation effects of providers for quality, especially physicians, have always been and surely will remain important, but it was often difficult for a layman to judge quality, especially the technical aspects of care. In principle, plans can and almost certainly do develop reputations, but the decrease in exclusive contracting between physicians and plans reduces the benefits of plan reputations.

A second potential advantage of integration is *improved efforts at prevention*. Physicians were traditionally trained to treat illness, and typically spent relatively little time counseling patients, in part because counseling was relatively poorly rewarded. But if a health plan is at risk for medical spending and if it expects the enrollee to remain enrolled, it has an obvious incentive to prevent illness. For example, one prominent cause of spending among the elderly is falls that result in hip fractures. Falls often occur in bathtubs, and relatively inexpensive nonslip bathmats can help prevent them. Assume for the sake of argument that such bathmats are cost-effective. It would have been almost unthinkable in an unintegrated system that a nurse or other provider would inspect the patient's home, and, if she lacked a bathmat, give her one. Indeed, there was no direct financial incentive to do so; if anything, the financial incentives militated against such an action. Yet it clearly could be efficient for an integrated plan to do so. In chapter 5 I explore this more formally.

In the RAND Health Insurance Experiment, 34 percent more preventive visits per person at the HMO occurred than in the fee-for-service system (Newhouse and the Insurance Experiment Group 1993, chap. 8). Despite this finding from the RAND experiment, the evidence that integrated health plans actually carry out more preventive activities than unintegrated plans is very thin. I comment in chapter 5 on why this may be so.

Agency and the Rise of For-Profit Entities

In addition to the greater integration of financing and delivery, American medical care has been characterized in recent years by a growth of for-profit relative to not-for-profit providers. This is true of integrated plans, where there have been well-publicized conversions of not-for-profit Blue Cross plans to for-profit plans, and it is true as well for home health agencies and skilled nursing facilities. The increase in for-profit firms has raised concern in several quarters (Cutler 2000; Institute of Medicine 1986; Kuttner 1996).

Furthermore, physicians have been selling their practices to integrated health care providers, often based in hospitals. Both these sales and the increase in for-profit firms raise the concern of whether the ability of the physician to act as the patient's agent (physician agency) has declined. For centuries physicians have taken the Hippocratic Oath to act in the best interests of their patients, meaning that they should be faithful to their principals, the patients. In the economics literature stemming back at least to Arrow's seminal article in 1963, provider agency has been seen as a device for overcoming patient ignorance. Nonetheless, it has only been in more recent years that agency has been incorporated into formal behavioral models of provider and plan behavior. I am now ready to take up more formally the issue of managing moral hazard and possible stinting in integrated health plans, which is the subject of chapter 3.

The Management of
Moral Hazard and
Stinting: Demand- and
Supply-Side Prices

Moral hazard classically refers to the weakened patient incentive to take measures to protect against, or reduce the probability of, an insured event. A textbook example is a homeowner, having insured his house against loss from fire, being less vigilant about keeping brush away from his house. In the health insurance context, however, moral hazard has come to connote consumption of a larger than optimal quantity or quality of services because of the demand-side subsidy from health insurance. What is the optimal quantity and quality of services? This question must be answered in order to define either moral hazard or stinting (a smaller-than-optimal quantity of services), and economists tend to answer it differently than clinicians do.

To most *clinicians* the optimal level of services is where the (expected) marginal product of additional services is zero or near zero. Clinicians are in fact trained to do everything possible to aid the patient. The cost of the services is traditionally not to be considered.[1] (For the moment, in contrasting the clinician with the economist I will ignore the private financial incentives facing clinicians.)

By contrast, an *economist* defines the optimal level of services to be where the value of the marginal service to the consumer equals its marginal cost, as shown in figure 2.1. In a competitive world the marginal cost reflects the value of the resources in their next best use; hence, the resources used to produce any service whose value is less than its marginal cost should be redeployed elsewhere. As a result, the economist's optimum level of medical services will generally be a lesser quantity or quality than the clinician's, so that a clinician may find underservice where an economist would not. Operationalizing the economist's optimum, of course, is extremely difficult because of difficulties in measuring marginal cost, much less the value of the marginal service. For now, however, I wish to set such measurement problems aside, although they clearly define what is feasible in practice.

I also set aside that in practice monopolistic competition, not perfect competition, is a more plausible description of the physician market (McGuire 2000). In some instances this may be an important limitation of the analysis, since monopolistic competition models imply that the physician sets quantities and therefore the patient will generally not be on a demand curve.[2] The welfare economics of a monopolistically competitive model, however, have not been addressed, and I do not address them here. The lack of realism from assuming competition is a matter of degree, however. As the number of competitors rises in a monopolistic competition model, results will tend toward those of a purely competitive model, and in most urban areas there are dozens, if not hundreds of physicians of a given specialty.

Demand-Side Moral Hazard

For an economist with no prior exposure to health care, the mere existence of the subsidy from health insurance is (almost) a sufficient condition to infer the existence of moral hazard or overservice.[3] Consider for simplicity a fully insured and informed patient who could choose from many physicians. That patient would demand all services with an expected positive value, the clinician's traditional definition of the optimal amount. If any physician failed to supply what the patient demanded, this informed patient would simply go to another physician. For the general economist who infers moral hazard in this fashion, the physician is merely the passive supplier of services to meet the consumer's demand. The assumptions of perfect competition and full patient information in the physician market are sufficient to bring about this outcome.

This is classic moral hazard (Pauly 1968), and it implies that the marginal unit of service is little valued by the consumer. In a standard market, one would describe the area bounded by the triangle DEF in figure 2.1 as deadweight loss.

In the case of health care, however, the usual measure might considerably overstate the deadweight loss. First, the marginal valuation curve is drawn on the assumption that the expenditures in question are small relative to income so that one can assume approximately constant marginal utility of income as price varies. For sufficiently large expenditures this will not be the case, and indeed the purpose of insurance is precisely to shift dollars to certain sick states so as to equalize the marginal utility of income across states (de Meza 1983). For example, one should not treat the additional spending on dialysis by an insured patient whose kidneys have failed relative to the spending by an uninsured patient entirely as a deadweight loss, because the costs for the uninsured patient may simply lie outside the budget constraint (Nyman 1999). In other words, for the insured patient the income effect from the resources transferred to the unhealthy state has shifted the demand curve; the additional spending does not simply reflect movement along a demand curve.

Second, and related to the first point, there are gains from risk aversion, as pointed out previously (Zeckhauser 1970). Third, the figure is drawn on the assumption that others do not value consumption of services by the individual; to the degree that others are willing to pay, the demand curve should shift upward, reducing the deadweight loss (Culyer and Simpson 1980; Evans 1984).

Although these qualifications reduce the deadweight loss shown in the simple diagram, they almost certainly do not eliminate it in the many cases in which income effects are small. As I pointed out, in all countries where measurements have been made, nontrivial quantities of services with zero or near zero value seem to be delivered, and the RAND experiment found little or no effect on health for the average person from a substantial variation in the use of services induced by varying cost sharing (Newhouse and the Insurance Experiment Group 1993, chaps. 6, 7). If there is no effect on health, others' willingness-to-pay may not be large. Moreover, the RAND group found that gains from risk aversion were small relative to moral hazard if there was a stop-loss provision in the policy (Newhouse and the Insurance Experiment Group 1993, chap. 4).

Supply-Side Moral Hazard

Despite the evidence that patients receive many services of little value, which appears consistent with the demand-side moral hazard story shown in figure 2.1, the theory behind figure 2.1 requires the assumptions of an informed patient and a competitive provider market. These assumptions are very strong in this context. Physicians do not think of themselves as passive suppliers of services, and with good reason. As Arrow pointed out in 1963, the service that the patient is buying from the physician is often information about the cause of her problem and the alternatives for treatment. As already described, in the fee-for-service system with fees above marginal cost, the physician's incentives are to deliver at least as many services as would a passive supplier. Moreover, given the patient's lack of information, the physician may be able to act on these incentives and deliver more services than an informed patient would have liked. This is moral hazard on the supplier side—namely, a response to the incentives offered by the supply prices in the insurance contract.

By contrast with the usual fee-for-service system, if fees are less than marginal cost—a capitation payment is the limiting case—the physician has an incentive to deliver fewer services than an informed patient would like, a phenomenon I term stinting.[4] Thus, unlike demand-side moral hazard, supply-side moral hazard can cause either too many or too few services.

If the patient is informed and the market for physician services is competitive, stinting would not be observed because the consumer can enforce his or her demands by threatening to use another supplier if there is any underservice. A hairdresser or barber may want to stint on the quality of the haircut, by taking less time for example, but since the consumer can readily observe the product, such a hairdresser is likely to soon be out of business. In medicine, however, consumers may not be well enough informed to prevent stinting if the supplier's incentives favor it. If so, the physician can be assumed to set both quantity and quality.

Stinting and moral hazard are usually modeled as affecting the quantity of services, but clearly they can affect quality as well.[5] If quality and quantity are both observable, the distinction between them is not important theoretically because one can always define a different quality as a different good. In what follows, however, I shall emphasize that some aspects of quality are not measurable or contractible, in which case the distinction between quantity and quality will matter.

If the physician is paid a capitation amount independent of the services delivered, for example, what are the incentives not to stint or underserve? On the nonfinancial side are medical ethics, which I discuss shortly. The financial incentive not to stint, however, stems from the possibility of discovery and consequent negative effects on reputation and future demand (Darby and Karni 1973; Dranove and White 1987). As a result, before devoting effort to issues of supply-price incentives, as well as nonfinancial incentives such as physician ethics, one must establish that demand incentives are not likely to be sufficient to lead to near optimal outcomes, that is, not sufficient to render supply-side moral hazard negligible.[6]

Demand, Consumer Information, and Quality

To the degree patients or consumers are well informed and can assess quality, issues of stinting are less important, as already pointed out. In the limiting case, as Mark Pauly (1980) noted several years ago, when patients are perfectly informed and can choose among competitive providers, reimbursement methods, whether fee-for-service or capitation, make no difference in outcomes, in which case there would be little point in the reader's continuing further in this chapter. In fact, several models in the economics literature focus on patient or demand-side incentives for reaching optimal quality (Allen and Gertler 1991; Dranove and Satterthwaite 1992; Glazer and McGuire 1994; Hodgkin and McGuire 1994; Ma 1994).

Many economists, however, and virtually all non-economists start from the presumption that consumer or patient information is poor.[7] Indeed, for precisely that reason several jurisdictions have actively pursued initiatives to improve consumer information (Eddy 1998). Might more resources devoted to such efforts suffice to reduce over- or underprovision to de minimis levels?

The most prominent American efforts to improve information have been in the states of New York and Pennsylvania, where attempts have been made to publicize mortality rates for cardiac surgeons. In New York there appear to have been positive results, because after the information was published, in-hospital mortality rates fell 21 percent from 1989 to 1992 (Hannan et al. 1990, 1994; Chassin, Hannan, and DeBuono 1996).[8] Risk-adjusted mortality rates fell even more, 41 percent.

Although not fatal to the notion that empowering the demand side makes supplier incentives uninteresting, it is somewhat disquieting that the New York result did not appear to stem from patients shifting from high- to low-mortality hospitals or toward high quality surgeons, but rather from improvement efforts at all hospitals, especially

poorly performing hospitals. Consistent with the lack of patient reaction in New York, few Pennsylvania patients knew about the effort
there, and few referring physicians used the data (Epstein 1998;
Schneider and Epstein 1996, 1998). These results cast some doubt on
the degree to which the market can be perfected through a strategy
of improved consumer information.

Indeed, there are doubters even about the favorable New York result. A nontrivial part of the estimated effect on risk-adjusted mortality stemmed from similar patients' being coded as having more
severe illnesses after the rating system went into effect (Green and
Wintfeld 1995). Nonetheless, the fall in the raw mortality rate would
be unaffected by any changes in coding. Others argue that the fall
can be attributed to surgeons' accepting better risks in order to lower
their observed mortality rates (Dranove et al. 2000), but in fact the
number of high risks undergoing surgery increased 73 percent.[9] Raw
mortality rates would also have fallen if the effort to publicize results
led some surgeons to refer some difficult patients out of state, but it
is not plausible that such behavior could account for a 21 percent fall
in the raw statewide mortality rate.

Even accepting that New York had a good result from publicizing
mortality rates by surgeons, it is not clear how much this result can
generalize past the surgery example. Surgery is typically a discrete
event with a few relevant and relatively easily assessed outcomes,
such as operative mortality and wound infection rates. It is more
difficult to measure outcomes for chronic diseases that are being
managed medically such as congestive heart failure.

Moreover, because it is virtually impossible for a third party to
measure well all the relevant dimensions of a hospital's or a physician's quality, publicity about only a few dimensions, such as cardiac surgery, runs the risk that resources will be allocated toward
those dimensions and away from unmeasured dimensions. For example, it is easier to measure quality of care for acute myocardial
infarction (heart attack) than many other diagnoses; as a result, if a
hospital's reputation is based on outcomes for heart attack patients,
hospitals may shift resources toward the care of acute myocardial
infarction.[10] The economics literature refers to this as the multitasking problem (Holmstrom and Milgrom 1990; Baker 1992; Hofer
et al. 1999).

Even without the multitasking problem, however, it would be
misguided to rely principally on reputation effects to assure quality.

Although reputation effects are doubtlessly important, both theoretical and empirical arguments suggest that they will not suffice to bring us close enough to an optimum to dismiss supply-side moral hazard.

Theoretically, although patients undoubtedly respond to certain aspects of care, such as interpersonal manner and waiting time, patients will not readily observe many other features of care that affect outcome. In particular, it will not be easy for a patient to distinguish whether a bad outcome was attributable to the quality of care received or to the underlying disease. Indeed, it is sometimes difficult for physicians to determine this; there are physician-experts on the opposite sides of every malpractice case who disagree on precisely this point. Moreover, in many instances the patient may have little choice of provider; for example, only one hospital may be nearby.

Beyond these theoretical arguments, three types of evidence suggest that the financial consequences of a diminished reputation would not suffice to allay concerns about stinting or underservice if there were nontrivial financial gains from doing so. The first has already been mentioned; there appeared to be no movement of patients toward hospitals with better cardiac surgery results in either New York or Pennsylvania. Instead, physicians and hospitals, whether for professional and ethical reasons or from fear of litigation or future patient shifting, improved performance across the board.

A second piece of evidence comes from studies of medical malpractice. Medical malpractice—meaning the physician's care fell below a professional standard and thereby resulted in damage to the patient—is the extreme end of poor quality care. As a result, it should be the area where the patient has the best chance of detecting poor technical quality of care, and, because the health consequences are often severe, where a physician could suffer most from reputation effects.

How much a successful malpractice claim or lawsuit against a physician diminishes future business is not known. But the data from a New York state study of medical malpractice suggest that this apparent signal of malfeasance comes with a great deal of noise. Specifically, only *1 to 2 percent* of the hospital admissions in which malpractice occurred resulted in a claim against the physician (Weiler, Hiatt, Newhouse et al. 1991). This low rate of claims suggests that patients are not good at detecting the most readily detectable form of poor quality. Consistent with the poor ability of consumers to assess quality, over half the claims of malpractice that were actually brought were in cases with no evidence of malpractice in the medical record. Thus, even the rate of claims against a physician has little association with the frequency of poor quality care.[11]

Malpractice claims might nonetheless provide some signal of quality if the court system effectively winnowed out the many claims in which there was no malpractice. But damages appear more related to the fact of disability than to negligence (Brennan, Sox, and Burstin 1996). In short, measuring quality by observing the signal of a malpractice claim, even a successful malpractice claim, is a highly error-prone process.[12] One can infer that if consumers or patients have difficulty monitoring the extreme end of poor-quality care and if reimbursement to the physician favors stinting, a substantial burden will fall on medical ethics and peer monitoring if stinting is to be at negligible levels.

A perhaps less compelling third piece of evidence comes from the RAND Health Insurance Experiment. In that experiment, patients faced varying out-of-pocket payments for care but physicians were paid similarly irrespective of the patient's insurance arrangements (in general, physicians were paid their billed fees). Patients in plans with different degrees of cost sharing differed substantially in the rate at which they sought care (i.e., initiated treated episodes), but the size of the treated episodes varied little (Newhouse and the Insurance Experiment Group 1993, chap. 4).[13] In other words, conditional upon seeking care, the demand curve shown in figure 2.1 appears to be little affected by price, at least over the variation in price in the RAND experiment. If the demand of informed patients were approximately as sensitive to variation in the number of services conditional on seeing a physician as to variation in their decision to obtain care, one should not have observed this.[14] In short, the experimental data accord with the common sense view that patients make the decision to seek care in the first place and thereafter to a great extent place themselves in the hands of their physicians, in which case the incentives the physician faces matter a great deal.

Before coming to the incentives of the physician, however, several caveats need to be made to the assertion that consumers, once having decided to seek care, are mainly at the mercy of the physician because of their inability to monitor quality:

1. A rational patient in deciding to seek care will anticipate what will happen subsequently, in which case the decision to seek care is not independent of what the patient thinks the physician will do. For example, if the patient has doubts about the physician's competence, she may seek care elsewhere or not seek care at all.

2. Patients often have some knowledge, so that the diagnosis and course of treatment is not entirely under the control of the physician. For example, it may be self-evident to the patient what ails her (e.g., she has a rash), or the patient may know from previous experience that a particular prescription drug will cure her problem.

3. Patients may be aware of alternative treatments given a diagnosis, or physicians may offer them treatment options. For example, patients may know that certain cancer chemotherapies could prolong their life but at a reduced quality level. The physician may simply explain treatment options without making a recommendation, but even if she makes a recommendation, the patient may elect another course of action. And patients in many instances do not comply with drugs or other treatment regimens that physicians prescribe.[15] Furthermore, the Internet is undoubtedly increasing patient information (though it is probably increasing misinformation as well).

In short, to suggest that the quantity and quality of treatment is solely a function of physician incentives once the patient has sought care surely oversimplifies the issue. Nonetheless, in sorting out incentive effects, it seems both useful and consistent with the evidence to think of financial and nonfinancial incentives directed at the patient—demand prices—as primarily affecting the decision to seek care and those directed at the physician—supply prices—as affecting primarily the course of treatment once the patient has sought care.

Consequently, I do not rely on the usual market incentive that patients will punish poor quality providers by not patronizing them, thereby making supply-side incentives irrelevant. Rather, I assume that patient actions may help shift services toward higher-quality providers, but that any such actions by themselves are insufficient to obtain the outcome that would be observed if all patients had good information about provider quality. Such was Kenneth Arrow's (1963) assumption as well.

Even if consumers are not sufficiently informed to monitor quality of care or outcomes, might health plans and other payers be? Health plans, for example, could pay more for higher-quality care. At the end of chapter 6 I take up several problems that a health plan faces in doing so. I believe that basing payment on measures of quality of care or possibly outcomes is an important avenue to explore, but payment on quality and outcomes is little used anywhere in the world, suggesting the problems in doing so may be large.

I now turn to the price incentives facing physicians and other providers that do not arise from patients' efforts to avoid low-quality providers. These incentives, which arise most often out of administered price systems, will not necessarily be optimal—and frequently may be far from optimal.

The Theory of Stinting: Ellis and McGuire

The economic theory of stinting is well illustrated in a model that was first put forward by Ellis and McGuire (1986, 1990). This model also shows how physician ethics potentially constrain stinting. In the Ellis-McGuire model, the context for which is the Medicare PPS described in chapter 1, the hospital is paid a lump sum per admission. The physician, however, controls the care the patient receives, and the physician is an agent for two principals, the hospital and the patient. In their 1986 formulation of the model, which I describe here, Ellis and McGuire assume that the patient is fully insured; thus, there is no role for demand-side cost sharing. Moreover, the patient is passive and simply accepts the decisions of the physician.[16] Although the setting for the Ellis-McGuire model is a physician treating patients in a hospital, the same model can be applied to a physician's contracting with a health plan to care for a patient, as I show in chapter 5.

The setup of the Ellis-McGuire model and its main results are as follows. The patient has a total benefit function $B(q)$, where q is quantity of hospital services, and a marginal benefit function $b(q)$. $b(q)$ can be negative because of iatrogenesis or medically induced illness. To keep matters simple, $B(q)$ measures full social benefit; thus, there are no externalities.

The profit to the hospital, denoted π, is revenue less cost, or

$$\pi(q) = R(q) - C(q). \tag{3.1}$$

If the context were physician instead of hospital services, of course, $\pi(q)$ would be the net income of the physician and $C(q)$ would include the cost of effort.

Physicians, who make the resource allocation decisions, all have utility functions $U(\pi(q), B(q))$.[17] Because the benefit to the patient, B, is an argument in the physician's utility function, agency on behalf of the patient is formally a part of the model. Define a parameter α that equals the rate at which the physician is willing to trade off a dollar of benefit (profit) to the hospital for a dollar of benefit for the patient.[18] In other words, α defines the degree to which the physician takes the patient's interests into account, and it is presumptively shaped by medical ethics.

One might ask why a physician should care about benefits to the hospital. Although not part of the Ellis-McGuire model, it is not hard to imagine how a hospital might be able to share profits with physicians, for example, by purchasing equipment so that the physician can undertake new and profitable procedures or providing funds for travel to conferences.

The parameter α, or the degree to which the physician is motivated by financial reward in ways that are not totally congruent with the patient's interest, may at first not seem to be a policy instrument. But further thought shows that several policy debates turn on this issue. For example, American physicians often leave medical school with debts of $100,000 or more. Although one study suggests such debt does not affect specialty choice (Bazzoli 1985), contrary to much anecdotal evidence, the degree of debt may affect the marginal utility of income to the physician—namely, affect the size of the agency parameter.

Extending such a model to other providers leads to the crux of the debate between those who wish to minimize the involvement of for-profit firms in medical care and those who see little difference between for-profit and not-for-profit firms. In terms of the Ellis and McGuire model, the disagreement could be characterized as whether α materially differs between the two types of organizations.[19] Of course, it may well matter what organization one has in mind. For example, the difference in α between not-for-profit and for-profit hospitals may differ from that between for-profit and not-for profit health plans or home health agencies. And α may differ between a firm or provider with some market power and firms in reasonably competitive markets. Sloan (2000), for example, suggests that for-profit and not-for-profit hospitals that compete with each other have few measurable differences.

Returning to the Ellis-McGuire model, under cost-based reimbursement, revenues equal cost by definition, so

$$\pi = R(q) - C(q) \equiv 0; \text{hence}, d\pi/dq = 0.$$

Since $d\pi/dq$ always equals zero, a physician treating a fully insured patient will, by the first-order condition shown in equation (3.2), always behave so as to make $dB/dq = 0$; that is, the physician will carry out all procedures that have any expected positive benefit, irrespective of cost. Thus, under cost-based reimbursement there are too many resources in hospital production relative to a socially efficient point. Although observationally equivalent to demand-side moral hazard, this results from supply-side moral hazard.

Consider now prospective payment. Assume first full prospective payment with revenue fixed at a; hence $R(q) = a$. In this case,

$$\pi = a - C(q). \tag{3.4}$$

In the general case, one can use this expression to show that at an optimum $\alpha b(q)$ equals marginal cost.[20] In the simpler case in which marginal cost is constant, one can write:

$$\alpha b = c. \tag{3.5}$$

Suppose $\alpha = 1$, or that, from a social efficiency perspective, agency is perfect. Note that at this socially efficient point the physician will not be acting as the "perfect" agent from the individual patient's point of view because the insured patient will want more services than he is getting, reflecting the inefficiency attributable to moral hazard.[21] Thus, this definition uses an economist's definition of an optimal amount of services, not a physician's.

When $\alpha = 1$, then from (3.5) at an optimum $b = c$, or the marginal benefit to the patient equals the marginal cost to the hospital. If the payer sets payments so as to cover a supplier's costs, as Medicare did for hospitals prior to the PPS, then hospitals will initially make profits from the implementation of a PPS while they cut back the level of services. In principle, however, the payer can recoup these profits by subsequently lowering rates, assuming that it knows about the profits and that hospitals don't "bury" them in expenses that yield utility to the medical staff or to the hospital administration. This reduction in cost to a socially efficient level is what Ellis and McGuire characterize as "the promise of prospective payment."

The story of hospitals' reducing services, making profits, and the payer's subsequently cutting rates roughly squares with the American experience immediately following Medicare's introduction of the PPS. In the first year, 1984, length of stay fell markedly and hospital margins were at historically high levels (table 3.1). Subsequently, the increases or updates in hospital rates were modest, as the government made an effort to recoup the overpayments and margins were substantially lower. As Ellis and McGuire emphasize, however, this may have been a move to an economically more efficient point. In addition to the changes at the time of the introduction of the PPS and its immediate aftermath, table 3.1 also shows major changes in the 1990s, which seem attributable to unbundling of services in the hospital stay to the post-acute sector (see chapter 1).

Suppose now that agency is not perfect. If $\alpha < 1$, the physician gives too much weight to hospital profits relative to patient benefits.[22] Then, using (3.5), there will be too little benefit to the patient since b will be greater than c, or at the stopping point, the marginal benefit of more services to patients will exceed the services' marginal cost. This represents the economist's (and physician's) concern about stinting in a fully prospective system; physicians, however, might think of any reduction in services from the point where marginal benefits are zero as stinting, whereas an economist would not.

Ellis and McGuire then turn from a fully prospective to a mixed reimbursement system in which

$$R(q) = a + rC(q), \tag{3.6}$$

where a is a fixed payment as before, and $0 \le r \le 1$ represents the fraction of cost that is reimbursed. Note, however, that $C(q)$ could represent a fee schedule rather than the cost of production; what matters is that reimbursement increases with the quantity of services delivered. Total spending by the payer, however, can be constant as r changes because the fixed amount a can be lowered as r is increased to maintain the same total payment per case.

Although the reimbursement formula shown in equation (3.6) is a generalization of fixed payment (equation 3.4), it too is a special case because it is linear in $C(q)$. A still more general formula would be

Table 3.1
Length of Stay, Medicare Inpatient, Total Hospital Margins, and Update

Year	Length of stay (days)		Medicare inpatient margin (%)	Total margin (%)	Update factor (%)
	All patients	Medicare patients			
1981	7.2	10.4	a	not available	a
1982	7.2	10.2	a	not available	a
1983	7.0	9.8	a	not available	a
1984	6.7	8.9	13.4	7.3	a
1985	6.5	8.6	13.0	6.6	not available
1986	6.6	8.7	8.7	4.3	not available
1987	6.6	8.9	5.9	3.6	not available
1988	6.6	8.9	2.7	3.5	not available
1989	6.6	8.9	0.3	3.6	3.3
1990	6.6	8.8	−1.5	3.6	4.7
1991	6.5	8.6	−2.4	4.4	3.4
1992	6.4	8.4	−0.9	4.3	3.0
1993	6.2	8.0	1.3	4.4	2.7
1994	6.0	7.5	5.6	5.0	2.0
1995	5.7	7.0	11.1	5.8	2.0
1996	5.6	6.5	15.8	6.1	1.5
1997		6.2	17.0	6.0	2.0
1998		6.1	14.4	3.9	0.0

Sources: All patient length of stay: Prospective Payment Assessment Commission, "Medicare and the American Health Care System: Report to the Congress," June 1997, 89; Medicare length of stay through 1996: *Health Care Financing Review: Medicare and Medicaid Statistical Supplement, 1998,* 206; 1997 and 1998 calculated from Medicare Payment Advisory Commission, "Report to the Congress," June 2000, Table C.1. Margins to 1993: Medicare Payment Advisory Commission, "Report to the Congress: Medicare Payment Policy," March 1999, 53, 55. 1993 and later: Medicare Payment Advisory Commission, "Report to the Congress," June 2000, Tables C.3 and C.8. The Medicare inpatient margin is the ratio of Medicare revenue to the allocated cost of Medicare cases; the total margin is the ratio of hospital revenue from all payers to total hospital cost. Operating updates from Medicare Payment Advisory Commission, "Report to the Congress," June 2000, Table C.1.
a Not applicable.

nonlinear in C(q). Lest this remark be thought of as an academic nicety, the outlier feature of the Medicare PPS described in chapter 1 is in fact a nonlinear reimbursement system. Because of their analytic tractability, however, the theoretical literature generally works with linear payment systems. Moreover, as pointed out in chapter 1, the element of additional reimbursement for performing certain procedures in the actual PPS means that the effective r in that system is on the order of 0.5 and that in practice the PPS is a mixed system.

Returning to the theoretical level, suppose the physician is an imperfect agent for the patient ($\alpha < 1$). In that case, Ellis and McGuire show that a mixed system such as that shown in equation (3.6) will induce the socially efficient level of services. Recall that α shows the physician's "tilt" toward patient benefit and away from hospital profit. That is, the further α decreases toward zero, the greater the weight the physician places on hospital profit and the lower the weight on patient benefit. The intuition of the Ellis-McGuire result is that the regulator can offset the physician's increased weight on hospital profit by increasing the proportion of reimbursed cost r (and decreasing a to keep total payment constant) to make the provision of additional services more profitable. In the case in which marginal cost is constant, r should equal $(1 - \alpha)$.[23]

The Ellis-McGuire papers (1986, 1990) have proved very important in the subsequent literature. Numerous models have built upon and extended their notion of an objective function that includes both benefits to patients and profits to hospitals.[24] One such effort is by Malcolm Chalkley and James Malcolmson (1998; see also Chalkley and Malcolmson 2000), who extend Ellis and McGuire's results to consider quality as well as quantity.

The Theory of Stinting: Chalkley and Malcolmson

Chalkley and Malcolmson (1998, 2000) take up the problem of a purchaser—either a public purchaser, such as the American Medicare program or a British local health authority, or a private purchaser such as an employer buying coalition—that contracts with a hospital to provide service to its beneficiaries. Ellis and McGuire measured services only by their quantity, but Chalkley and Malcolmson distinguish the quantity and quality of services because they assume quantity is observable by the purchaser and hence contractible, whereas quality is not.[25] As a result, the purchaser cannot contract for quality because a third party or a court cannot determine if the contract has been properly carried out.[26]

Even if a third party cannot contract for quality, a consumer or patient can observe some aspects of it and potentially seek care from higher-quality hospitals. Nonetheless, following Arrow (1963) and my previous assumption, Chalkley and Malcolmson assume the consumer is imperfectly informed about quality. As a result, the purchaser cannot rely on consumers to demand services from the highest quality provider and thus leave it to the market to police quality.

Total costs paid by the purchaser, however, are a function of the observed quantity and the unobserved quality, as well as the unobserved effort of the hospital to keep costs down, analogous to the models of the firm discussed in Laffont and Tirole 1993. When some elements of a service (quantity) are contractible and others are not, one has the multitasking problem discussed earlier in the context of paying only on some measures of quality. Achieving a first-best outcome is generally not possible.

The purchaser wants the hospital to serve the right number of patients, as well as offer the right quality, and make the right effort for cost reduction. The purchaser naturally wants costs low to minimize the deadweight loss from financing the necessary payments. For example, if the purchaser finances its payments through taxes, as Medicare does, taxpayers will inefficiently expend resources to avoid taxes.[27] The purchaser is assumed to wish to maximize net social welfare, that is, the benefit to patients plus the surplus if any at the hospital, less the deadweight loss of the taxes and premiums necessary to finance hospital payments. Because any surplus at the hospital must be paid for with taxes and premiums, the purchaser will attempt to keep the surplus at the minimum level necessary for the hospital to be willing to provide care. Given these assumptions, Chalkley and Malcolmson consider how the hospital's objective function affects the type of contract that the purchaser should offer the hospital.

Rather than reiterate here the mathematics of Chalkley-Malcolmson results, I simply state them and motivate their intuition. First they show that Ellis and McGuire's conclusion that the payer can simply adjust the cost sharing fraction r and obtain optimal results (i.e., get to the first-best) does not survive their more general assumptions. Unless the contract provides for full cost reimbursement, the hospital will generally provide too little quality. In other words, the hospital will stint on those aspects of service for which it is not paid and which are not observed. This result holds even if the hospital exhibits a degree of altruism or agency.

Full cost reimbursement, however, carries with it two drawbacks. A hospital will make too little effort to reduce cost because there is no reward for efforts to reduce cost. The resulting higher costs will mean more deadweight loss in financing hospital payments. Second, with cost reimbursement physicians and patients will maximize moral hazard from quality, as well as from quantity to the degree that quantity is not specified in the contract, which will further increase cost and hence the deadweight loss.

On the other hand, full cost reimbursement has the advantage of offering the hospital no incentive to select good risks, a phenomenon that Chalkley and Malcolmson do not consider and that I come to in chapters 4–6. Cost reimbursement thus trades off higher costs against both no (or less) stinting on quality and minimizing selection.

The advantages of cost reimbursement may explain why it was the method initially used by the American Medicare program to reimburse hospitals.[28] But, as explained in chapter 1, starting in October 1983 cost reimbursement gave way to the PPS in order to give Medicare greater control of costs.

Like Ellis and McGuire, who model the physician as valuing patient benefit, Chalkley and Malcolmson also emphasize the importance of agency, which they term the benevolence of the supplier. With agency explicitly in the hospital's objective function, they obtain a second result: If the supplier has a sufficient degree of agency or concern for the patient's welfare, it is in general better for the purchaser to move away from cost reimbursement.

Specifically, Chalkley and Malcolmson show that if the hospital's objective function is influenced in part by benefits to the patient (as assessed by the purchaser, however, not by the patient) and by the quality of services, the purchaser can do better than simply reimbursing costs if the purchaser writes a contract that mixes partial cost reimbursement with a fixed payment per patient. Moreover, the greater the altruism of the hospital, the more the purchaser should move away from cost reimbursement. The intuition is simple. Altruism reduces the hospital's willingness to stint on quality and patient benefit even if it is not reimbursed for the resulting costs. As a result, by moving away from full cost reimbursement, the purchaser can reduce the deadweight loss from financing the costs incurred under a cost reimbursement contract and still obtain the quality the purchaser seeks.

If altruism is sufficient, this conclusion from their model is consistent with the Congress's mandating in 1997 that Medicare move away from full cost reimbursement (subject to upper limits) for home health services, skilled nursing facilities, and hospital outpatient departments. But as noted in chapter 1, whereas the home health agencies serving the Medicare population were once entirely not-for-profit, a majority are now for-profit firms. Thus, the assumption of sufficient agency or altruism on the part of current home health agencies is problematic. Two-thirds of skilled nursing facilities also are for-profit.[29]

The fundamental reason the purchaser cannot achieve its aims in the Chalkley-Malcolmson model is that it has three goals: quantity of services, unobserved quality, and cost-reducing effort. To achieve those goals, however, it has only two instruments or bases for rewarding the hospital, the quantity of services and total cost, because that is all it observes.

Chalkley and Malcolmson proceed to derive results for the optimal contracting form, which depends upon the degree to which altruism enters the objective function of the hospital. I begin with the case in which the hospital is purely self-interested, that is, exhibits no altruism, as would customarily be assumed for a for-profit firm. In this case the purchaser can achieve the quantity of services it wishes, because it is observable, and also one of the other two goals, either the efficient level of quality or the efficient level of effort. Chalkley and Malcolmson assume that the unchosen third goal, either quality or effort, will be at the minimum enforceable level because the self-interested firm will either exert minimal cost reduction effort or provide minimal quality depending upon the nature of the contract.

For example, suppose the purchaser cares more about the level of effort the hospital devotes to efficient production than about the quality of care. Then the purchaser should write a contract of the form $pq + b$, where q is the (observed) number of units of quantity, p is the price paid per unit, which should equal marginal cost, and b is a constant, which is sufficient to make up for any loss if the hospital is paid marginal cost.[30] On the other hand, if the purchaser cares more about the quality of care than cost reduction effort, the purchaser should use a cost reimbursement contract. Effort being at the minimum enforceable level will then mean an upper limit on unit cost or total cost. In general, the intuition is that the self-interested hospital will not work to reduce cost unless it keeps the cost savings (which it does not under cost reimbursement), but if there is no element of cost reimbursement, it will not increase quality above the minimal level, since that increases cost without increasing revenue.

In the case of partial altruism or benevolence—probably a reasonable assumption for many not-for-profit hospitals not in competitive markets—the optimal contract includes an element of cost reimbursement, assuming that the verification of cost is not itself too costly.[31] The reasoning comes from an envelope theorem argument. In the reimbursement formula $pq + b$, the purchaser can increase b with the hospital's costs rather than keep it constant. Doing so will sacrifice some effort at cost reduction and thus increase the purchaser's cost, but it will also gain some quality, because the benevolent firm will use some of the increased revenue to increase quality. Because cost-reducing effort was optimized when b was a constant, however, a small move away from the optimum and the resulting increase in cost will be a second-order effect on social welfare. By contrast, the increase in quality from moving away from a contract in which b is a constant will result in a first-order effect on quality, because quality was far from its optimum.

Thus, Chalkley and Malcolmson reach the same conclusion as Ellis and McGuire from a considerably different setup. Under reasonably general assumptions, both conclude that an optimal contract will include an element of cost reimbursement.

Neither Chalkley and Malcolmson nor Ellis and McGuire, however, consider the alternative of a very detailed fee schedule rather than cost reimbursement. If sufficiently detailed, such a schedule may be an attractive alternative to cost reimbursement. It will reimburse for many services that, if not delivered when the hospital is paid a fixed, lump sum, might lower unobserved quality (e.g., a particular diagnostic test). Relative to pure cost reimbursement, however, it will preserve an incentive to produce each of those services efficiently. A seeming drawback of using a fee schedule is that the actual level of the administratively determined fees may approximate marginal cost to varying degrees and so may induce distortions; in particular, rents in the fees may induce overservice (see chapter 1). But cost reimbursement contracts typically have some sort of clause about reimbursing "reasonable" costs or have explicit limits (e.g., the contract will reimburse costs up to $X per day), so that in practice a cost- reimbursement contract may be similar to a fee schedule. Another drawback of fee schedules relative to literal cost reimbursement is that fee schedules will not reimburse for many costly actions that improve quality or outcomes because they will not be observable or contractible services.

To those familiar with the procurement literature in economics, these conclusions will have a familiar ring. They are similar to those of Laffont and Tirole (1993), who conclude that contracts should generally contain an element of cost sharing. Laffont and Tirole, however, came to their conclusion for a different reason; in their model the provider/supplier has better knowledge of cost than the purchaser. The one extreme of a full cost reimbursement contract does not offer the provider any incentive to reveal its true costs, whereas the other extreme of a fixed price contract will be excessively costly if set at a level that will keep all firms in business, which Laffont and Tirole assume is desired. In their model some element of cost sharing can improve matters for reasons similar to the envelope-theorem reasoning in the Chalkley-Malcolmson model. In the Chalkley-Malcolmson case, however, the role of cost sharing is not to reveal the hospital's cost but rather to give the hospital some incentive to increase either quality or cost-reducing effort above minimal levels.

The Chalkley-Malcolmson model also sheds light on an important institutional detail of American and Canadian medical organization, the split in decision making between physicians and hospital administration (Harris 1979; McClellan 1993). Suppose that physicians were to choose higher quality and less cost-reducing effort than hospital administrators would; this is, in fact, Chalkley and Malcolmson's characterization of Fuchs's (1974) technological imperative. Such an assumption works in the purchaser's favor in a world with a fixed budget and self-interested hospital administration, because physicians will push quality above the minimum enforceable quality. On the other hand, it works against the purchaser in a cost reimbursement world. This is a possible rationale for Medicare's leaving physician reimbursement outside the PPS and paying physicians through the much lower-powered method of the RBRVS; because physicians are generally paid more for doing more, they provide a check on the hospital's incentive to stint.

Empirical Evidence of Stinting

Although there is considerable fear of stinting among the American public—witness the political demand for patient protection legislation—there is remarkably little evidence that stinting has been a problem. In chapter 1, however, I cited considerable evidence that providers respond to variation in fees. In addition to the studies cited there, Decker (1993) showed that physicians adjust along a quality dimension to financial incentives. In the American Medicaid program, many states keep office visit (and other) fees below private market fees. Decker found that time spent by the physician in a Medicaid visit was reduced in a fashion to keep payment per minute more nearly equal to that of other payers. (Within certain limits, the Medicaid program simply pays an amount per visit, irrespective of the actual time spent.) Similarly, Weissman and Epstein (1989, 1993, 1994) found that Medicaid patients who were otherwise similar to commercial patients but for whom reimbursement was lower were less likely to receive certain procedures. For all hospital procedures the reduction was 6 percent, but for coronary angiography, bypass grafting, and angioplasty the reductions were from 33 to 60 percent.[32]

Moving from Medicaid fees to a capitated setting, one observes considerable evidence of fewer services being delivered in HMOs that are paid a capitated amount. In the RAND experiment the rate of hospital-days was 39 percent less in the HMO and the rate of imputed expenditure was 28 percent less (Newhouse and the Insurance Experiment Group 1993; see also Miller and Luft 1994).[33] The reduction in services did not appear to affect the health of the average person; nonetheless, it appears to have been a substantial response to financial incentives.

Changing from fee-for-service to managed care arrangements in mental health care has had dramatic effects on utilization (Huskamp 1999). Indeed, the demands of many American mental health advocates for "parity" in mental health benefits do not seem to recognize the importance of supply-price incentives. Once not all medically efficacious services are delivered, it is not clear that parity between mental health services and other medical care can be readily assessed.[34]

Reduced utilization, however, is not the same as stinting, especially since no systematic outcome effects have been observed between HMOs and fee-for-service medicine (Miller and Luft 1997).

There may be at least three reasons for the lack of observed outcome effects. First, all-inclusive capitation at the level of the individual physician is still rather rare, so that capitation at the level of the insurance plan may be considerably moderated by lower-powered incentives at the level of the provider.[35] Second, capitation may simply lead to services being at the minimum enforceable level, and the additional services in the fee-for-service system may have little or no effect on health status. Third, because of the historical predominance of the fee-for-service system and the resulting fear of overservicing, methods for detecting overservicing are much better developed than those for detecting underservicing (Kerr, Mittman, Hayes et al. 1996).

Finally, I remind the reader that this discussion of capitation and stinting is in the context of dimensions of care that are unobservable to the patient.[36] For dimensions that are observable, such as the time of the visit, capitation may lead to overservicing in two contexts: (1) competitive supply and rents in the capitated payment, as in the earlier discussion of supplementary benefits by Medicare health plans (table 1.7); (2) decisions to provide additional services that differentially attract low-risk patients, which I cover in chapter 6.

Stinting, Dispute Resolution, and Welfare Economics

The contracts consumers have with American health plans typically call for the provision of all "medically necessary services." The meaning of this term, of course, is open to interpretation, and American courts are currently struggling to reach an acceptable definition in cases in which disputes arise over what is medically necessary. Given the transactions costs of resolving disputes through the courts, it would be highly desirable if some kind of alternative dispute resolution mechanism could be found.[37] Events, however, seem to be moving in the other direction (Studdert and Brennan 2000).

Even more important from the point of view of efficiency, the ambiguity of the contract means that rationing in health plans may well occur in a way not envisioned in traditional welfare economics. In standard theory when the price of a good rises, consumers will stop purchasing the least-valued units, thereby minimizing their welfare loss. Although I assume in chapter 6 that health plans do ration in such a fashion, in fact there is typically no mechanism at the time of service for the patient to express how much he or she values the service. Instead the physician or other health care provider is choosing who is to receive what services in accordance with clinical criteria.

Physician ethics state that the patient's ability to pay for services should not affect whether he or she receives them. Even if physicians paid no attention to this ethical dictum, however, the inability of patients in managed care to reveal the intensity of their preferences through the usual market mechanisms suggests that physicians in fact ration on some basis other than willingness-to-pay or at least that if they attempt to ration on willingness-to-pay criteria they will make mistakes. For those who believe that services should be rationed according to clinical need and that clinical need is in fact how physicians ration, there is nothing amiss with such a situation (Hurley 2000; Williams and Cookson 2000).[38] But conventional welfare economics assumes rationing on the basis of willingness-to-pay (a demand price).

This means that, as conventionally measured, stinting or rationing of services may impose a greater welfare loss than might at first appear. In other words, there is no reason to think that supply-side measures to control moral hazard will reduce only those services for which marginal cost exceeds the marginal benefit. Moreover, the nature of the rationing probably depends upon the method of contracting; that remains for the future research agenda. But that rationing may occur among high-valued services underscores the importance of dispute resolution mechanisms and potentially of patient protection legislation. It also implies that the greater the denial of services valued above marginal cost, the more the optimal balance between supply-side cost sharing (or other rationing methods) and demand-side cost sharing should tilt toward the latter.

Provider Ethics, One-Class Care, and the Limits of the Market

Can Traditional Ethics Be Maintained?

Provider ethics favoring one-class medicine evolved at a time when medical services were not very expensive. A hundred years ago, treating all patients in the same fashion tended to mean that the physician should allocate her own time and perhaps dispense a few inexpensive nostrums without regard to income. But medical services now can be very expensive, and much of the expense is associated with nonphysician inputs, so that donations of physician time do not address the issue. This inevitably means that the higher-income groups in a society will have to pay for the lower-income groups if the latter are to receive certain medical services. Indeed, institutions to make the necessary resource transfers, whether through insurance or direct delivery mechanisms, are in place in every developed society.

The cost-increasing technological change in medicine, however, has meant that the price to higher-income groups of providing the class of care that they wish to have for themselves has steadily increased. Thus, even though national income has everywhere increased, one would expect that societies would adhere less to the principle of one-class care. In effect, altruism has its price. One measure of equity is the degree of equality in the receipt of medical services across income classes controlling for health status (Wagstaff and van Doorslaer 2000). On the basis of this criterion one would expect that medical services would have become less equally distributed in recent years, but I have not found data that test this proposition.

The Limits of Payment Incentives

Although this book focuses on optimal contracts and optimal payment incentives, there is clearly a limit to what payment incentives can accomplish. Inevitably many services that a patient values will not appear on even the most detailed fee schedule. For example, some of a physician's efforts to remain current with the literature or a home health aide's effort to be kind to the cognitively impaired or to terminally ill patients are not likely to be rewarded financially under any plausible fee schedule, except possibly through increased future demand.[39] Of course, standard forms of simple cost reimbursement will not reimburse such efforts either. Thus, if such services are to be attained through the market—and if patients either cannot judge whether in fact they are being delivered, as might be the case if the physician fails to keep up with the literature and thus recommends a suboptimal therapy, or if patients cannot readily change suppliers, as might be the case for the home health aide treating the cognitively impaired patient—one must rely on some combination of norms instilled in training and provider altruism. This underscores Arrow's (1963) emphasis on the importance of professional ethics. The imperfection of professional norms and provider altruism suggests why many services may be provided by family members or friends rather than through the market.

4   Selection and the Demand Side

For many years selection or cream skimming was a more popular subject with actuaries and health plan managers than with economists. This situation has changed dramatically in the past few decades.

In the health insurance context, selection often connotes effort by health plans to obtain good risks and exclude poor ones. In fact, however, selection can arise from efforts of plans, providers, consumers, or employers or other sponsors of health plan menus (including government), or all four. More formally, one can define selection as actions of economic agents on either side of the market to exploit unpriced risk heterogeneity and break pooling arrangements, with the result that some consumers may not obtain the efficient amount of insurance (Newhouse 1996b). In some models there is simply no market for insurance; in others consumers cannot obtain insurance at a price that reflects their actuarial risk plus a competitively determined loading fee, even though the insurance market is competitive. In this chapter I focus on consumer demand and its role in selection. That is, I treat the menu of plan characteristics (other than price) from which the consumer chooses as given and focus solely on the consumer's choice among plans.[1] In chapter 5 I turn to actions of plans, and in chapter 6 to actions of sponsors.

Some economics literature appears to treat the possibility of selection as theoretically possible but not likely in practice because it would only appear when prices are regulated and therefore not free to clear markets.[2] Implicit in this view is that were it not for such regulation, insurance would be priced at the level of the individual's expected risk plus any loading charge. Yet insurance markets with no regulation do not price at the level of the individual. For example, the plans I am eligible to elect as an employee of Harvard University all charge the same rate to any individual who enrolls in the plan.[3]

Neither Harvard nor any public agency forces the plans to price in this fashion.[4] And this manner of pricing is scarcely unique; rather, it is virtually universal in the American group insurance market. Although health plans almost always have one rate for individual subscribers and another for families, sometimes distinguishing families with and without children, it is uncommon in the American group health insurance market to distinguish further among subscribers, even using characteristics that are readily observable, such as the number of children or the age of household members. This failure to distinguish among individuals does not come from any regulatory constraint. To underscore that the issue is not a regulatory constraint, the individual health insurance market, which in fact is subject to much more regulation than the group market, uses substantially more information about individuals, including their initial health status, in setting a price.[5]

Pricing that is independent of an individual's disease state obviates the risk that one's premium may change when a chronic illness strikes. If, for example, premiums were rated on an individual basis, diabetics would surely pay more than nondiabetics, other things equal. But nondiabetics have some chance of becoming diabetic or having a diabetic child. If premiums were adjusted for expected spending, they would rise if one became diabetic, but then one could not insure the financial risk of becoming diabetic.

This seeming market failure arises because insurance contracts are written on an annual rather than a lifetime basis (Cochrane 1995). In the American context a lifetime contract would seem to pose insuperable obstacles. For those under 65 years of age insurance is mostly employment based, and all employers do not offer the same plans. Thus, a change of job or a child's leaving home and entering the labor market often entails a change of insurance plan. Lifetime insurance would therefore mean abandoning the employment-based system. Abandoning the system may or may not be a good idea, but it does not seem likely to happen any time soon. Similarly, many managed care plans are not national in scope, meaning that a change in location may mean a change in plan even in the individual market.

As a remedy Cochrane (1995) proposes that insurers be allowed to charge more if individuals fall ill with a given disease, but that insurance contracts have either lump sums or periodic payments that would hold individuals harmless against such premium increases. An important problem with such a proposal is the rapid change in medical technology. The lump-sum payment that may have held one harmless against the premium increase from a diagnosis of coronary artery disease in 1980 or even in 1990 may not be nearly sufficient today. In any event, such an insurance feature is not observed anywhere in the world (to my knowledge), which suggests that there are important problems in adopting it.

Selection and Asymmetric Information

For a quarter of a century economists have understood that if information between suppliers and demanders of insurance is asymmetric, an equilibrium in the insurance market may not exist (Akerlof 1970; Rothschild and Stiglitz 1976). Because health insurance markets exist, however, the tone of some literature has been to treat the theoretical possibility of no equilibrium or the nonexistence of certain insurance markets as an intellectual curiosum and of little practical consequence.

But in fact there are three types of evidence that health insurance markets do exhibit selection and market failure. The first has to do with two features of health insurance policies, preexisting condition clauses and upper limits, which are hard to understand unless selection is at play. Policies, especially in the individual and small group markets, often have preexisting condition clauses; that is, the policy will not cover expenditures related to medical conditions existing at the time of purchase for some initial period of time (e.g., for one year). This "refusal to sell at any price" means the buyer is unable to insure against any random expense connected with the condition. Such clauses may "lock-in" individuals to current insurance contracts and have given rise to a literature in labor economics on how health insurance may inhibit job mobility (Madrian 1994; Kapur 1998; Gruber 2000).

Upper limits are similarly difficult to understand unless selection behavior is at play. Policies often have both annual and lifetime upper limits beyond which the policy will not pay. A risk-averse consumer, however, should not want such a policy (Arrow 1963). Unless the insurance company (or possibly the employer) is protecting itself against bad risks' demanding the policy, it is hard to understand why policies with such clauses would be bought, much less be common.[6]

Table 4.1
Cost and Actuarial Value of Insurance Policies

Percentile	Individual policy		Family policy	
	Cost	Actuarial value	Cost	Actuarial value
10	$1220	$1740	$2760	$4220
25	1670	1910	3950	4600
50	2100	2100	5070	5070
75	2620	2260	6090	5450
90	3220	2440	7670	5890
Difference 90–10	164%	40%	178%	40%

Source: Cutler 1994, Table 2.

Indeed, the existence of such clauses in private insurance may have been the explanation for their unfortunate appearance in the Medicare program. I know of no economic rationale for the upper limits in Medicare's hospitalization policy: no coverage after 90 days in a hospital in one episode of illness, except for 150 "lifetime reserve" days.[7] This feature probably was mimicking the terms of 1960s private insurance contracts, but it had the unfortunate side effect that 35 percent of Medicare beneficiaries buy individual supplementary insurance at a high (perhaps 30 percent) loading charge in order to provide themselves with "back-end" protection.[8] Clearly it would have been cheaper to provide this back-end coverage through Medicare in the first place, but there is a natural political reluctance at this point to abolish an existing industry.

A second and important piece of evidence supporting selection comes from demand for insurance policies with different degrees of coverage; when offered choice, consumers tend to sort themselves by their expected risk. Not surprisingly, those with higher expected spending prefer policies that have greater coverage when policies are priced in proportion to their expected payout. As a result, premiums for policies with different degrees of coverage, for example, policies with different coinsurance rates, differ by much more than would be implied simply by the difference in payout if the same set of risks chose each plan.

Table 4.1 demonstrates this point. It shows the cost or premium for insurance policies ranked at varying percentiles of generosity; thus, policies at the 90th percentile cover a much higher fraction of health care spending than those at the 10th percentile. The Actuarial Value column shows estimates by actuaries of the cost of the policies if an average group of risks bought each policy.[9] These reflect demand elasticities. As can be seen, the spread in the premiums is much greater than could be accounted for simply by demand elasticities applied to the relevant plan provisions. The spread in premiums not accounted for by demand reflects selection.

A third and related piece of evidence is the phenomenon of premium or death spirals. These have only recently been studied formally in economics, although they have been well known in the actuarial literature for decades. A premium spiral is a case in which better risks leave a plan, whereupon its premium goes up to cover the now higher average claims expenses, but this precipitates further withdrawal from the plan, and so on.

David Cutler and Sarah Reber (1998) have constructed a formal model of a death spiral, which is shown in figure 4.1.[10] Their model was constructed in the context of an employer who offered multiple health insurance plans to employees, but it also applies to the at-risk or HMO side of Medicare. In this model plans are passive; their characteristics are given from outside the model and are unchanged except for repricing to accommodate a change in the risk mix enrolled in the plan.[11] Plans cannot or do not price differently for different individuals—the price is the same for all persons who choose to enroll—and they must accept all persons who choose to enroll. As emphasized at the outset of this chapter, this is the usual arrangement in American group insurance markets.

Figure 4.1 shows the death spiral process with two health plans, one of which is relatively more generous. Cutler and Reber illustrate with the more generous plan being a PPO and the less generous one an HMO, but it is only important that there is some difference in the plans and that the more generous plan is relatively more attractive to those expecting to spend more. Individuals are arrayed on the horizontal axis in terms of their health risk as measured by expected spending h in the more generous or PPO plan; as one moves to the right, one finds less healthy (higher spending) people.

The incremental value of the PPO to the each employee is summarized by the willingness-to-pay line $g(h)$; that the line slopes up $(g'(h) > 0)$ indicates that the less healthy employees on the right of the figure value the PPO more highly. In practice there will not be the perfect correlation between expected spending and plan

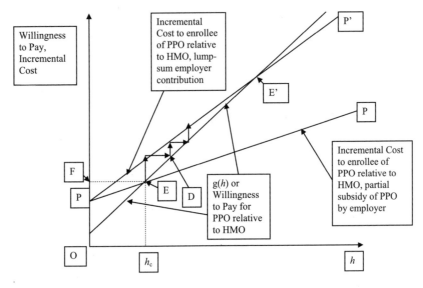

Figure 4.1
A premium death spiral. The PP line is the incremental cost of the PPO; the $g(h)$ schedule reflects willingness to pay for the PPO relative to the HMO. Those in worse health, found on the right of the Figure, are willing to pay more. See text for additional explanation.

preference shown in the figure, but any positive correlation will lead to similar results.

Under these assumptions, for any given set of out-of-pocket prices that employees pay for the two plans, there will exist a critical value of h, denoted as h_C, such that all employees with health better than h_C or equivalently with expected spending less than h_C (i.e., those to the left of h_C on the horizontal axis) will prefer the HMO and all others will prefer the PPO. One example of h_C is shown in figure 4.1. If, for example, the difference in out-of-pocket price is at a level OF, then all those to the left of h_C will choose the HMO. Let the mean healthiness of the HMO enrollees, the conditional mean of h for enrollees with $h < h_C$, be h_L and the mean healthiness of the PPO enrollees be h_H.

The out-of-pocket price to the employee is determined by the employer's schedule of subsidies. It does little violence to reality to assume a linear price schedule for the employer; that is, the employer's payment for insurance plan k is $E_k = \alpha_k + \beta P_k$, where P_k is the premium charged by plan k. A traditional payment rule was for the employer to pay a fixed percentage of the premium, say 80 percent, in which case $\alpha = 0, \beta = 0.8$. An increasingly common arrangement is for the employer to pay a lump sum toward any plan the employee chooses, perhaps an amount equal to 80 percent of the lowest cost plan. If the HMO is the lowest cost plan, one has $\alpha = 0.8P_{HMO}$, $\beta = 0$, where P_{HMO} is the price of the HMO.

In a competitive market the plan's premium will reflect the mix of enrollees in the plan, so $P_{PPO} = h_H(h_C)$ and $P_{HMO} = \lambda h_L(h_C)$, where λ reflects any efficiencies of the HMO and h_C appears in the expression to denote that h_H and h_L are functions of h_C. A change in the premium difference that employees face will change the value of h_C. Suppose, for example, the PPO becomes more expensive to the employee relative to the HMO. The marginal person will move to the HMO (h_C moves to the right). The premium in the HMO will rise because the person moving to the HMO spends more on health care than the average of those already enrolled, but so will the premium in the PPO because the person leaving the HMO spends less than the PPO average.

For a premium spiral to occur, the difference in the premiums must rise as enrollees shift to the HMO (as h_C moves to the right). For these purposes the relevant difference in premiums is the difference paid by the employee, which depends on the subsidy rule. For simplicity assume that the subsidy rule is a fixed proportion of the difference in the plans but less than a full subsidy ($\beta < 1$). In that case whether the difference rises as enrollees shift to the HMO depends on the distribution of health spending. Empirically the distribution of health care spending is approximately lognormal, conditional upon some spending (Newhouse and the Insurance Experiment Group 1993). For the lognormal distribution the difference in premiums rises as people shift to the HMO; that is, the PPO average spending increases more than the HMO average spending.

The rising difference in premiums is reflected in the positive slope of the line PP, which is the out-of-pocket premium for the PPO. PP, of course, is conditional on a given α and β, as well as on how the premium differential of the PPO changes with h_C.

If the difference in premiums between the plans to the employees is OF, the equilibrium is at point E; employees have optimally selected plans since E is on $g(h)$, and premiums are consistent with those selections since E is on PP. This equilibrium may or may not be stable; stability requires that if the marginal person moves from the

PPO to the HMO, the resulting increase in premium at the HMO relative to the PPO will deter the new marginal person from moving (i.e., the increase in PPO premiums is less than the increase in the reservation value for the PPO of the new marginal person). This condition will hold if $g(h)$ is more steeply sloped than PP. As drawn, the slope of PP is markedly less than one, indicating that β is positive (the employer subsidizes the PPO).

Now suppose the employer changes the subsidy policy from paying a percentage of each plan's premium to a lump-sum rule ($\beta = 0$). The line PP will rotate to look like PP′. One possible new equilibrium is at E′, with a lower PPO enrollment. Notice that PPO enrollment may change by a large amount even with a modest subsidy change because enrollment reflects both the price elasticity for the PPO and selection. Indeed, there may be no PPO enrollment in equilibrium. If, for example, the $g(h)$ schedule were somewhat less steeply sloped than shown in figure 4.1, then everyone would be enrolled in the HMO.

If the employer changes the subsidy rule, the subsequent dynamics depend upon insurer and individual behavior. If, as is usually the case, insurers set prices for each year based on the past year's experience and employees select plans on the basis of current year prices, there will be a discrete transition process, shown by the stair-step line away from point E in figure 4.1. When the employer changes the subsidy rule from PP to PP′, the out-of-pocket premium for the PPO rises, shown by the line going straight up from the initial equilibrium at E. This causes some employees to switch to the HMO, shown by the move to the right to point D, whereupon the process repeats until the point E′ is reached. If there is no equilibrium short of everyone in one plan, this process is literally a death spiral.

Ignoring risk, the efficient price would reflect the resource savings of the HMO. Suppose the HMO saves a fixed proportion $0 < \lambda < 1$ on each enrollee. If, for example, the HMO saved 10 percent with equivalent quality care, λ would equal 0.1. Under these conditions for any given employee h^* the efficient price for the HMO would be $(1 - \lambda)h^*$.

An equal contribution (lump-sum) rule will generally not achieve this price. The difference in out-of-pocket premiums with a lump-sum rule is $(1 - \lambda)h_L(h_C) + (h_U(h_C) - h_L(h_C))$. The first term is the efficiency savings from the HMO; that is, even on same risks, the HMO costs less (assuming $\lambda > 0$). The second term reflects adverse selection; spending is higher at the PPO because the mix of health risks it attracts is not as favorable. The second term creates a wedge with efficient pricing; it is zero only if people are distributed randomly across plans or if people are identical with respect to expected spending.[12]

This reasoning also makes clear that the employer subsidy rule that achieves the efficient price depends upon the desired value of h_C, the proportion of employees in the HMO.[13] For any given value of h_C, the employer can in principle subsidize the PPO by an amount that offsets any selection and makes the difference in premiums that the employees face equal to $(1 - \lambda)h_C$. If the employer does this, the marginal employee at h_C will face the true cost difference in choosing between the HMO and PPO. Unfortunately employers have little ability to determine λ in any actual situation and thus there is no expectation that they will in fact achieve an efficient subsidy. One important corollary of this reasoning, however, is that an employer can in principle offset selection that arises from the demand side—namely, from employees choosing among passive health plans—just as the regulator could offset a physician bias toward hospital profits in the Ellis-McGuire model.

Cutler and Reber (1998) use the framework shown in figure 4.1 to examine a premium spiral at Harvard University. This case study has lessons about selection, death spirals, and welfare loss.

A few years ago Harvard University offered its approximately 10,000 employees a set of several HMO plans and a more generous PPO plan. Although Cutler and Reber do not observe expected spending by each employee, they do observe the employee's age, which correlates with expected spending. Cutler and Reber show strong suggestive evidence that individuals choose plans in accordance with their expected spending. In the initial year of observation the average age of the employees in the HMO plans was 41, and the average age in the more generous PPO plan was 50. Thus, there was evidence of substantial selection.

In 1995 Harvard changed its subsidy rule from one paying around 80 percent of the premium of each plan to a lump sum, thereby greatly increasing the employee portion of the premium for the PPO. For example, for employees enrolling as individuals rather than as families, the employee share of the premium for the PPO more than doubled (from $555 to $1152), whereas the premium for the HMOs offered only increased about 50 percent (from $277 to $421).

This change induced switching among plans; the average age of those who switched from the PPO to the HMO was 46. This accords with figure 4.1, because the marginal group of plan switchers should have an age between the average of those who began in the PPO and those who began in the HMO.[14] This switching increased the difference in average age between the two groups from ten to eleven years.

The switching was substantial enough to result in a rather quick death spiral. By 1996 the insurer offering the PPO felt it was no longer competitive with the HMO plans and converted the PPO to a new HMO option in 1996. Thus, the PPO "died." But enough of the older, sicker enrollees remained with the new HMO option that in 1997 the insurer who initially offered the PPO withdrew from the Harvard market altogether.

What was the welfare loss? Two considerations operate, selection and pricing by the health plans. In terms of selection, Cutler and Reber estimate that the prior regime at Harvard, in which Harvard paid 80 percent of each plan's premium, was approximately equal to the expected cost difference of the two plans for a given risk (i.e., λ was approximately 0.2) and therefore that the plan switching induced by the new lump-sum regime could be construed as almost entirely a welfare loss. I have more to say about this type of welfare loss in chapter 5.

Lump-sum employer payments, however, in contrast to a fixed percentage of total premium, increase the elasticity of demand between competing plans and therefore lower optimal insurer markups. Thus, any full analysis needs to account for an effect on plan markups. In the Harvard case it appears that the markup response amounted to about a 10 percent once-and-for-all decline in premiums. Cutler and Reber find that the resulting welfare gain was substantially greater than the welfare loss from greater selection; that is, on net there was a welfare gain from the pricing change.

There are two reasons, however, why this conclusion about the change in welfare might be incorrect in the Harvard case and another reason why, even if it is correct about Harvard, it might not generalize. Cutler and Reber note one of the two reasons; their calculations only account for only short-run welfare losses; long-run losses will be greater as more individuals exit from the generous plans.

Second, Cutler and Reber assume that preferences for health plan are solely a function of the individual's expected spending. But at a given level of expected spending, preferences undoubtedly differ. Individuals in the same health state, for example, may value a larger network differently. In that case there can be a further welfare loss from selection, especially if certain classes of plans disappear. I come to that in chapter 5.

Finally, in their simulations Cutler and Reber, like Keeler, Carter, and Newhouse in the simulations reported in chapter 6, assume plans do not respond to changes in subsidy arrangements in ways other than in their pricing. In the context of the Harvard case study this assumption almost certainly is valid; because Harvard was only a small part of the Boston market, its change to lump-sum employer payments would not likely affect plan characteristics.[15] Even if that were not the case, however, reconfiguring the health plan to induce greater selection is presumably costly, so one would not expect it to occur immediately. But when an employer or public purchaser is a large portion of a plan's business, one might expect some reaction in how plans configure themselves if the employer changes its subsidy rule. I now turn to plan actions.

Selection and the Supply Side

If selection were solely a demand-side phenomenon, it could in principle be countered by appropriate subsidies from the sponsor of a given menu of health plans, as just shown. In practice, however, this observation is not especially helpful. First, even if the appropriate subsidies were known, they weaken the incentives for efficiency among the plans, as the Harvard example in chapter 4 showed. Second, the subsidies are like any other administered price; they will contain errors because in practice it is difficult if not impossible to know the degree to which higher health plan costs are attributable to poorer health risks, inefficiency or a product difference. Finally and most important, health plans and provider groups paid by capitation are themselves economic agents and will presumably respond to incentives to select; it is not plausible that selection is solely a demand-side phenomenon.

In this chapter, therefore, I turn to active selection efforts by both health plans and providers such as physicians and hospitals, as opposed to consumer self-selection among a given set of plans or physicians with given characteristics. In other words, plans and physicians are now allowed to choose the characteristics of the "product" that they offer patients. A key point of this chapter is that in contract theory terms, actions that plans take to accomplish selection become noncontractible when consumer sovereignty over choice of plan is honored. Even if regulations require open enrollment, meaning that plans must accept all who apply, many plan characteristics could be chosen so as to induce low-cost consumers to select and high-cost consumers to avoid a plan.

This chapter's principal model, however, emphasizes the role of the physician rather than the plan, thereby allowing the physician to be an important actor. There are three reasons to do so. First, groups of physicians and sometimes even individual physicians are paid by capitation, both in the United States and elsewhere. Such physicians will have financial incentives to engage in selection. Second, the physician has greater medical knowledge of the patient's future health care costs than does the plan and is therefore in a position to implement a more sensitive selection regime. Third, law or regulation may restrict somewhat the design of plans, but it is much more difficult to restrict actions of physicians.

The chapter's main focus is on a model developed by Karen Eggleston; in her model plans and physicians choose the privately optimal amount of selection.[1] At the end of the chapter I turn to empirical data demonstrating the importance of selection. The evidence does not distinguish selection originating on the supply side from that originating on the demand side, nor that from plan design rather than from physician action. I have made these conceptual distinctions to allow for an orderly exposition, but they are not very meaningful in practice.

An Initial Model of Selection

One of the best-known models of selection behavior in insurance markets, developed by Michael Rothschild and Joseph Stiglitz (1976), was motivated by plan behavior. Because it is so well known to economists, I do not describe it here, but simply summarize two of its main results:

1. If consumers differ in their expected spending in ways that are not known or cannot be adjusted for by varying premiums and if most consumers have lower- than-average expected spending (i.e., the spending distribution is right skewed, as health care spending is), then an equilibrium may not exist in an individual insurance market.

2. If an equilibrium exists, it will not involve pooling individuals with different expected spending, because it will pay an insurance firm to offer the individuals with low expected spending a new contract that they will find more attractive, but that those with high expected spending will not. Rothschild and Stiglitz implicitly assume that firms can costlessly offer such a contract.

These results appear to explain much about insurance markets, most important why individual and small group markets often seem to fail. The model obviously does not apply to universal public programs that offer only one option, nor does it apply to cases in which groups form for reasons other than obtaining health insurance and a premium can be paid for the entire group that reflects its costs, as in the case of the employees of a large firm.[2]

The Rothschild-Stiglitz model also explains that a regulator or an employer may improve welfare by charging above expected cost for plans that attract low risks and using the funds to subsidize plans that attract high risks.[3] This result corresponds to an often observed American arrangement in which employers provide a greater subsidy to those enrolling in a high premium plan.[4] The result, however, assumes that the subsidy has no effect on the efficiency with which services are produced or priced, contrary to the Chalkley-Malcolmson model and the empirical evidence of Cutler and Reber.

Useful though it has been, the Rothschild-Stiglitz model has two implications that do not correspond to what is observed. The first is its prediction of no pooling of heterogeneous risks within a given insurance plan. But almost no group insurance plan in the United States varies its premium to each individual or family in a way that corresponds to that specific individual's or family's risk, yet plans have heterogeneous risks enrolled. This is not only the case within the group insurance market, but it is also generally the case within the individual market, where premiums often do vary by age, sex, and geographic location, but usually not by disease. Although those with a disease may not be able to obtain insurance at any premium because of either medical underwriting or preexisting condition clauses, premiums rarely increase when an already insured person contracts a chronic disease.[5]

Second, if there is an equilibrium in the insurance market, the model predicts that the poor risks (sicker individuals) will obtain their desired amount of insurance, while the better risks would like to buy more insurance but cannot. In reality it is exactly the opposite; it is poor risks who have trouble purchasing insurance at all or who would like more complete insurance than is offered them, for example, insurance without preexisting condition clauses. By contrast, good risks tend to have little trouble finding their preferred insurance arrangement.

If selection is costly to plans, however, the two troublesome implications of the Rothschild-Stiglitz model are reversed. A limited degree of pooling of risks within plan emerges, and it is the poorer risks who do not obtain their desired degree of insurance (Newhouse 1996b).[6] How important, therefore, are costs to plans or physicians of selection?

Unfortunately I know of no empirical evidence on this point, but costs could differ between the plan and the physician. On the one hand, medical ethics and altruism are undoubtedly more important among physicians, but on the other physicians have more information about an enrollee's expected cost. If the plan controls benefit design, the assumption of costless selection methods (i.e., offering a contract that would appeal to the healthy but not the sick) could be a good approximation to reality, because changing many aspects of the benefit design is straightforward. For example, it would seem nearly costless for an insurer to introduce a plan with a larger deductible, yet such a plan would clearly appeal more to those with lower expected spending.

Precisely for this reason, one form of regulating or "managing" competition to minimize selection calls for the employer or government (the "sponsor") to standardize the benefit design across competing plans (Enthoven 1988). For example, competing plans might be asked to cover all medically necessary hospital and physician services, with a specified copayment for a visit.

Although sponsors can standardize the benefit up to a point, it is impossible to do so fully, especially if the plan is an HMO that integrates insurance and the delivery of services.[7] If, for example, there is a drug benefit, plans typically have a formulary, or list of preferred drugs. Because the marginal cost of another pill is often negligible, drug companies will deeply discount price if large numbers of users can be moved to a given drug, just as airlines will deeply discount otherwise empty seats to group tours. In the drug case, this means that if an insurance plan or HMO will generally use one particular drug within a class of drugs such as anti-hypertensives, it can obtain a favorable price.

But using only one drug offers an opportunity for selection. Certain high-cost patients may need drugs that are not on the formulary. If they have to pay relatively large amounts out of pocket to obtain such drugs, those patients may seek another plan. Nor is the answer necessarily abolishing the formulary. Although doing so would end selection of this nature, it would also raise the price of drugs and hence the price of the plan.

Similarly, if a plan makes referrals to specialists hard to come by, patients who want such referrals will look for another plan. This could be accomplished by simply having few specialists in the plan's network. In that sense the network of physicians is analytically identical to the drug formulary, and costs of selection could still be small.

If, however, primary care physicians could be persuaded to make it differentially difficult for poor risks to obtain referrals, selection could potentially be still more profitable. Or if physicians could be persuaded simply to be rude to poor risks, those persons would want to seek their care elsewhere. Although further examples are given in what follows, this discussion makes clear that plans may wish to seek physician participation in selection methods.

Physician participation in selection, however, is likely costly to the plan, partly because physicians are trained that such activities are unethical and will therefore not want to engage in them.[8] Plans can and do offer physicians financial rewards for delivering fewer services, however, of which the simplest is capitated payment. Because sicker patients require more services, if reimbursement does not account for how sick a physician's group of patients is—and it typically does so very imperfectly if at all—the physician or physician group will have a financial incentive to select.

Such arrangements with physicians, however, make selection less rewarding to the plan, because some gains from selection must be shared with the physician. In the limiting case of full capitation to the physician, all the gains from selection, at least in the short run, will accrue to the physician or physician group. How gains are distributed in the long run will depend upon assumptions about competition and information in both the physician and plan markets. If patients tend to remain with their physicians and if plans and other physician groups have little ability to monitor the degree to which a physician or physician group has selected good risks, the gains could remain with the physician even in the long run.

The Welfare Implications of Selection

Selection is important because a fundamental result of the standard competitive model does not necessarily hold if it is present. In the standard model an entrepreneur who brings a profitable new product to market makes both herself and consumers better off and hence improves social welfare. In the case of a profitable new health plan that attracts good risks, however, the entrepreneur makes the good risks better off, but the poor risks worse off. As a result, one cannot insure against becoming a bad risk and economic efficiency has potentially decreased. Efficiency also decreases to the extent that marketing and other costs are incurred.[9]

Suppose that, to take a concrete example, the new plan is like the old plan but has a modest feature that appeals differentially to better risks. For example, suppose the two plans are similar, but the new one provides worse access to cancer specialists and therefore appeals differentially to those without cancer. The new plan could therefore break a Rothschild-Stiglitz pooling equilibrium. Those with cancer will remain in the plan with the better access, but some of those without cancer may not want to pay the additional premium for that access and move to the new plan, thereby raising the premium of the plan with the good access. If, ex ante, other risk-averse consumers wished to insure against the possibility of becoming a future bad risk (e.g., being diagnosed with cancer in the future, which would imply higher expected costs), then those consumers now face a riskier environment and will be worse off. There is a form of market failure; the resources the entrepreneur spent to bring the new plan to market (i.e., reducing the access to cancer specialists) could be social waste, depending on the balance between those who do and those who do not wish to insure the future risk.

Implicit in the foregoing scenario was that medical care prices were at competitive levels given the degree of pooling in the insurance market. But I noted earlier that the actual medical care world relies substantially on administered prices. This creates further opportunities for selection. For example, the method Medicare uses to reimburse both health plans and hospitals, described in chapter 1, gives agents substantial incentives to engage in selection.

Medicare pays health plans the same amount for individuals with different expected spending, and so plans have a financial incentive to want certain individuals and not want others. Plans have several tools at their disposal to attract those they desire. They choose the nature of their network, including the location of participating physicians, hospitals, and other providers. They have considerable choice of how to market themselves.[10] They can potentially offer providers incentives to appeal to low cost patients. I show in what follows that favorable selection into Medicare health plans has been substantial.

An analogous situation arises for hospitals under the PPS, because they make losses on some patients, for example outlier patients, and profits on others. Dranove (1987) and McClellan (1997) both show that there is substantial heterogeneity among patients within a given DRG; for example, coefficients of variation of spending within a DRG often exceed 1.[11] Although physicians, not hospitals nominally control admissions, hospitals may still be able to exert some degree of selection by their choice of which physicians to have on their staff (so-called economic credentialing takes into account differences in the average costliness of a physician's patients), or by creating incentives for their staff to admit certain patients at their hospital and other patients elsewhere. Hospitals also control the choice of services they offer, for example, whether they have an emergency room that might attract uninsured patients. In short, hospitals that have been paid a fixed amount for a heterogeneous group of patients also have an incentive to configure themselves to attract those with positive profits and conversely. Nonetheless, the evidence of selection at the hospital level is much weaker than at the plan level.

Provider Agency

Any discussion of plan and provider behavior requires an assumption about what these agents are trying to achieve, namely, their objective functions. In the standard competitive model one assumes firms are trying to maximize profit, but that is not necessarily a good assumption in health care (Cutler 2000; Sloan 2000). Like the Ellis-McGuire model described in chapter 3, Eggleston's model permits physicians to have a more general objective function than profit maximization, although profit maximization remains as a special case of the model.

As already described, physicians have a code of ethics embodied in the Hippocratic Oath, which asks them to do everything possible to help patients. Everything possible presumably includes activities whose marginal cost exceeds a positive benefit, so an ethical physician is not necessarily economically efficient, as noted earlier.

Other health care agents may also exhibit a degree of agency. In the American health plan market, as well as in the markets of other countries, one finds nonprofit or public institutions, especially hos-pitals, but also some health plans. Like the physician, these entities also may not necessarily act like profit-maximizing firms, although those in competition with profit-maximizing firms can presumably only depart from profit-maximizing behavior to the degree they can obtain subsidies for such behavior or to the degree that consumers have a preference for nonprofit firms (Weisbrod 1988).

Agency may also be facilitated by public subsidies. Public institu-tions usually obtain direct subsidies from the public treasury. In the United States differential tax treatment of nonprofit firms exists (Frank and Salkever 1991; Sloan 2000). Such tax subsidies, however, confer only a limited advantage. Beyond subsidies and tax exemp-tions, therefore, one needs some kind of market power or rents in administered prices for agency considerations to be interesting. But rents in administered prices are widespread in health care markets, making the question of how providers spend them important. For example, although providers could lower prices, they could also use the rents on perquisites for management. In any event, profit maximization by physicians emerges as a special case in Eggleston's model, to which I now turn.

Provider Selection Behavior: The Eggleston Model

Karen Eggleston (1999, 2000) has developed a model that includes physicians and health plans and yields an optimal amount of selec-tion behavior, though the "health plan" is perhaps better thought of as a group of physicians who are paid by capitation and who value profits highly. In Eggleston's model selection occurs through actions by individual physicians, who maximize utility. Because of medical ethics, physicians dislike engaging in selection efforts, and greater selection efforts reduce their utility. Physicians' utility functions are similar to those in the Ellis-McGuire model described in chapter 3, so physicians are agents for patients.[12] Health plans, which are assumed to maximize profit, determine the terms under which physicians are reimbursed.

The most important property of Eggleston's model for the pur-poses of this chapter is an expression for the privately optimal amount of selection activity, a feature I have found in no other model.[13] Her model also suggests underprovision of services (stint-ing) when physicians share in the cost of services and overprovision when they profit from providing more services (fee-for-service). Stinting, however, is the subject of chapter 3; because her model adds no new insights to the discussion there, I do not emphasize that aspect here.

In Eggleston's model medical care is a local public good; physicians treat all patients in the same way.[14] Selection occurs ex ante with the population of applicants to plans or those designating a physician group as their source of primary care. Physicians' actions make some patients not want to enroll in a given plan or with their group. Because physicians do not like to engage in such actions, a higher degree of physician agency toward patients, or concern for patients' welfare, decreases selection.

Like the Rothschild-Stiglitz model, Eggleston postulates two types of persons, high (H) and low (L) risk, who differ in their probability of illness, but not in their severity of illness should they become sick. The proportion of high risks in the population is common knowledge. A coinsurance rate is set exogenously by a regulator or a sponsor. This assumption describes not only Medicare but also most American employer-provided plans; more generally, this corresponds to efforts to standardize benefits across plans, a feature of managed competition.[15]

Plans take as given the price they are paid for insuring enrollees. This clearly fits an administered price setting such as the Medicare program, but it is also compatible with perfect competition. Assume for the moment, however, that only one managed care plan with no competitors exists, an assumption I relax later.

Selection is represented by a variable t, which ranges between 0 and 1. In the Medicare context t might be a measure of the time a physician spends discussing with a patient whether to remain in traditional Medicare. A physician's selection effort t has a utility cost to the physician of $\gamma(t)$ that is increasing and convex in t. If there is no selection, there is no disutility to the physician, so $\gamma(t=0) = \gamma'(t=0) = 0$. Perfect selection, meaning that all profitable patients are enrolled in the plan and no unprofitable patients are enrolled, occurs if t = 1, but it is assumed to be infeasible, so that $\gamma(t=1) = \gamma'(t=1) = \infty$.

Assume there is a potential enrollee whose risk type is unknown. If the enrollee is a high-risk person and a physician exerts selection effort t, probability t exists that the applicant will be excluded or will choose not to enroll.[16] Let the proportion of high risks in the population be μ; thus, if all physicians exert selection effort t, a proportion of the population $t\mu$ finds it not utility maximizing to enroll in the plan. This description could apply to physician organizations that accept an imperfectly risk-adjusted capitation payment from private health plans (so-called delegated risk), or more generally to individual physicians whose payment includes some financial incentive to keep utilization low.[17]

Let the probability of illness in the population be δ; then the average risk of illness in the population is $\delta = \mu\delta_H + (1 - \mu)\delta_L$, where H and L index the high and low risk classes respectively. Normalize the population N to equal 1. Then with selection effort t the population enrolled in the health plan is

$$N(t) = (1 - t)\mu + (1 - \mu) = (1 - t\mu), \tag{5.1}$$

and the average risk mix in the health plan is

$$\delta(t) = [(1 - t)\mu\delta_H + (1 - \mu)\delta_L]/N(t). \tag{5.2}$$

If risk selection is zero $(t = 0)$, the average enrollee risk in the plan is the population average δ. If risk selection were perfect $(t = 1)$, enrollees would be entirely low risk $\delta(t = 1) = \delta_L$; no high risks would be enrolled. Average enrollee risk and thus expected treatment costs decrease as selection effort increases:

$$\partial\delta(t)/\partial t = [-\mu(1 - \mu)(\delta_H - \delta_L)]/N(t)^2 \le 0. \tag{5.3}$$

If the population is homogeneous $((\delta_H = \delta_L)$ or $\mu = 0)$, then the numerator of the previous equation is zero. By definition, selection does not—indeed cannot—arise in such a case. But if the population is heterogeneous, selection effort will reduce average enrollee risk and thus potentially raise profit (net of any selection cost) if price is administratively determined, as in Medicare, or if the market exhibits competitive behavior. Whether selection emerges in Eggleston's model depends on physicians' objective functions.

As noted earlier, Eggleston assumes physicians are agents for the patient in the sense of Ellis and McGuire.[18] Thus, physicians have a utility function that is separable in patient benefit and profit, namely, $V(X) = \alpha B(X) + \pi(X)$, where α is the degree to which the physician is willing to trade off patient benefit and profit, B is the function relating patient benefit to medical services X, and π is profit. Eggleston parameterizes $B(X)$ as $aX - 0.5bX^2$, with $a, b > 0$. Although it seems strained to think of physicians as seeking to earn profits for health plans, plans might motivate physicians to do so by using profit as one criterion in forming a network. And it seems less strained to treat V(X) as the objective function of a physician who is an equity partner in a capitated physician group.[19]

Like Ellis and McGuire, health plans pay physicians partially on the basis of observed costs. Let s be the fraction of the physician's cost paid for by the plan. Unlike Ellis and McGuire, Eggleston allows a profit per unit in fee-for-service reimbursement, so $-m \leq s \leq 1$, where m is the profit margin per service, rather than $0 \leq s \leq 1$ as in the Ellis and McGuire model.[20]

Recall that δ measures not only the average risk but also the average probability of illness. Because a fraction δ of the enrollees in the plan become sick and seek care and because δ is a function of selection effort t, $1 - \delta(t)$ is the fraction of enrollees who use no services. Because she subsequently treats cost as endogenous, Eggleston relaxes the Ellis-McGuire normalization that cost is 1 and denotes unit cost as c; thus, c is the cost (or in some contexts the fee) for each unit X of services that an ill person receives. It simplifies matters, however, to treat c as exogenous for the moment. Thus, scX is the physician's share of the cost of services per enrollee and $\delta(t)$ is the probability that an average enrollee seeks care.

Putting all this together, the physician's profit π per person enrolled is $R - \delta(t)scX$, where R is the amount of any capitation paid the physician.[21] The capitation is set to cover the loss on the average risk in the population.

The physician's expected utility E(V) is a separable function of both total patient benefits and profits, which in turn are a function of the number of enrollees N(t) and the average enrollee risk $\delta(t)$. These determine both the expected profit per patient and the utility gain from agency for patients. Specifically, using the Ellis-McGuire utility function and adding a term $\gamma(t)$ reflecting the disutility from selection effort gives

$$E(V) = N(t)[R - \delta(t)scX + \delta(t)\alpha B(X)] - \gamma(t)$$

$$= N(t)[R + \delta(t)\{\alpha B(X) - scX\}] - \gamma(t). \qquad (5.4)$$

The term in brackets in the first line is profit per enrollee plus the agency effect per enrollee; that is, $\delta(t)\{\alpha B(X)\}$ is the provider agency benefit per user of services. This can be thought of as the utility benefit to the physician of making sick persons well.

Equation 5.4 yields the privately optimal amount of selection t. Differentiating E(V) with respect to t and setting the resulting expression equal to zero gives a first-order condition: [22]

$$\gamma'(t) \geq \mu[\delta_H\{scX - \alpha B(X)\} - R]. \tag{5.5}$$

To understand this equation, suppose the condition holds with equality and remember that selection is practiced only on the high risks. As selection increases from zero, the health plan drops a fraction μ of the high risks (recall that $\partial N(t)/\partial t = -\mu$). The loss that would have been incurred by enrolling this fraction is given by $scX - R$, which is positive for high risks. Thus, if agency α is zero, the term in brackets is strictly positive, and the expression is strictly positive. For the first-order condition to hold, $\gamma'(t)$ must be positive, meaning there is selection. Thus, in this model a purely profit maximizing physician—meaning there is no agency effect—*always* engages in selection. Furthermore, as the degree of physician cost sharing s increases, the term in brackets becomes more positive and the degree of selection increases.

This formalizes one reason for controversy over the role of profit in medical care, especially as the role of capitation has increased. Generalizing to providers other than physicians, whether α is materially different between for-profit and not-for-profit providers such as nursing homes and hospitals—indeed, whether it can differ in a competitive market—is a point of serious contention in the United States, as noted previously.

Similar to the Chalkley-Malcolmson model, agency mitigates selection. A provider who is a better agent for the patient has a higher α, which makes the term in brackets less positive and decreases selection. Selection is also not practiced if $B(X)$ is sufficiently large relative to $R - scX$ (for a given $\alpha > 0$). This corresponds to the notion of rendering aid to a seriously ill patient.[23] In this case the right-hand side of the first order condition is negative, but since $\gamma'(t)$ is assumed to always be nonnegative, the first-order condition holds with an inequality. In fee-for-service medicine, assuming s is negative, the provider never selects.

There is also a consumer side of the model, which is used to determine the actual quantity of services delivered. Here Eggleston uses a bargaining model similar to that of Ellis and McGuire (1990) to derive the quantity of services delivered. Theoretically one must either give the consumer some bargaining power or rely on physician altruism to avoid the conclusion that a physician paid a purely capitated amount will supply no services. I have put the mathematical details of this part of the model into the appendix to this chapter.

In sum, the key points developed thus far are that capitated physicians will engage in selection behavior unless agency is sufficiently great or, for a given degree of agency, unless patient benefit from treatment is sufficiently great. Likewise services may be underprovided when physicians share in the cost of services and overprovided when they earn a profit on each unit of service (pure fee-for-service reimbursement).

The Sponsor or Regulator in the Eggleston Model

Eggleston posits a sponsor who chooses demand- and supply-side cost-sharing values θ and s to maximize social welfare or the welfare of the employment group. In the Medicare context the sponsor is the government, but more generally the sponsor could be an employer or a coalition of employers. Like community rating, consumers are charged an actuarily fair premium, which is based on pooled population risk, or the unit cost c and expected utilization $E(X)$. Any rents in provider payment carry a deadweight loss τ ($0 < \tau < 1$). In the context of a tax-financed health insurance program such as Medicare, τ would be the deadweight loss from the taxes necessary to finance the program. In the employer context, any rents in provider payments would come from cash wages and thus make the firm less attractive in the labor market.

Selection in this model is the inability of high risks to enroll in the health plan. In a first-best world, where a sponsor or regulator can directly control utilization and selection, profits π would be zero and first-best utilization X^{FB} would be set where marginal benefit equals marginal cost. Demand-side cost sharing would be zero to minimize risk. Selection t would be zero and so γ would also be zero. Again mathematical details appears in the appendix to this chapter.

When the sponsor has four goals—efficient health care utilization X, efficient risk spreading, zero risk selection t, and zero deadweight loss from financing—the availability of only two cost-sharing instruments, one on the demand side and one on the supply side, means that in general the sponsor cannot achieve all four goals.[24]

Rather Eggleston assumes that demand- and supply-side cost sharing will be set to minimize losses subject to the reaction functions of providers and consumers.

When the physician appropriately balances patient benefit and profit (meaning at the same rate as the regulator or sponsor) so that an efficient outcome is achieved, Ellis and McGuire (1986, 1990) find full supply-side cost sharing optimal. They do not, however, consider selection, which lowers the optimal amount of supply-side cost sharing. Moreover, Ellis and McGuire assume that the optimal degree of patient cost sharing is zero, because positive cost sharing imposes risks on consumers while providing no offsetting benefit because utilization can be fully controlled through an appropriate choice of provider cost sharing. Once provider cost sharing is allowed to affect selection, however, there is a role for patient cost sharing.[25]

Competition in the Health Plan Market in the Eggleston Model

All of what precedes is in the context of a monopoly managed care plan that selects and a default fee-for-service plan like traditional Medicare that does not. Consider now competition between two health plans that both select. The main result here is that selection makes the possibility of entry attractive. Assume that selection efforts at the two plans are independent. The risk mix at a given plan now depends on the risk mix of the other plan, which in turn depends on selection efforts of physicians affiliated with that plan. Eggleston shows that, given Cournot assumptions, if selection effort increases at one plan, it increases at the other. The intuition behind this result is that if selection effort increases at one plan, the marginal payoff from selection effort increases at the other.

Suppose now a second health plan enters a market with one plan, but that insured high risks stay with their existing plan to avoid the likelihood they may be turned down ("discovered" to be high risk) by the new plan.[26] Another reason to remain with their plan is that they may have established relationships with physicians who are not in the new plan's network. Assume, however, that all uninsured high risks apply to the new entrant and that some fraction of the existing low risks also apply; the low risks, of course, are now insured with the existing plan. The new entrant will not enter if the fraction of high risks in the applicant population renders entry unprofitable; this will depend upon the selection efforts of the incumbent plan and the fraction of low risks that switch plans. If the existing plan has enrolled everyone (i.e., not engaged in selection) and if only low risks switch, then the entrant who is paid a capitation based on population-wide risk makes an even greater profit in the short run than the existing monopoly plan (i.e., before any further entry or response from the monopolist), because the entrant gets only low risks without paying any selection costs. This is analogous to a second health plan entering the Medicare market, when some members of an existing, well-established plan have developed both a loyalty to the plan as well as a chronic disease. A new entrant can try to attract the good risks away from the well-established plan.

Endogenous Cost and Cost Reduction Effort in the Eggleston Model

Suppose now that cost is a function of the effort made by the physician to reduce it. The result is a trade-off between devoting greater efforts to achieving efficiency in the production of services and the degree of selection behavior. Under this assumption Eggleston makes more formal the trade-off between selection and efficiency-in-production discussed in Newhouse (1996b). Again, I have put the mathematical details in the appendix.

Risk Adjustment

I deal more extensively with risk adjustment in chapter 6, but having described Eggleston's model here, it is convenient to show how it incorporates risk adjustment. Eggleston assumes that the goal of risk adjustment is to pay the physician the expected cost of the patients in the physician's practice. The absence of risk adjustment corresponds to simply paying the average cost in the population; as risk adjustment improves, it approaches the goal of paying the cost of the patients in the practice. Although traditional Medicare does not risk-adjust physician payment because it uses fee-for-service reimbursement, payment of expected cost is Medicare's intent in both its payment of health plans and hospitals.

Not surprisingly, improved risk adjustment reduces selection efforts; as reimbursement more closely approaches the cost of the patients enrolled, selection efforts diminish for any given degree of effort to make production efficient. The appendix demonstrates this conclusion formally. In the appendix I also point out that greater risk adjustment can in theory reduce the plan's or the physician's incentives to prevent illness, similar to Ehrlich and Becker's (1972) argument that health insurance can reduce the consumer's incentives to prevent illness. In practice this incentive is likely to be unimportant, because many preventive services such as immunization are verifiable and contractible and the costs of pain and suffering are uninsured, as I describe in greater detail in the appendix.

The Evidence of Selection

The empirical data suggesting the importance of selection come from both the Medicare program and from private insurance. Glied (2000) reviews twenty-four studies of selection. The studies differ both with respect to how selection or health risk is measured and their findings.

Most studies do not make contemporaneous comparisons of the utilization of those enrolled in HMO and fee-for-service plans, because contemporaneous comparisons confound selection and any economies of the HMO. In the RAND Health Insurance Experiment, individuals were successfully randomized to one HMO, thereby avoiding the selection problem, and a control group of those who selected it on their own was also drawn. After controlling for age and other observable variables, those randomized to the HMO had the same use patterns as those in the control group, so there was no evidence of selection on unobserved variables (Newhouse and the Experiment Insurance Group 1993, chaps. 2, 8).

The RAND experiment had data on use of services in the HMO; such data, however, are often unavailable, so a common methodology is to compare the use of those who enroll in an HMO immediately before they enroll with those who do not enroll, or those who disenroll immediately after they disenroll with those who have not disenrolled.

A number of such studies have been done using data from the Medicare program, and they have yielded some of the strongest evidence of selection. As described in chapter 1, Medicare enrollees in the past have been allowed to change health plans monthly, whereas in private insurance annual changes are the norm. More frequent changes make selection behavior easier, since an enrollee who becomes sick can change to a more generous plan more quickly.

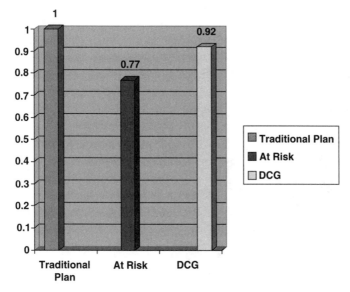

Figure 5.1
Second column: Ratio of prior spending, at-risk enrollees relative to controls, Medicare, 1997. Those enrolling in at-risk-plans had spent 23 percent less in the twelve months before they enrolled when they were in the traditional plan after controlling for age, sex, institutional status, welfare status, and county of residence. Third column: Ratio of prior spending after controlling for age, sex, welfare status, county of residence, and diagnostic cost group. (*Source*: Medicare Payment Advisory Commission 2000.)

Figure 5.1 shows the results of such a study in the Medicare program. Adjusting for age and sex and the other variables in the payment formula, those Medicare enrollees who left traditional Medicare and enrolled in HMOs in 1997 spent 23 percent less in the twelve months before they enrolled than those who did not enroll, as shown in the first two columns of the figure. (The results in the last column will be discussed in chapter 6.) Those who disenrolled and changed back to traditional Medicare, however, used about the same amount of services. In other words, the relatively healthy were enrolling, although those disenrolling seemed approximately representative.[27]

Although use was not observed after enrollment in the HMO, mortality was. Consistent with the use data, after adjusting for age and sex, those enrolling in HMOs had a 15 percent lower mortality rate than did those who remained in traditional Medicare (figure

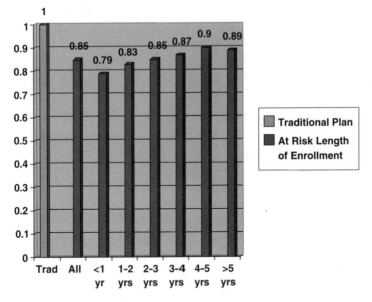

Figure 5.2
Mortality of enrollees in at risk plans, 1997, by years enrolled, relative to those remaining in the traditional plan after controlling for age, sex, and welfare status. Overall, there is a 15 percent reduction in mortality. (*Source*: Medicare Payment Advisory Commission 2000.)

5.2).[28] Although in principle this mortality advantage could have come from better care in the HMO, it is implausible to believe that any change in medical care could have resulted in more than a few percentage points change in the mortality rate.

The favorable selection just described implies that the Medicare program has overpaid at-risk plans. The CBO estimates that the overpayment is on the order of 8 percent (Congressional Budget Office 1997). This is much less than the difference described in figure 5.1 for two reasons. First, as more fully described in chapter 6, spending tends to regress toward the mean; over time those who change plans move toward the average of those already enrolled in the plan to which the individuals move, whereas the value in figure 5.1 is only for the immediate pre-enrollment period. Second, because the Medicare program wishes to share in the savings, it only pays plans 95 percent of the comparable average in the traditional plan. Beeuwkes Buntin, Garber, McClellan et al. (2001) find that in 1997 about half of the overpayment can be attributed to the difference in mortality experience shown in figure 5.2, and the resulting avoidance of high end-of-life spending among those enrolled in health plans.

Notice, however, that selection in Medicare implies there could be a type of death spiral in plan payments, similar to that described in chapter 3. As explained in chapter 1, prior to 1997 Medicare payment of health plans was 95 percent of the average payment in traditional Medicare in the beneficiaries' county of residence. If those who are better risks were to continue to move to at-risk plans, the fee-for-service average payment would continue to increase. Hospital payments, for example, would increase proportionately with the Case Mix Index, but at-risk plans would also receive this increase because their payments were tied to the average payment in the traditional plan. The 1997 Balanced Budget Act changed this feature by breaking the link between the updates in at-risk plan payment and the traditional plan; both updates are now set administratively.[29] Thus, a death spiral can no longer occur formulaically.

A similar selection is present in traditional individual insurance markets (see the data in table 4.1). Selection has also been observed in the individual plans that supplement Medicare (so-called Medigap plans). Market performance was sufficiently poor that in 1990 the American Congress mandated that plans in this market would be standardized to ten types.[30] Three of these ten plans provide an outpatient pharmaceutical benefit. These three plans both show substantial evidence of selection; that is, those with above-average spending for drugs choose such plans (McCormack, Fox, Rice et al. 1996; Rice, Graham, and Fox 1997).

The foregoing discussion concerns selection of insurance plan, but in principle selection can occur at the hospital and physician level as well. Newhouse (1989) examined whether hospitals seemed to shun or "dump" unprofitable cases following the introduction of the Prospective Payment System in 1984. That study found limited evidence of such behavior; patients in DRGs with negative accounting profits, however, substantially shifted to hospitals of last resort, which would be consistent with dumping.[31] The test was not fully satisfactory, however, because few DRGs at that time had negative accounting profits; the DRG system when introduced was mis-normed and hospital margins were therefore large in the first few years (table 3.1).

A further piece of evidence comes from Newhouse and Byrne (1989). They showed that patients with long stays, who were most likely unprofitable under the PPS, were disproportionately shifted to hospitals that were exempt from the PPS, such as psychiatric, long-term, and rehabilitation hospitals. Although these hospitals were paid on a per admission basis following the PPS, the amount paid was typically higher than a general hospital received for the patient, so that it was not necessarily true that the case was unprofitable at such a hospital.[32]

Health plans can select by offering benefits that differentially appeal to healthy individuals. An example of such a benefit is a subsidized membership in a health club. Frank, Glazer, and McGuire (2000) show that in the Medicaid population it is especially attractive to select by providing poor mental health services.

This chapter has established that selection frequently does emerge in competitive insurance markets, described the welfare loss from selection, and presented a model of selection behavior, which shows that payment methods that minimize selection decrease efficiency-in-production. It also shows theoretically that better risk adjustment methods improved welfare. Chapter 6 focuses on risk adjustment methods and other methods for decreasing selection.

Appendix to Chapter 5

Derivation of Equations in Chapter 5

Equation 5.5 is derived as follows for the case in which the condition holds with equality:

$$\gamma'(t) = -\mu[R + \delta(t)\{\alpha B(X) - scX\}] + N\{\alpha B(X) - scX\}\partial\delta/\partial t.$$

Substituting in for $\delta(t) = [(1-t)\mu\delta_H + (1-\mu)\delta_L]/N(t)$ and $\partial\delta/\partial t = [-\mu(1-\mu)(\delta_H - \delta_L)]/N(t)^2$, one gets on the right-hand side:

$$-\mu[R + [((1-t)\mu\delta_H + (1-\mu)\delta_L)/N(t)]\{\alpha B(X) - scX\}]$$

$$+ N\{\alpha B(X) - scX\}[-\mu(1-\mu)(\delta_H - \delta_L)]/N(t)^2.$$

$$= -\mu R + \{\alpha B(X) - scX\}[-\mu^2(1-t)\delta_H - (\mu(1-\mu))\delta_L]/N(t)]$$

$$+ \{\alpha B(X) - scX\}[-\mu(1-\mu)(\delta_H - \delta_L)]/N(t).$$

Collecting terms in δ_H and δ_L, one has the following:

$$= -\mu R + \{aB(X) - scX\}[-\mu^2(1-t)\delta_H - (\mu(1-\mu))\delta_L - \mu(1-\mu)\delta_H$$

$$+ \mu(1-\mu)\delta_L)]/N(t).$$

$$= -\mu R + \{aB(X) - scX\}[-\mu^2(1-t)\delta_H - \mu(1-\mu)\delta_H]/N(t).$$

$$= -\mu R + \{aB(X) - scX\}[-\mu^2 + t\mu^2 - \mu + \mu^2)\delta_H]/N(t).$$

$$= -\mu R + \{aB(X) - scX\}[(t\mu^2 - \mu)\delta_H]/N(t).$$

$$= -\mu R + \mu\{aB(X) - scX\}[(t\mu - 1)\delta_H]/N(t).$$

$$= -\mu R - \mu\{aB(X) - scX\}[(1 - t\mu)\delta_H]/N(t).$$

$$= -\mu[R + \{aB(X) - scX\}[(1 - t\mu)\delta_H]/N(t).$$

$$= -\mu[R + \{aB(X) - scX\}(\delta_H)].$$

$$= \mu[\delta_H\{scX - aB(X)\} - R].$$

The details of the consumer bargaining model are as follows. Eggleston begins by deriving an expression for the consumer's expected utility. Recall that there is a single illness of uniform severity that anyone can contract. The probability of contracting the illness, however, varies within the population; it is δ_H for the high risks and δ_L for low risks. The benefits B from treating the illness with a quantity of medical care X are $aX - 0.5bX^2$. When ill, the consumer's utility is a function of money income and health. Expected utility when ill is $\delta(\lambda(Y - P - \theta cX) + B(X) - K)$, where δ is the probability of being ill, λ is the marginal utility of income when ill, Y is money income (assumed to be unaffected by illness), P is the premium for health insurance, θ is the coinsurance rate (the share of medical costs paid by the consumer) and K is the nonpecuniary loss from illness.[33] When well, X and K are zero and expected utility is only a function of money income; thus, expected utility when well reduces to $(1 - \delta)\eta(Y - P)$, where $(1 - \delta)$ is the probability of being well and η is marginal utility of money when well. Normalizing the marginal utility of income for the average risk to be 1, one has $(1 - \delta)\eta + \delta\lambda \equiv 1$. Using this normalization, one can derive an expression for the expected utility of the consumer:[34]

$$E(U) = [Y - P + \delta(B(X) - \lambda\theta cX - K)]. \tag{5.6}$$

As stated in this chapter, in Eggleston's model the actual amount of services delivered, X, reflects a bargaining relationship that is similar to the one in Ellis and McGuire (1990). She develops her model under the assumption of equal bargaining power, in which case the outcome is halfway between the provider's and the patient's preferred outcome. For simplicity I follow that assumption here, although if physicians anticipate this outcome, they would include it in their calculations on selection, something that is not part of Eggleston's model. An alternative assumption would be that the patient has no bargaining power, but that physicians weight patient utility in such a way that the outcome resembles the bargaining model with equal weight on the physician's and patient's utility. As pointed out in the text, either some kind of patient bargaining power or physician agency is needed to avoid the outcome that physicians supply no services when paid a capitation.

The patient's preferred outcome comes from maximizing $E(U)$, which yields for the patient

$$X^*_D = \max(0, (a - \lambda\theta c)/b), \tag{5.7}$$

where the subscript D denotes demand, so services demanded are decreasing in the coinsurance rate θ and cost c.[35] The provider's preferred outcome comes from maximizing $E(V)$, which yields

$$X^*_S = \max(0, (\alpha a - sc)/b), \tag{5.8}$$

where the subscript S denotes supply, so services supplied are decreasing in supply-side cost sharing s and cost c.[36] If $\alpha = 0$ (pure profit maximization), then providers prefer to take the capitation and provide no services. In that case the assumption of equal bargaining power by the patient leads to the outcome that $X = X^*_D/2$.

The sponsor or regulator is interested in social welfare. That is modeled as follows. Without loss of generality, normalize the utility of not being in the health plan to be zero.[37] Social welfare W is the sum of consumer and provider welfare.[38] Thus,

$$E(W) = \mu\{tE(U_H(\text{not enrolled in the health plan}))$$

$$+ (1 - t)E(U_H(\text{enrolled in the health plan}))\}$$

$$+ (1 - \mu)E(U_L) + E(V) - N\tau\pi, \tag{5.9}$$

where the first three terms on the right-hand side sum to $E(U)$ (recall that μ is the proportion of high risks in the population and that a fraction t of them are out of the health plan from the selection efforts of physicians). π is the profit per enrollee, so the last term is the deadweight loss from provider profits or rents. Substituting in the expressions derived previously for $E(U)$ and $E(V)$, one has

$$E(W) = N[Y - P + \delta\{B(X) - \lambda\theta cX - K\} + (1 - \tau)\pi] - \gamma. \tag{5.10}$$

Note that this framework uses the consumer's valuation of the services as the social valuation. Not everyone accepts this assumption, on the grounds that either others may also value one's health or consumers are ignorant (e.g., Evans 1984; Rice 1992, 1998), but it is consistent with standard welfare economics.

In the first-best world the expression for $E(W)$ simplifies to

$$E(W) = N[Y - \delta cX + \delta\{(B(X^{FB})) - K\}]. \tag{5.11}$$

The first-best level of X is $(a - c)/b$. Consider now fee-for-service reimbursement, in which s is negative. Since $X^*s = \max(0, (\alpha a - sc)/b)$, for negative s and $\alpha \geq 1$ this will exceed the first-best level, namely, there will be demand inducement. The first-best level will also be exceeded—that is, there will be inducement—whenever $s/\alpha < 1$; in this case, the provider cost sharing is not sufficient to offset the physician's agency on behalf of the patient.

One can formalize the trade-off between efficiency-in-production and selection as follows. In order to bring efficiency in the production of services into the model, treat the formerly exogenous unit cost c as the cost that would be realized with no effort at cost reduction; denote it as c_0. Alternatively, it can be thought of as the price in a fee schedule. Eggleston models cost-reducing effort e similarly to selection cost t; thus, let $\gamma(e + t)$ represent the disutility from cost-reducing effort e and selection effort t, and let cost-reducing effort e have the effect of reducing costs to $c(e) = (1 - e)c_0$.[39] As with selection efforts, assume that e varies between 0 and 1, but that 1 is infeasible because it implies zero cost. Hence even if $t = 0$, $\gamma(1) = \gamma'(1) = \infty$.

The first-best level of cost reduction effort is given by minimizing the total cost of physician services:[40]

$$\delta(1 - e)c_0X + \gamma(e + t). \tag{5.12}$$

This first term in this expression is simply the probability of any service δ times $c(e)$, or cost per unit, times the number of units. To derive the first-order conditions (FOCs), first optimize X with respect to e. This yields[41]

$$X(e) = (a - (1 - e)c_0)/b. \tag{5.13}$$

Let e^* be the optimal e. The FOC for the optimal cost reduction effort e^* is the rather formidable expression:

$$N(t)\delta(t)(sc_0X(e^*) + [(c_0(\lambda\theta + s)/2b]\{a(a - bX) - s(1 - e)c_0\})$$

$$= \gamma'(t + e). \tag{5.14}$$

I will formally derive this expression in what follows, but I first explain the intuition of the FOC. The term in brackets, $[(c_0(\lambda\theta + s)/2b]$ is dX/de, or the trade-off between the quantity of services and cost-reducing effort.[42] One can see from inspection that this term is positive if θ, the coinsurance rate, is positive. A positive dX/de means the greater the effort, the greater the treatment. Moreover, inspection of equation 5.14 shows that the greater the coinsurance rate θ or the greater the agency a, the greater must be γ' to maintain equality and hence the greater the cost-reducing effort.

A commonly heard argument against health plans that compete on price is that the possibility of selection means health plans will devote resources to selection rather than to the efficient production of treatment for a given patient. Equation 5.14 shows this trade-off between selection and efficiency-in-production more formally.

The trade-off between selection and efficiency-in-production is given by de^*/dt^*. That de^*/dt^* is negative is demonstrated in what follows.

But before doing so, an intuitive way to see the trade-off as supply-side cost-sharing increases is to start with either fee-for-service ($s < 0$) or cost reimbursement ($s = 0$). In that case both the optimal selection effort t^* and the optimal cost-reducing effort e^* are zero. As s becomes positive, investment in selection and cost-reducing effort (efficiency-in-production) both increase at decreasing rates.

Equation 5.14 is derived as follows. Substitute $X(e^*)$ into the FOC from differentiating the total cost of services

$$\delta(1 - e)c_0X(e^*) + \gamma(e + t)$$

with respect to e, and set the result equal to zero, which gives

$$-\delta c_0X(e^*) + \gamma'(e + t) = 0, \quad \text{or}$$

$$\gamma'(e + t) = \delta c_0X(e^*) = \delta c_0(a - (1 - e^*)c_0)/b.$$

This expression holds at the first-best outcome. Go back now to the optimal cost-reducing effort of a monopoly provider. The FOCs for the optimal selection effort t^* and cost reduction effort e^* are similar to those derived in the text for the case of exogenous cost. In particular, the provider's expected utility is

$$E(V) = N(t)[R - \delta(t)sc(e)X + \delta(t)aB(X)] - \gamma(t + e),$$

where this expression is as before except that c is now a function of e and e has been added as an argument to the γ term. The FOC for t^*, the optimal degree of selection, is also essentially the same as before but now takes account of e as an argument:

$$\gamma'(t + e) = \mu[\delta_H\{sc(e^*)X - aB(X(e^*))\} - R].$$

Now use from the previous that equal bargaining results in $X = (X^*_D + X^*_S)/2$, where

$$X^*_D = \max(0, (a - \lambda\theta(1 - e)c_0)/b, \qquad \text{and}$$

$$X^*_S = \max(0, aa - (s(1 - e)c_0)/b).$$

Thus, one has

$$X = [(a - \lambda\theta(1 - e)c_0) + (aa - (s(1 - e)c_0))]/2b.$$

Differentiating this expression with respect to e gives

$$dX/de = (\lambda\theta c_0 + (sc_0))/2b = (c_0(\lambda\theta + s)/2b.$$

Going back now to $E(V)$ gives

$$E(V) = N(t)[R - \delta(t)sc(e)X + \delta(t)aB(X)] - \gamma(t + e)$$

$$= N(t)[R - \delta(t)s(1 - e)c_0X + \delta(t)aB(X)] - \gamma(t + e).$$

Differentiating this with respect to e and setting the result equal to zero gives

$$d[E(V)]/de = N(t)\delta(t)[sc_0X - s(1 - e)c_0(dX/de) + a[dB(X)/de]]$$

$$- \gamma'(t + e) = 0.$$

Shifting the last term to the right-hand side, one has

$$d[E(V)]/de = N(t)\delta(t)[sc_0X - s(1 - e)c_0(dX/de) + a[dB(X)/de]]$$

$$= \gamma'(t + e).$$

Now $dB(X)/de = (dB/dX)(dX/de) = (a - bX)(dX/de)$, so one has

$$d[E(V)]/de = N(t)\delta(t)[sc_0X - s(1 - e)c_0(dX/de) + \alpha(a - bX)(dX/de)]$$

$$= \gamma'(t + e).$$

Factoring out dX/de, one has

$$d[E(V)]/de = N(t)\delta(t)[sc_0X + \{\alpha(a - bX) - s(1 - e)c_0\}(dX/de)]$$

$$= \gamma'(t + e).$$

Substituting in for dX/de, one has

$$N(t)\delta(t)(sc_0X(e^*) + [c_0(\lambda\theta + s)/2b]\{\alpha(a - bX) - s(1 - e)c_0\}) = \gamma'(t + e),$$

which is equation 5.14.

The demonstration that de^*/dt is negative is as follows. Assume α and θ are zero. Then the general FOC for t^*,

$$\mu[\delta_H\{sc(e^*)X - \alpha B(Xe^*))\} - R] = \gamma'(t + e),$$

reduces to

$$\mu[\delta_H\{s(1 - e^*)c_0X\} - R] = \gamma'(t + e).$$

If one differentiates this expression with respect to t and uses asterisks to denote optimal values of e and t, one gets

$$-\mu\delta_H sc_0X(de^*/dt^*) = \gamma'' + \gamma''(de^*/dt^*).$$

Collecting terms in de^*/dt^*, one gets

$$-\gamma'' = (\mu\delta_H sc_0X + \gamma'')(de^*/dt^*).$$

Solving for (de^*/dt^*), one gets:

$$de^*/dt^* = -\gamma''/[\mu\delta_H sc_0X + \gamma''] < 0, \text{ since } \gamma'' \text{ is positive.}$$

The mathematics of risk adjustment in the Eggleston model are as follows. Eggleston introduces a parameter β bounded by 0 and 1 to represent the accuracy of risk adjustment. With risk adjustment β in effect, define a linear combination of $\delta(t)$, the average risk mix of the patients in the physician's practice, and δ_P, the average risk in the entire population:

$$\delta(t, \beta) = \beta\delta(t) + (1 - \beta)\delta_P. \tag{5.15}$$

The better the risk adjustment methods, the more the capitation payment to the physician R will approximate the physician's expected costs. Thus, with risk adjustment of accuracy β, define R in the payment formula as

$$R(t, \beta) = \delta(t, \beta)scX = [\beta\delta(t) + (1 - \beta)\delta_P]scX. \tag{5.16}$$

If $\beta = 0$, the capitation payment is based on the average population risk; that is, there is no risk adjustment. If $\beta = 1$, risk adjustment is perfect and capitation is based on the average risk mix of the patients actually being treated in the practice, $\delta(t)$. Using the earlier definition for E(V),

$$E(V) = N(t)[R - \delta(t)sc(e)X + \delta(t)\alpha B(X)] - \gamma(t) \tag{5.17}$$

$$= N(t)[R + \delta(t)\{\alpha B(X) - sc(e)X\}] - \gamma(t). \tag{5.18}$$

Define $c(e) = (1 - e)c_0$ to account for endogenous c and substitute the risk-adjusted capitation payment for R in the formula for E(V). One then has

$$E(V) = N(t)[R + \delta(t)\{\alpha B(X) - sc(e)X\}] - \gamma(t + e)$$

$$= N(t)[(scX(\beta\delta(t) + (1 - \beta)\delta_P) + \delta(t)\{\alpha B(X) - sc(e)X\}] - \gamma(t + e). \tag{5.19}$$

The payment schedule for R has an exogenous c, and therefore the c in the first term in brackets is not a function of e. The c in the last $sc(e)X$ term in brackets, however, is endogenous because the supply-side cost sharing is applied to the practice's observed cost. If this last assumption were changed to have the supply-side cost sharing fixed, as in a fee schedule, then the last term would have c rather than $c(e)$ in it, and the following derivation would change correspondingly.

Gathering the terms in $\delta(t)$, one has

$$E(V) = N(t)[\delta(t)(scX\beta + \alpha B(X) - sc(e)X) + (1 - \beta)\delta_P scX] - \gamma(t + e)$$

$$= N(t)[\delta(t)(\alpha B(X) + sX(c\beta - c(e))) + (1 - \beta)\delta_P scX] - \gamma(t + e). \tag{5.20}$$

To derive the optimal level of selection in the case of a monopoly physician one wants to differentiate this expression with respect to t and set the result equal to zero. After the manipulation shown in what follows, the result is

$$\gamma'(t^* + e^*) = \mu[\delta_H\{-scX(\beta - 1) - \alpha B(X)\} + (\beta + e - 1)\delta_P scX]. \tag{5.21}$$

Using this FOC, one can show how selection changes as risk adjustment technology improves. Subtracting $\gamma'(t^* + e^*)$ from both
sides of the equation gives

$$\mu[\delta_H\{-scX(\beta - 1) - \alpha B(X)\} + (\beta + e - 1)\delta_P scX] - \gamma'(t^* + e^*) = 0 \quad (5.22)$$

Totally differentiate this, first with respect to t^* and then with respect
to β, yielding:

$$-\gamma''(t^* + e^*)(dt^*) = 0 \quad\quad\quad\quad\quad\quad\quad\quad\quad\quad\quad\quad\quad\quad (5.23)$$

$$\mu(-\delta_H(scX) + \delta_P scX)d\beta = \mu scX(\delta_P - \delta_H)d\beta = 0. \quad\quad\quad (5.24)$$

Setting the two expressions on the left-hand side equal and manipu-
lating, one gets

$$dt^*/d\beta = -\mu scX(\delta_P - \delta_H)/\gamma'' < 0, \quad\quad\quad\quad\quad\quad\quad (5.25)$$

so as risk adjustment technology improves, selection diminishes.

When risk adjustment technology is perfect ($\beta = 1$), then selection
is zero because the capitated portion of the reimbursement is based
entirely on the risk of the enrolled population (this follows from the
formula for $R = scX(\beta\delta(t) + (1 - \beta)\delta_P) = scX\delta(t)$ if $\beta = 1$). In this case
there is no gain from engaging in selection efforts.

With population heterogeneity and insufficient degrees of agency,
however, the optimal payment system trades off selection and
efficiency-in-production. For a given state of risk adjustment technology, the optimal system may well not remove selection entirely
(i.e., may well not establish a fee-for-service system), because to do
so invites moral hazard or induced demand; hence, the optimal system is likely to involve some supply-side cost sharing. Ignoring preventive efforts for the moment, improved risk adjustment, however,
always improves welfare by allowing the amount of supply-side cost
sharing to increase while holding selection constant.

Allowing supply-side cost sharing to increase has two welfare
improving effects. As stressed initially by Ellis and McGuire (1986),
it allows lower demand-side cost sharing for a given amount of
moral hazard and hence imposes less risk. It also improves production efficiency.

There is a cloud on the horizon, however. Improved risk adjustment does not necessarily improve welfare if the physician or the
health plan can invest in prevention and thereby lower the risk δ of a
given group of enrollees, because better risk adjustment means the

physician or health plan gets less financial reward from an investment in prevention. A higher degree of agency on the part of the physician or health plan, of course, would serve to counteract any incentive to reduce the volume of efficacious preventive services.[43]

There are, however, two reasons to think that the incentive to reduce preventive services from improved risk adjustment is not important empirically.

1. Even in the absence of risk adjustment, many preventive services may be contractible or verifiable, for example, immunizations or physical examinations. Unlike therapeutic services, where ex ante some patients may benefit and others may be harmed by a specific procedure and thus there is an allocation problem, a preventive service is ex ante likely to be provided to all or none in an observable class (e.g., mammography to all women over 50). Moreover, the patient can typically observe whether the preventive service is delivered. Under these conditions the service is contractible. Indeed, fee-for-service insurance typically pays physicians a fee for performing preventive procedures.

2. Also in the absence of risk adjustment, the physician or health plan may not find it worthwhile to deliver preventive services for two reasons. First, the greater the turnover rate among the physician's or health plan's enrollees, the less its ability to recoup any investment in prevention in future years (Phelps 1978). Second, preventive efforts by the physician or plan, as opposed to consumer's own efforts, may not be very effective in any event. For example, the consumer has to decide to exercise; the physician can counsel that exercise is good for one's health, but it is not clear that such counseling actually increases exercise sufficiently to justify the costs of the counseling.[44]

The conclusion that better risk adjustment will little affect the physician's preventive efforts mirrors a similar empirical conclusion that better health insurance will little affect a consumer's preventive efforts. On the consumer side, the analogous theoretical argument is that health insurance increases classic moral hazard by reducing consumer incentives for healthy behavior (Ehrlich and Becker 1972). But the nonpecuniary (pain and suffering) costs of illness are uninsurable and often substantial; as a result, the marginal decrement in incentives for healthy behavior that health insurance produces are likely ignorable on the consumer side. In fact, in the RAND Health Insurance Experiment, less consumer cost sharing did not materially change health habits such as smoking, exercise, and diet (Newhouse and the Insurance Experiment Group 1993).[45]

The expression for equation 5.21 can be derived as follows. Equation 5.21 comes from adapting the result for the FOC that did not consider e. The objective function in that case was

$$E(V) = N(t)[R + \delta(t)\{\alpha B(X) - scX\}] - \gamma(t).$$

Ignoring the term in γ, the new objective function

$$E(V) = N(t)[sX(c\beta - c(e)) + \delta(t)(\alpha B(X)) + (1 - \beta)\delta_P scX] - \gamma(t + e)$$

is similar with two differences: $sX(c\beta - c(e))$ has replaced R, and $(1 - \beta)\delta_P scX$ has replaced $-scX$. Neither of these changes is a function of t, and so neither of them affects the FOC that was derived without considering risk adjustment. That first-order condition from earlier was

$$\gamma'(t^* + e^*) = \mu[\delta_H\{scX - \alpha B(X)\} - R].$$

Making the substitutions for R and scX and substituting $(1 - e)c$ for $c(e)$ in the term $sX(c - c(e))$ to get $sX(c\beta - (1 - e)c) = scX(\beta + e - 1)$ yields the FOC shown previously.

Risk Adjustment, Market
Equilibrium, and
Carveouts: Pulling a
Rabbit Out of a Hat?

In this chapter I deal with the empirical aspects of risk adjustment. I begin by describing the degree of potential profit from being able to select good risks and then turn to the performance of risk adjusters that are in use and those coming into use. I conclude there may not be a rabbit in the hat, at least given the state-of-the-art today. But even this is uncertain because of the limited degree to which risk adjustment has been implemented.

In the beginning of the chapter, I use the term *risk adjustment* as it is conventionally used in the literature: namely, adjusting a fully prospective payment conditional upon some observed characteristics of an individual. Subsequently I broaden the definition to encompass non-fully prospective schemes. At the end of the chapter, I take up directions for risk adjustment that are now only glimmers in theoreticians' eyes.

The Skewness of Spending and the Profits of Selection

The extreme skewness of health care spending suggests that there will be substantial profits to a health plan if it can disproportionately enroll good risks and be paid at something approximating the cost of an average risk. For example, in the United States the top 1 percent of spenders in 1987 accounted for 30 percent of all spending and the top 5 percent for 58 percent (Berk and Monheit 1992). At the other extreme, the lowest 50 percent of the population accounted for only 3 percent of the spending. Clearly a plan that can avoid or "dump" the high spenders and enroll or "cream" the low spenders can substantially reduce its cost. To the degree health spending is random, however, a health plan will be unable to select better-than-average risks. Much turns, therefore, on the health plan's ability to predict spending and willingness to act on its predictions.

Some help in assessing the health plan's ability to predict spending is available from a five-year panel data set that John Chapman (1997) analyzed. Because Chapman's results are both important and not widely available and because I rely heavily on them in the next several pages, I take a moment here to describe the data from which they come.[1]

Chapman's data come from 49,201 persons who were continuously enrolled in an Independent Practice Association (IPA) model HMO between 1989 and 1993 inclusive.[2] Ninety-eight percent of this cohort was enrolled through contracts with employer groups; the remaining 2 percent were Medicaid beneficiaries. Chapman analyzes the amount actually paid by the HMO for medical care services, excluding spending on drugs. Because drugs only accounted for 13 percent of total national spending on hospital, physician, and drugs in 1998, it is unlikely that any conclusions I draw are affected by the omission of drug spending (Levit, Cowen, Lazenby et al. 2000). Copayments by patients are also not counted, but they are small and would not importantly affect the results. Because he is interested in comparing spending across years, Chapman deflates each individual's expenditure by the average expenditure in that year.[3]

Because of the large sample, almost all of the estimates I use from Chapman's data are significantly different both from zero and from other values shown in the tables at the 1 percent level or better. To avoid cluttering up the tables, therefore, I have omitted indications of statistical significance.

I begin with some descriptive statistics, which show that these data are similar to those in national probability samples. Fifteen percent of Chapman's sample has no spending in a year, whereas the highest 5 percent of spenders account for 54 percent of the dollars in a year, very similar to the national figure of 58 percent.[4] Table 6.1 shows the skewness of spending in a somewhat different fashion. It shows the amount of spending over both a one- and a five-year period. The table shows the "loss," or the difference between mean spending in the given group and average spending (as a percentage of average spending), on the assumption that a plan is paid the average amount of spending.

The first row of table 6.1, for example, shows that in 1991 among the top half percent of spenders, mean spending less overall average

Table 6.1
Difference between Spending in Stratum and Average Spending ("Loss"), for One- and Five-Year Periods

	Distribution of 1991 loss, by strata of 1991 loss		Distribution of 1989–1993 loss, by strata of five-year loss	
Loss stratum (percentile of spending)	Avg loss as multiple of mean spending	Loss as % of total spending	Avg loss as multiple of mean spending	Loss as % of total spending
99.5+	34.3	17.2	21.1	10.6
99 to 99.5	13.9	6.9	9.4	4.7
98 to 99	8.5	8.5	6.1	6.1
95 to 98	4.6	13.9	3.4	10.1
90 to 95	1.94	9.7	1.65	8.2
80 to 90	0.37	3.7	0.63	6.3
0 to 80	−0.75	−60.0	−0.58	−46.1

Source: Chapman 1997.

spending was 34 times the average rate of spending and that that the loss among this group was 17 percent of total spending. Over the five-year period, those in the top half percent of spending had a loss 21 times the mean, which was 10.6 percent of total spending. Thus, spending over longer periods is less skewed.[5]

Chapman also calculated the profit a health plan might earn if it were paid an amount equal to the spending of the average person in the population, if it could costlessly choose which individuals to enroll, and if it had perfect foresight, that is, if it knew what each person was going to spend in the future. This is clearly the upper bound on potential profit. Chapman calculates that in this case the profit margin, or (revenue-cost)/cost, will be 75–80 percent.

Such a high rate of profit should not be surprising; if the plan is reimbursed an average rate but can avoid the high spenders, it can clearly do well. Elsewhere I have likened the plan's incentives to those that players of the game of Hearts have to avoid possessing the queen of spades at the end of the game (Newhouse 1986).

These numbers, however, do not clinch the case that plans will engage in selection efforts for at least three reasons, the last two of which are related. First, as emphasized in chapter 5, selection may be costly. Obviously if it is sufficiently costly, one would not expect to observe it, although the data at the end of chapter 5 suggest that cost is not a bar to some selection.[6] I have no direct evidence, however, on the cost of engaging in selection.

Second, as already mentioned, actual spending contains a random element. No one can know, for example, if a given person will be in an auto accident or have a heart attack in the future, although some individuals are surely at greater risk of an accident or a heart attack than others. If the random element in spending accounts for most of the variation across individuals in their spending, then it would not be possible for a health plan or group of providers to know in advance who would be in the top and bottom percentiles of spending and hence efforts at selection would be futile. The importance of the random element is reduced, the longer the time period over which health care spending is measured, because the random events tend to average out.

Third, individuals' health status does not remain static; over time, even if there were no random element, spending may regress to the mean as individuals recover from whatever ails them. As a result, any profits from selection activity may be dissipated quickly.

The policy import of these last two arguments depends on the period for which individuals are enrolled. In the United States, most commercial health plans enroll persons for one year; traditionally, however, as described in chapter 1, the Medicare enrollment period has been one month. Both because of the shorter enrollment period and the greater (absolute) variance in spending among the elderly, one might expect selection to be greatest among the elderly, but they are excluded from Chapman's data.

In any event, because individuals rarely if ever contract for health insurance for periods longer than one year, data on spending for periods longer than a year are only relevant to the degree individuals tend to remain in a plan. Neipp and Zeckhauser (1985) have pointed to the substantial inertia of individuals with respect to plan choice, even if they have the option of changing, and this is likely to be particularly true of healthy individuals who make little use of the medical care system, that is, those whom plans would find profitable if paid an average rate.[7] Thus, even if individuals can change plans each year, data on both how much of the variance in health care spending is random and how spending persists over time periods longer than a year are important.

The Unpredictability of Random Spending and the Evaluation of Risk Adjustment Methods

How much would these estimated profit rates be reduced if one made the more realistic assumption that the plan could not predict the random variation in spending? Chapman begins to answer this question by calculating a five-year mean rate of spending for each person. He then calculates the profit rate if a plan that is paid at an average rate enrolls all individuals whose five-year average spending is less than this mean. Five years is too short a time to average out all the randomness, so this method also includes an element of knowing the future. Nonetheless, and disconcertingly, the profit rate only falls from the range of 75–80 percent to 69 percent.

To make further headway on this question, I find it helpful to introduce a decomposition of actual medical care spending into four components: an individual-specific, time-invariant component; a first-order autoregressive component; an individual-specific, time-varying cost; and a random term, or

$$\text{Actual Cost}_{it} = \mu_i + \rho \, \text{Actual Cost}_{it-1} + v_{it} + \varepsilon_{it}, \tag{6.1}$$

where μ_i is the time-invariant term, ρ is the autoregressive feature $(0 \leqslant \rho < 1)$, and v is potentially estimable, whereas ε is not.[8] In most applications, including those discussed in what follows, the time period t is taken to be a year.

To provide some intuition for this expression, the first term on the right-hand side of (6.1), μ, represents among other things routine spending for a chronic disease. An example might be routine physician visits and medications for a disease such as hypertension. These continue at roughly the same rate year after year. The second term represents, among other things, continuing spending from an acute event in the prior period, as well as the reality that certain acute events raise the likelihood of subsequent costly events. Those who have had a heart attack in one year, for example, have higher expected spending in the following year in part because they are at greater risk of a subsequent heart attack.

An example of variation in the v term is obstetrics; in a given year, a woman may be pregnant with a delivery date in the following year. This would raise her expected spending in the year of her delivery, but because she will not be pregnant in every year, expected maternity spending in most years will be zero. Thus, maternity spending is captured in neither the first nor the second term. But the fact of a delivery can be anticipated, so the spending for the delivery is not random. The last term, ε, represents random and unpredictable events, such as whether an individual actually has a heart attack in a given year conditional on some level of underlying risk.

The value of this decomposition is the insight it offers on how much variation an ideal adjuster, one that would eliminate selection, might explain; that is, how much variation is in the first three terms and how much is in the last. Several analysts have estimated the variation attributable to the first term on the right-hand side, generally by averaging individual spending across years, as Chapman did. By doing so they can typically account for about 15 percent of the variance in annual spending.[9] Some of the between-person variation that this term captures is attributable to differences in the intensity with which the providers the individual uses treat illness rather than to patient characteristics, but most data sets have too few patients per provider to estimate a provider effect reliably, so confounding the two causes has been unavoidable.

More specifically, Newhouse et al. (1989) used data from the RAND Health Insurance Experiment to estimate the first term for adults under 65; in their data that term explained 14.5 percent of the variance. In Chapman's data it explains 16 percent. McCall and Wai (1983) estimated a value of 14 percent. The estimates of ρ in the literature generally cluster around 0.2 (Newhouse et al. 1989; Beebe, cited in Welch 1985a; Welch 1985b). Most analysts have not attempted to estimate the amount of variation in v, although a portion of the variation explained by the diagnostic adjusters described in what follows is part of that variation. The amount of variation in v, of course, will depend upon the observable measures one includes. In any event, estimates based only on the first two terms of (6.1) underestimate the amount of predictable variance.

Equation 6.1, however, leads to one criterion for evaluating risk adjustment methods, the proportion of explainable variation in cost across individuals that an adjustment method captures, or some similar measure of squared forecast error. Although squared forecast error is not the only criterion one might use, it is a principal criterion used in the literature, and I shall focus on it here.[10] Other measures that the literature uses are the amount of forecast bias (when the method is used on a sample other than the one used for estimation), mean absolute error, and performance in various subsamples of individuals.

The criterion of explainable variation begins with the notion that risk adjustment cannot and should not seek to explain all variation across individuals in observed or actual cost. It *can* not explain all such variation because some of the variation is inherently unpredictable or random; although one person might be at higher odds for a heart attack than another, no one can know before the fact whether either of them will actually suffer an attack and incur the expense of treating it. It *should* not explain all variation because any method that did so would be cost reimbursement.

Instead of explaining variation in the actual cost of treatment across individuals, then, traditional risk adjustment has sought to explain variation in their *expected* cost of treatment, or the sum of the first three components in equation 6.1. As noted previously, the first two components explain around 20 percent of the variance in actual cost.[11] Thus, an ideal risk adjuster should be able to explain *at least* a fifth of the variance across individuals in annual spending.[12] Before turning to how well current risk adjustment methods stack up against this criterion, I take up the argument that the profits of selection are transitory because of regression to the mean.

The Persistence of Health Care Spending and Plan Profits and Losses over Time: Regression to the Mean

The Medicare data presented at the end of chapter 5 indicate that health plan enrollees spent on average 13 percent less than enrollees in traditional Medicare after adjusting for several observed variables.[13] This strongly suggests that regression to the mean is not sufficient to eliminate incentives to engage in selection, though it does not fully prove it since Medicare enrollment in health plans cannot be assumed to be in a steady state.[14]

With Chapman's longitudinal data, however, one can quantify the regression to the mean. As a simple descriptive statistic, the top 5 percent of spenders in 1989 in Chapman's data, who accounted for 54 percent of the 1989 spending, accounted for only 14 percent of the dollars five years later. Nonetheless, the 14 percent figure implies that this cohort remains well above average in spending.

A more relevant figure for the profitability of selection is how subsequent profits are affected by various hypothetical selection rules.

Table 6.2
Profit Margins, by Year, by Selection Mechanism

1989 subgroup	1990	1991	1992	1993
Top 30% fully excluded	37%	31%	29%	28%
Top 30% underrepresented by half	15%	13%	12%	12%
Top 5% underrepresented by half	6%	5%	5%	5%

Source: Chapman 1997.

Table 6.2 shows values from Chapman's data from some strategies that a plan might have followed in 1989: excluding the top 30 percent of 1989 spenders; excluding a random half of the top 30 percent of 1989 spenders; and excluding half of the top 5 percent of 1989 spenders.[15] Table 6.2 shows the results on profits in the subsequent four years.

Recall that the profit rate from perfect forecasting was 75–80 percent. The results in table 6.2 show healthy future profit rates from simply excluding current high spenders, even though not all of them will be high spenders in future years. Interestingly, however, the higher profits appear not from just excluding the currently very sick, the top 5 percent of spenders; future profits are greater if not only the currently very sick but also the somewhat sick, those in the top 30 percent of spending in the base year, are excluded.

Another way to describe the data in tables 6.1 and 6.2 is as follows. The top 5 percent of spenders, who accounted for over half the spending in 1989, accounted for nothing like that amount subsequently; much of their high spending in 1989 was therefore random or, if predictable in 1988, stemmed from a nonrecurring event. They did, however, remain above-average spenders. The top 30 percent of spenders, who accounted for 75–80 percent of the spending, also remained above-average spenders, and the plan can profit even more by underenrolling in that group than by focusing its efforts only on the top 5 percent of spenders in a given year.[16]

Table 6.3 provides more detail on regression to the mean in Chapman's data by showing one-year and five-year transition matrices. "Quantile" is in quotation marks because the quantiles in the table are not uniform in size, as described in the note to the table.

Further insight on the persistence of spending over time can be gathered from the raw correlations of individual spending across years in Chapman's data, shown in table 6.4. The last two columns

Table 6.3
Persistence in Health Care Spending (%)

1989 "quantile"	% in 1989	"Quantile" in 1990					"Quantile" in 1993				
		1	2	3	4	5	1	2	3	4	5
1	40	60	18	12	7	2	55	18	14	9	3
2	20	37	28	22	11	3	36	25	22	13	4
3	20	24	22	30	18	5	29	22	25	18	5
4	15	18	15	25	32	10	24	17	25	25	8
5	5	18	13	21	29	19	25	15	21	25	14
Total	100	40	20	20	15	5	40	20	20	15	5

Source: Chapman 1997. The "quantiles" are defined as 1: 0–39th percentile; 2: 40–59th percentile; 3: 60–79th percentile; 4: 80–94th percentile; 5: 95–99th percentile.

Table 6.4
Correlation of Spending across Years Commercially Insured Population in Massachusetts, 1989–1993

Year	1989	1990	1991	1992	1993	Pair	Average R^2
1989	1					t, t	1
1990	0.317	1				$t, t + 1$	0.300
1991	0.183	0.262	1			$t, t + 2$	0.182
1992	0.169	0.193	0.338	1		$t, t + 3$	0.156
1993	0.135	0.144	0.171	0.281	1	$t, t + 4$	0.135

Source: Chapman 1997.

show the average R^2 for years of varying distance apart. For example, the 0.300 figure in the second row of the far right column is the average correlation for the four correlation coefficients that are one year apart (0.317, 0.262, 0.338, 0.281). The regression to the mean is shown by the falling R^2 values as the interval between the years increases; for example, the average correlation between spending in year t and year $t + 1$ is 0.30, whereas between year t and year $t + 2$ it is 0.18. Note that as the intervals increase the values are estimated less precisely because there are fewer observations; for example, the 0.135 figure for the t, $t + 4$ pair is based on only one observation.

These results are similar to those derived by Newhouse et al. (1989) using data from the RAND Health Insurance Experiment. The corresponding correlogram from those data is shown in table 6.5.[17]

Finally, analysts at the Health Care Financing Administration computed numbers similar to those in the last column of tables 6.4

Table 6.5
Correlation of Spending across Years RAND Health Insurance Population, United States, 1974–1982

Year	1	2	3	4	5	Pair	Average R^2
1	1					t, t	1
2	0.090	1				t, t + 1	0.192
3	0.054	0.221	1			t, t + 2	0.105
4	0.044	0.195	0.265	1		t, t + 3	0.114
5	0.045	0.184	0.065	0.192	1	t, t + 4	0.045

Source: Newhouse et al. 1989.

and 6.5 for Medicare beneficiaries. The resulting values were 0.22, 0.14, 0.12, 0.13, and 0.11 (Beebe, cited in Welch 1985a).[18]

The data in tables 6.4 and 6.5 suggest three conclusions:

1. Expenses regress toward the mean, but they do not regress all the way to the mean, at least not over the time periods studied here. In none of the three studies cited previously did the correlations become zero after five years; the correlation coefficients were 0.14, 0.05, and 0.13 in the three studies, respectively. Thus, profits from selection can persist for at least up to five years.

2. There is substantial persistence of spending over time (i.e., someone who spends a lot in one year is likely to spend a lot in future years and conversely) and that persistence is not just due to a few high spenders.

3. There is a subgroup that it is particularly lucrative to exclude.

The Costliness of Selection

So far this chapter has provided some quantitative information on the gains to a health plan if certain subgroups could be favored or disfavored in enrollment choices and the degree to which that profitability maintains itself over time. As I have already mentioned, another key determinant of the degree of actual selection is its cost, about which there is no direct evidence.

Even without such evidence, however, some observations seem pertinent. The previous two chapters show that the observed selection activity could proximately arise solely from actions of beneficiaries, as in the Cutler-Reber model described in chapter 4. Thus, selection does not have to arise from active efforts of health plans to discourage specific individuals from joining or remaining with the plan. But of course plans choose the dimensions of the product that they offer consumers. Thus, the issue is the cost to plans of adjusting their product in order to influence consumer choice.[19]

Although product adjustments in indemnity insurance seem almost costless (such as increasing a deductible), in a world of capitation and managed care, selection may be more costly. As the theoretical models of the prior chapter suggest, the physician who is contracting with the plan is in part an agent for the patient and may well resist incentives to dump the sick. Still, plans have moved toward partial or full capitation of physicians, and, if one ignores the ethical issues, it would seem less costly for physicians than plans to engage in selection activities. Physicians, for example, should have better information than plans about future health care costs, because they observe the patient firsthand. And they can alter their effort in a patient-specific manner if they choose to; for example, they could cut short their visit with a patient whom they wish to encourage to seek care elsewhere. Or they could simply advise such a patient that he or she would be better served to seek care from someone more specialized. The latter claim, of course, may be truthful, in which case the physician might serve both her own and the patient's interests.

Moreover, it is not sufficient to know just the financial incentives facing the individual physician. Suppose, for example, a plan contracts with a group of ten physicians and pays the group a capitated amount. Suppose that the ten physicians divide revenues among themselves on a fee-for-service basis using the RBRVS described in chapter 1, with fees set at a level that exhausts total revenue. Because revenue to the group itself is fixed by the capitation amount, each physician's ordering of services affects the income of all the others in the group.[20] Under such circumstances one might expect the group to develop norms of appropriate treatment to which physicians in the group would be expected to adhere. Thus, knowing how the individual physician is being paid—for example, on a fee-for-service basis—is not sufficient to predict the outcome. The relevance of incentives at all levels of contracting makes studying the effects of financial incentives on selection difficult.

In sum, the data presented earlier in this chapter establish that incentives for selection are strong if a health plan or group of physicians is simply paid an average rate for all enrollees. The standard

Table 6.6
Correlations of Spending among Different Years as High-Spending Individuals Are Eliminated from the Sample, for One- and Five-Year Distributions of Spending

Upper percentile limit	Sample size	$t, t+1$	$t, t+2$	$t, t+3$	$t, t+4$
100 (all observations)	49,201	0.29	0.17	0.14	0.13
99—1 yr[a]	48,709	0.21	0.11	0.08	0.06
95—1 yr[a]	46,741	0.19	0.09	0.07	0.05
99—5 yr[b]	48,709	0.15	0.10	0.07	0.06
95—5 yr[b]	46,741	0.13	0.09	0.07	0.05

Source: Chapman 1997.
[a] For the row labeled 99 percent, the top 1 percent of spenders in 1989 (492 individuals) are eliminated from the sample, and for the row labeled 95 percent the top 5 percent are eliminated.
[b] For the row labeled 99 percent, the top 1 percent of spenders over the entire five-year observation period (492 individuals) are eliminated from the sample, and for the row labeled 95 percent the top 5 percent are eliminated.

solution in the literature to remedy these incentives is not to pay an average rate for everyone but to vary the payment in accordance with the expected cost of the person, in other words, to risk-adjust the payment. Unfortunately, the technology for risk adjusting has to date not been up to the task assigned it. I turn now to risk adjustment and begin with a particularly simple form, an outlier or reinsurance scheme.

Is an Outlier Scheme Sufficient to Deal with the Selection Problem?

Partly because of the skewness of annual health care spending and partly because of the precedent of the outlier system in the hospital PPS, use of an outlier scheme may seem like a natural starting point for a risk adjustment scheme. In such a scheme a certain percentage of total payments, 5 percent in the PPS hospital scheme, is set aside as an additional payment for very expensive cases. Specifically, as described in chapter 1, if the cost of a case exceeds a certain amount (the outlier threshold), a percentage of the additional costs are paid by the scheme (80 percent of the costs above the threshold in the PPS). An outlier scheme might also be considered reinsurance.

The data shown in table 6.6 appear to support the efficacy of an outlier system. They show how correlations over time change as the highest spenders are eliminated from the sample. Both one-year and five-year distributions of spending are used to define high spenders; the conclusions are the same for both definitions.

These Pearson correlations clearly decline as high-spending individuals are eliminated from the sample, which suggests greater intertemporal correlation among the very high spenders.[21] Because an outlier scheme operates to reduce the loss for exactly that group, it might seem that it would be effective in reducing selection.

A related argument that appears to support an outlier scheme is based on the spending of the group that is in the top 5 percent of spenders for *each* of the five years. They represent 2 percent of the entire population and almost certainly have a serious chronic disease. If a plan could exclude just that 2 percent, its profit rate would be nearly 40 percent, or about half of the maximum profits from selection with perfect foresight. Thus, if selection costs rise with the numbers being selected against, this chronically ill population is an attractive target for selection efforts. An outlier scheme, however, makes this target less attractive.[22]

Outlier schemes, however, are unlikely to resolve the selection problem. First, as typically conceived, they provide additional payments for only a small percentage of cases: in the case of the hospital PPS, about 3 percent. Even for that percentage of cases, however, plans suffer a loss on each case because no payments begin until the outlier threshold is reached.

Second, and more important, for the great majority of cases, outlier schemes do nothing to change the incentives. Plans still will incur a loss on each nonoutlier case whose cost is above the mean (assuming reimbursement at the mean). Moreover, they still will make money on cases whose costs are below the mean, so the incentives to cream or dump for 97 percent of the cases are unchanged (ignoring uncertainty about who after the fact will be an outlier). Incentives for the good risks matter, because the results in table 6.3 show persistence of spending at the lower quantiles, not just among the top 5 or the top 20 percent of spenders. For example, over half of those in the bottom 40 percent of spenders in 1989 were in the bottom 40 percent of spenders in 1993.

But suppose that a larger outlier scheme than the PPS scheme were in place and reached the top 30 percent of spenders in a year. Further, suppose the outlier scheme completely prevented a loss among this group, which is far from the actual case. Ignoring the financing of the outlier payments, table 6.2 shows that enrolling only the bottom 70 percent of spenders in 1989 would still yield a profit rate of 28 percent in 1993. Enrolling the bottom 95 percent of spenders in 1989 would yield a 20 percent profit rate in 1993. To the degree that outlier payments are financed by reducing reimbursement for the bottom 70 percent, however, actual profit rates would be lower.

A variant of an outlier scheme is the ceding ex ante of expected high-cost patients to a common pool (van Barneveld, van Vliet, and van de Ven 1996). This proposal potentially improves on a simple outlier scheme by targeting payment on cases that the plan expects to incur the highest losses, thereby not spending outlier funds on nonforeseeable events. It leaves incentives in place, however, to skim and dump for all other cases, and, as just seen, these incentives are substantial.

Thus, an outlier scheme is only a partial answer. Indeed, I show in what follows that formal risk adjustment and outlier schemes are complements rather than substitutes. I am now ready to turn to more formal risk adjustment methods.

Demographic Adjusters: No Pain, No Gain

If an ideal adjuster should explain at least 20–25 percent of the annual variation in medical spending, how well do the usual adjusters stack up?

As described in chapter 1, Medicare has employed a simple form of risk adjustment from the mid-1980s to 2000, namely, adjustment on the demographic variables of age, sex, institutional status, welfare (low-income) status, and county of residence. For example, Medicare pays health plans more for enrolling a 70- to 74-year-old noninstitutionalized woman who is not on welfare than it does for a similar 65- to 69-year-old woman who lives in the same county.

Such demographic adjusters have the advantage of being inexpensive; all the required data are readily available in administrative files and cannot be easily manipulated or gamed to increase reimbursement to the plan. As a result, little downside exists to using such adjusters. But unfortunately the readily available and relatively inexpensive demographic variables explain only around 1–2 percent of the overall variation in annual spending across individuals, or less than 10 percent of what an ideal adjuster would explain, assuming such an adjuster would explain at least 20 percent of the variance. Given the previous chapter's description of the amount of selection observed in the Medicare program, one might say that use of demographic adjusters is a case of no pain, no gain.

Moreover, because Medicare beneficiaries could elect a new plan every month rather than once a year, any risk adjustment mechanism carried an additional burden. Given the small amount of variance they explain, it should not surprise anyone that demographic adjusters have not reduced selection in the Medicare program to negligible levels.

Diagnosis-Based and Other Adjusters

Although the demographic variables have not sufficed to reduce selection in the Medicare program to negligible levels, it is not clear how close to the ideal in terms of explained variation an adjuster must come in order to do so. To the degree that selection is costly or impractical, an imperfect adjuster will suffice, which is fortunate since one will never have an ideal adjuster. Alas, no one knows how imperfect an adjuster can be and still do an adequate job. The answer will surely depend in part on institutional arrangements, such as how often individuals are allowed to change plans and how plans structure contractual arrangements with physicians and others who can influence patient choice.

In the near term the largest gain in the explanatory power of the risk adjustment formula comes from incorporating diagnostic information into it. Thus, for example, a plan would receive more for a woman with breast cancer than for an otherwise similar woman without the disease. As I show in what follows, using diagnostic information only from inpatient stays appears to raise R^2 to the 0.06–0.07 range, whereas using information from both inpatient and outpatient claims raises it to the 0.09–0.11 range (Ellis, Pope, Iezzoni et al. 1996; Weiner, Dobson, Maxwell et al. 1996; Pope, Ellis, Ash et al. 2000). Whether these increments in explanatory power will suffice to render selection minimal is not known.

A leading system for incorporating diagnostic information is Principal Inpatient-Diagnostic Cost Groups (PIP-DCG), which are based on inpatient diagnoses only and which are now being implemented in Medicare. The group that developed this system also has developed a Hierarchical Co-existing Conditions (HCC) system, which exploits outpatient as well as inpatient diagnostic data. Other prominent systems include the Ambulatory Care Group (ACG) system, the Disability Payment System (DPS), and Clinical Diagnostic Groups (CDGs). Other than whether the system uses outpatient data, the differences among these systems are not important for my purposes. They vary essentially in how they aggregate the detailed diagnostic information, and they tend to change somewhat over time in their detail; the reader can refer to Ellis, Pope, Iezzoni et al. 1996; Weiner, Dobson, Maxwell et al. 1996; Kronick, Gilmer, Dreyfus et al. 1996; and Pope, Ellis, Ash et al. 2000 for expositions of the systems as of those publication dates.

Chapman used his data set to ascertain the effect of diagnosis-based risk adjustment on incentives to select.[23] He first estimated weights for his population for each adjustment method (e.g., the DCG method) using a sample of 65,000 persons who were continuously enrolled for three years (calendar years 1990–1992) but not for five years. Thus, there is no overlap with the sample used in the results already cited. He then used those weights to generate the following results on the sample of 49,000 persons who were enrolled continuously for five years, the same sample used in the preceding tables.

Chapman computed how potential profit rates are affected by various risk adjustment methods.[24] Although he used versions of these systems that are no longer current, it is unlikely that the inferences I draw from Chapman's results would change if more current versions were used.[25]

A key issue with respect to the use of diagnostic information to risk adjust is the timing of how the diagnostic information affects payment. Chapman distinguishes three ways of incorporating the information. The *retrospective* method uses diagnoses from the concurrent period to establish weights. For example, if a person has a heart attack in year t the increased spending from the (average) heart attack in year t enters the weight for the class or group of diagnoses that includes heart attacks. The *prospective* method uses diagnoses from a past period (and not the current period) to predict spending in the current period. Thus, a diagnosis of a heart attack in year t would not change the weight assigned a person in year t, but it would increase the weight in year $t + 1$. Then, however, the weight would only increase by the amount of average spending in year $t + 1$ among those who had had heart attacks in year t. As a result, in the prospective method the cost of the hospitalization for the (average) heart attack in year t does not affect the weight in year t. This is the method the HCFA has adopted for Medicare. Chapman also defines

Table 6.7
Average 1991–1993 Adjusted R^2

	Adjustment method	Retrospective	Prospective	Group prospective
No stop loss	Demographic	0.016	0.016	0.016
	HCC	0.355	0.066	0.037
Stop loss at 25 × mean	Demographic	0.027	0.027	0.027
	HCC	0.432	0.106	0.064

Source: Chapman 1997.

a *group prospective* method, which does a "retrospective" analysis of the past period at the individual level (i.e., uses characteristics from the past period to predict that period's spending) and then uses a group average of past period weights to predict group spending in the current period. Although I have left the group prospective results in the tables, I do not focus on them.[26]

The following data compare demographic and HCC adjusters because demographic adjustment is the most common type (other than none), and among the diagnostic-based adjusters the current version of HCCs does marginally better than other systems in most data sets.[27] Table 6.7 shows the R^2 values achieved by the two adjusters. Several things are apparent.

1. Exploiting the diagnostic information in the HCCs substantially improves performance relative to demographic adjusters. As in other data sets, demographic adjusters in this data set explain 1.6 percent of the variance (2.7 percent if losses are truncated at 25 times the mean), clearly not a stellar performance if the criterion is 20 percent of explained variance or better. Used prospectively, HCCs explain about four times as much variance as demographic adjusters, but even that does not come that close to 20 percent. As mentioned earlier, Ellis, Pope, Iezzoni et al. (1996) obtain somewhat better results on another data set. Of course, selection has costs, so how good predictions have to be to render selection minimal is still an open question—and one that data such as these cannot settle.

2. When used retrospectively, the HCC method generates much higher R^2 values and clearly seems to be picking up some of the random variation from new diagnoses. As a result, I do not have a criterion by which to judge how well retrospective adjustment would perform. The demographic values are invariant to prospective or retrospective adjustment.

Table 6.8
Average 1991–1993 Subgroup Profit Rates from Various Selection Mechanisms and with Various Risk Adjustment Methods

	Demo-graphic	HCC—individual prospective	HCC—group prospective	HCC—retrospective
Perfect selection (maximum profit rate)	0.66	0.47	0.28	0.19
1989 < mean	0.17	0.08	−0.01	0.00
1989 1st quintile	0.38	0.09	−0.15	−0.10
1989 5th quintile	−0.75	−0.32	0.05	−0.01
1989 hospitalization and heart diagnosis ($n = 399$)	−1.55	−0.31	0.80	0.57

Source: Chapman 1997.

3. A stop-loss or outlier scheme, even at twenty-five times the mean, has a substantial effect on the calculated R^2. The sensitivity to a truncation factor at twenty-five times the mean in a sample of nearly 50,000 persons indicates the "lower bound" that at least 20 percent of the variance can be explained may not be very precisely estimated, although similar results have been found by a number of investigators using different data sets.

4. Although a stop-loss value increases the R^2, it does not change the relative effect of diagnostic risk adjustment. As a result, one can infer that diagnosis-based adjusters are measuring something other than the probability of high-cost cases. Thus, they complement a stop-loss feature rather than substitute for it. I deal with this issue in more detail in what follows.

Table 6.8 translates the R^2 values shown in table 6.7 into profit and loss values. In particular, it shows how risk adjustment using HCCs changes average 1991–1993 profit rates if plans use various selection strategies on 1989 data. Several things are apparent.

1. Even after risk adjustment using the HCC prospective method, large *potential* profits remain on the table. For example, the 0.47 value in the first row means that if all those who were profitable with HCC risk adjustment were enrolled in the 1991–1993 period and the plan were paid the average amount, the plan would have a 47 percent profit rate.

2. But such large profit rates are not attainable because they require perfect foresight and costless selection. Strategies that do not

rely on foresight, such as enrolling only those whose 1989 spending is below the mean, generate only an 8 percent profit rate with HCCs, compared to 17 percent using demographic adjustment. Likewise the losses from not enrolling the high spenders (5th quintile) in 1989 are reduced, although they are still substantial.

3. The HCC retrospective method performs better than the prospective method in reducing the profit potential from certain skimming and dumping strategies. In fact, it overcorrects if the selection strategy is to aim for those in the first quintile (low spenders) and avoid those with heart disease, as shown by the negative profit rate on the low spenders and the positive profit rate on those with heart disease.

4. The last row shows the group of 399 persons who had a diagnosis of heart disease during 1989 and were hospitalized. Both the retrospective and group prospective methods overadjust for this group, meaning that they convert them into being profitable.[28]

Will the Game Continue?

A further question is whether diagnostic-based risk adjustment simply creates new opportunities for selection by changing the identities of who is profitable and who is not. In other words, in assessing how profitability will change with new risk adjustment schemes, most analytical efforts (e.g., Ellis, Pope, Iezzoni et al. 1996) assume plan managers do not react to new schemes. But one has no reason to suppose this is the case and therefore Chapman asks whether risk adjustment will "stick."

To answer this question, Chapman takes two steps. He first measures how profitability within individuals changes over time using various risk adjustment methods. The intuition is whether those persons who are profitable in a base period with, say, demographic risk adjustment remain profitable under a risk adjustment scheme. To the degree that they do, one would expect selection methods to remain directed at those individuals and conversely.

Chapman finds that profitable patients in one year tend to be profitable in a subsequent year using demographic risk adjustment but not using diagnosis-based risk adjustment. The Spearman rank order correlations between individuals' profitability in 1990 and in the three years 1991–1993 with demographic adjustment are 0.51, 0.45, and 0.41, respectively. With this substantial correlation, plans might continue to use similar selection methods.

By contrast, the correlations of 1990 and 1991–1993 profits using HCCs as prospective adjusters are much lower, 0.06, 0.15, and 0.16, respectively. In other words, with diagnosis-based risk adjustment little correlation exists between profitability in 1990 and in subsequent years. Because the gains from risk selection are more transitory and hence selection efforts less rewarding using HCCs, these low correlations suggest that selection strategies may change.

Second, and more directly, Chapman asks how the 1993 profitability of favorably selected groups (such as all those who are profitable in 1990) that are formed *after* risk adjustment compares with groups formed on the same criteria *before* risk adjustment. Ignoring any costs from selection, the gains from selection naturally increase in the *after* case, because the groups are reformed after accounting for the risk adjustment method. The increase in profitability is greater for retrospective adjustment, suggesting that selection strategies are more likely to change and risk adjustment is less likely to stick with retrospective than with prospective adjustment. Nevertheless, for the specific variant of the HCC method that its developers recommend (using those diagnoses least susceptible to moral hazard), the increase in profits from post-adjustment selection even with retrospective adjustment does not appear to be large.[29]

Moreover, the absolute profit rates after risk adjustment can still be substantial. For example, when payment is adjusted by the HCC model, the group that is in the bottom 5 percent of profitability in 1990 (after adjustment by HCCs) has a profit rate that is about −80 percent of the mean in 1993. The group in the top 5 percent in 1990 has a profit rate that is about 25 percent of the mean. This emphasizes that risk adjustment at its present stage of development is not a panacea.

In sum, the gains from improved risk adjustment may be less than they first appear. Because plans will have incentives to alter their selection methods, the data presented earlier in this chapter *understate* the potential for skimming and dumping after risk adjustment. It is like simulating the revenue effects of a tax law change without considering behavioral change.

Retrospective versus Prospective Adjustment

The data in tables 6.7 and 6.8 show a substantial gain in predictive accuracy for the retrospective method relative to the prospective method. But the higher R^2 values generated by the retrospective method are to be expected, because a diagnosis is recorded when a patient seeks treatment and the cost of that treatment is therefore included in the weight. In other words, the retrospective method adjusts for that expense on average, whereas the prospective method does not. Some, perhaps much, of the gain in R^2 from the retrospective method, however, does not mitigate selection, because it comes from predicting random variation. If a person has a first heart attack, for example, most of the additional spending is random, and the retrospective method picks up the average spending among people with heart attacks, whereas the prospective method does not. Even more important, moral hazard is greater with the retrospective method precisely because the retrospective method reimburses the average cost of the hospitalization that generates the diagnosis.

Nonetheless, one might expect selection incentives to be less with retrospective adjustment. Individuals will differ in their expected spending in ways that may be known to the plan or physician but not the risk adjustment scheme. Some individuals, for example those who smoke, will be at greater risk of having a first heart attack than others, and those who fail to wear helmets when riding a motorcycle will be at greater risk of trauma. If risk adjustment is prospective, the plan is at risk for the additional expected spending from the person at higher risk, whereas with the retrospective adjuster it is not. For example the average heart attack in Massachusetts in the 1993–1995 period cost just under $40,000 to treat (Cutler, McClellan, and Newhouse 2000). If heart attacks were entirely random, this would not matter for purposes of selection. But suppose one person's expected risk of having a heart attack is 10 percentage points higher than another's in ways that are not captured in the risk adjustment formula. That is a difference in expected spending of $4,000, a figure roughly equal to the average spending in the population. With this large a difference in expected spending, a plan is not likely to want the person who has a 10-percentage-point higher risk of having a heart attack as an enrollee.

That retrospective adjusters pick up systematic variation and not just random variation is supported by Chapman's data. If retrospective adjusters were explaining only random variation in the current year, their performance in future years would be the same as the prospective adjusters in future years, but this is not the case. In table 6.8 the data for groups with spending less than the 1989 mean and those in the highest spending quintile show the retrospective adjuster does better in reducing incentives to skim and dump than the prospective adjuster. For the last group (heart disease with a hospitalization) the retrospective adjuster does worse, but this is a relatively small group of people, and this result does not appear to generalize.[30] In short, retrospective adjustment appears to reduce the incentives to select relative to prospective adjustment. Thus, Chapman's results imply a trade-off between the incentives for selection and the degree of moral hazard in the risk adjustment system.

By contrast, two groups other than Chapman analyzed the difference between the retrospective and prospective methods and did not find substantial differences in their ability to predict spending for selected groups.[31] If these results were accepted, it would imply that there is no gain from using retrospective adjusters. Dunn, Rosenblatt, Taira et al. (1995) formed a group of low (and also a group of high) spenders in 1991 and examined the degree to which retrospective and prospective methods overpaid (underpaid) for this group in 1992. They used several risk adjustment methods, including demographic, DCGs, and ADGs. They found little difference between the retrospective and prospective methods in the degree of overpayment (underpayment) in 1992. Ellis, Pope, Iezzoni et al. (1996) found some differences but interpreted them as minimal. Like Dunn, Rosenblatt, Taira et al., Ellis, Pope, Iezzoni et al. used only two adjacent years of data.

Chapman replicated the findings of these two studies when he restricted himself to data from the two adjacent years of 1989–1990, but, as described previously, found substantial differences between the two methods when using the full five years of data. Chapman was thus able to confirm a speculation of Dunn, Rosenblatt, Taira et al. (1995) that using only two years of data is not a good test of the difference between the two methods, because the prospective method uses some of the same information (diagnosis in 1991) as is used in the construction of the low- and high-spending groups (spending in 1991).[32] This biases the finding toward no difference between the two methods. Thus, I conclude that retrospective adjustment does a better job of reducing the incentives to select than does prospective adjustment.[33]

This implies that the HCFA's decision to use prospective risk adjustment impairs the ability of risk adjustment to reduce selection. Although it has not been done, the welfare loss from the reduced ability to select needs to be compared with the loss from the increased moral hazard.

To sum up with respect to empirical work on diagnosis-based adjusters: These risk adjusters do much better at predicting current and future spending than demographic adjusters do, but much of the explainable variation remains unexplained and considerable potential for skimming and dumping therefore remains. Moreover, the introduction of diagnosis-based adjusters is not a panacea, except perhaps for consultants, because it will create new profitable opportunities that will offer incentives to change selection methods. Finally, relative to prospective adjusters, retrospective adjusters do reduce the incentives to select at the price of increasing moral hazard.

Risk Adjustment and the Clinical Treatment of Disease

Both the risk adjustment literature and the results reported here have used weights calculated from treatment under fee-for-service plans. Although potentially an issue even for demographic adjustment, the use of such weights could be a serious issue for diagnosis-based adjustment. It is known from work spanning many years that some diagnoses have essentially one method of treatment while others leave the physician substantial discretion. Moreover, the method of treating discretionary admissions varies substantially from place to place (Phelps 2000).

For diseases such as appendicitis and the associated treatment of an appendectomy, which show rather little variation from place to place, a weight based on average fee-for-service treatment is likely satisfactory. For diseases such as depression, however, whose treatment varies substantially from place to place, there is no assurance that a weight based on the average fee-for-service treatment is optimal. Frank, Berndt, and Busch (1999) and Berndt, Busch, and Frank (2000), for example, document that managed behavioral health care not only reduced the cost of treating depression around 30 percent but also improved outcomes from doing so. In light of this result, treatment for depression that was less intense than the fee-for-service average would probably be optimal, but one can imagine that for other diseases the opposite result would obtain. In the latter case pricing at the average for fee-for-service treatment would mean that the plan would incur a loss by using the optimal treatment because the average reflects a mix of the high- and low-cost treatment.

There is no simple answer to this issue, because the risk adjustment weight is inherently an administered price and how that price is set may affect the way in which a particular disease can be treated. Failing to employ diagnostic-based weights does not solve the problem either, because it implicitly sets an equal weight for each diagnosis class.

A similar issue arose when the DRGs were first introduced into the Medicare program and the weight for the relevant DRG was not adjusted to account for the cost of cochlear implants. As noted in chapter 1, this decision temporarily kept cochlear implants off the market (Kane and Manoukian 1989). That may or may not have been optimal; the point is that any risk adjustment scheme, including no risk adjustment, creates incentives to treat particular diseases in particular ways.

Risk Adjustment and Medicare Policy

As described in chapter 1, the Balanced Budget Act of 1997 mandated that the HCFA introduce "health-status based adjusters" into the Medicare payment method for health plans, and the agency is phasing in PIP-DCG-based payment. It has chosen not to rely on diagnosis from outpatient records, however, because of the incompleteness of those records (table 1.6).

The use of outpatient data is further complicated by the difficulty of establishing a diagnosis for many patients when they first present. For minor problems this is probably not a serious issue because grouping them in the lowest category will not be an important error. For more expensive diseases, however, there is a question of how the timing of the diagnosis affects payment. This is in part a question of prospective versus retrospective payment, already discussed, but it poses a further administrative problem if the intent is to pay for an episode that includes services, especially expensive diagnostic tests, before a diagnosis is established.

Auditing outpatient records is yet another administrative issue if outpatient diagnostic data are ultimately used. There are both mundane issues, such as the legibility of handwriting, and more substantive ones, such as the verification of information in the record. In an inpatient setting, where numerous individuals examine a medical record and use it for treatment of often seriously ill patients, fraud seems unlikely. In an outpatient setting, however, many fewer people may examine the record, and information may be more difficult to verify, particularly diagnoses that are made on the basis of what the patient tells the physician, that is, the medical history. It seems clear that incorporating outpatient diagnoses into a risk adjustment method poses difficult administrative problems.

This is unfortunate, since it is clear that use of only the inpatient diagnosis creates substantial moral hazard if the disease could be treated as effectively on an outpatient basis. The moral hazard will also be present if outpatient diagnoses must be introduced initially with little weight because of the coding problems just described.

The HCFA was certainly aware of the moral hazard problem when it introduced PIP-DCGs. As a result, it took the three steps described in chapter 1 to limit moral hazard.[34] Furthermore, initially only 10 percent of the plan's payment was based on the PIP-DCG-adjusted payment. Thus, the initial financial incentives for hospitalizing only to maximize reimbursement are minimal. Indeed, the cost of the hospitalization will outweigh the additional reimbursement in virtually all cases. Over time, however, the HCFA has proposed to increase the weight on the PIP-DCG, so the moral hazard will increase.

In addition to reducing potential moral hazard, the HCFA adopted prospective rather than retrospective reimbursement because most health plans favored it. The health plans argued that prospective reimbursement was superior because they would have a predictable revenue stream, whereas with retrospective reimbursement their revenues would vary with random illnesses (Academy of Actuaries 1993).

This argument is puzzling. What should matter more to plans than the variance in revenues is the variance in profit (or margin). Assume for the moment that all costs are variable. Then the greater the amount of risk adjustment, the greater the positive covariation of revenue and cost. As a result, the variance in profit will be less under retrospective risk adjustment. If costs are mostly fixed, however, the picture is more complicated. Retrospective risk adjustment could then make profits more variable.

But at the level of the health plan or the HMO one would expect costs to be mostly variable. Most costs are for treating enrollees' illnesses, and they will of course vary with enrollees' use of services. Most HMOs, for example, contract with providers on a per use basis;

for example, they pay hospitals per day or per admission.[35] A crude calculation from data in Wholey, Feldman, Christianson et al. 1996 confirms that the great majority of costs are variable.[36]

Instead of the predictability of revenues, the more likely reason HMOs do not favor retrospective risk adjustment may follow from the favorable risk selection that most (but not all) HMOs that now contract with Medicare enjoy. Not only will they lose revenue and profit from any risk adjustment method, Chapman's results show that they will lose more with retrospective risk adjustment. When the current Medicare risk adjustment scheme was proposed, HMOs lobbied strongly against it. Their representatives indicated to me privately, however, that they would offer little opposition if the HCFA would introduce the risk adjustment scheme on a budget-neutral basis.

Risk Adjustment Using Patient-Reported Information

Another potential improvement in risk adjustment might come from adding information on functional status (Gruenberg, Kaganova, and Hornbrook 1996; Medicare Payment Advisory Commission 1999). Information on functional status could be particularly important if capitation arrangements are to extend to cover chronic care for institutionalized populations, as Medicare is doing by expanding such programs as the Program of All-Inclusive Care for the Elderly (PACE). In addition to information on functional status, some have proposed using self-rated general health status (e.g., "How would you rate your health?" with choices of excellent, very good, good, fair, or poor) or scales based upon the same concept (Hornbrook and Goodman 1995, 1996).

There are several problems, however, with moving in this direction, starting with the degree of benefit. Over the entire population and not just the institutionalized, the increment in R^2 from including this information in addition to diagnosis is rather low, perhaps an increment of 0.01 (Newhouse et al. 1989). Because the gain from incorporating functional status seems limited to certain subsets of the population, such as the elderly, one might therefore want to use such measures only for those populations.

And there are important operational problems in trying to incorporate self-reported information. The most important is the cost of gathering information and keeping it current for each plan. For items such as "How would you rate your health?" data must be collected from beneficiaries. There will be problems of refusal, which may lead to bias; one would expect greater refusal among the more frail and functionally impaired. Furthermore, it is not clear how data will be gathered about the cognitively impaired. If the information is not frequently updated, plans could still temporarily profit from selection. Moreover, self-report is potentially vulnerable to fraud; although there may be no direct incentives for the consumer to overstate his or her disability, the group obtaining the higher capitation may find a way to share the gains with consumers.[37]

In the case of functional health status (but not overall self-reported health), one could potentially avoid both nonresponse and fraud by using third parties to report, but that would substantially raise the cost, especially if the nonelderly or the younger elderly were included. Finally, initial calibration will be problematic because neither functional status nor self-rated health are available in administrative data, which precludes the usual form of setting weights for cells. Such data are available for Medicare beneficiaries as part of the Current Beneficiary Survey, but with a sample size of around 12,000 persons this is a very small survey to use to set weights. Furthermore, data from the Current Beneficiary Survey suggest that the increment in payment as the number of functional limitations (Activities of Daily Living) increases is both nontrivial and lumpy; that is, payment can increase substantially for one additional limitation. This suggests there may well be an upcoding problem.

The Complementarity of Risk Adjustment and Reinsurance

The data in table 6.9 show that risk adjustment and reinsurance or pooling complement each other. Begin by examining the last three columns of the table, which show average loss rates as a percentage of age-sex-adjusted revenue. Loss is defined as spending less revenue. Positive numbers are loss rates; for example, 0.10 means the plan loses 10 percent on average for each person in that group. A zero means average revenue equals average expenditure, so that risk adjustment is perfect. Revenue to the plan is always adjusted by age and sex (demographic adjustment).

The first column shows results from three possible selection criteria for forming subgroups from the 49,201 persons in Chapman's sample. The first four rows are formed by perfect *unfavorable* selection

Table 6.9
Loss Rates on High-Risk Groups under Various Risk Adjustment and Outlier or Pooling Schemes, 1990–1993

Selection pattern	Group size	High-cost exclusion method	Base method	Four-year average loss		
				No exclusion	Exclude top 1%	Exclude top 5%
Perfect	13,027	Reins[b]	Demog[c]	1.79	1.40	0.87
unfavorable		MHRP[d]		1.79	1.69	1.55
selection[a]		Reins	HCC	1.20	0.82	0.33
		MHRP		1.20	1.14	1.07
1989 loss	9,575	Reins	Demog	0.78	0.59	0.39
		MHRP		0.78	0.69	0.57
		Reins	HCC	0.25	0.09	−0.06
		MHRP		0.25	0.19	0.13
Not lowest	39,362	Reins	Demog	0.109	0.116	0.123
quintile[e]		MHRP		0.109	0.101	0.093
		Reins	HCC	0.032	0.042	0.053
		MHRP		0.032	0.026	0.021

Source: Chapman 1997.
[a] Assumes person must be enrolled for the entire four-year period; that is, a plan cannot exclude a person who is on average profitable for only the year(s) in which the plan suffers a loss.
[b] Reins = Reinsurance. The top 1 or 5 percent of spenders in the current year is placed in the high-risk pool and financed from the base rate.
[c] Demog = Age and sex adjusters. The age adjustment uses dummy variables for each five-year age-sex group, except under 5 years of age is subdivided into under 1 year of age and 1–4 years of age, and the over 65 years of age are collapsed into one age group.
[d] MHRP = Mandatory High Risk Pooling. The top 1 or 5 percent of spenders in the prior year is placed in the high-risk pool and financed from the base rate.
[e] Not Lowest Quintile excludes lowest 20 percent of spenders in 1989.

—that is, the persons who, over the 1990–1993 period will ex post have spending exceeding their age-sex-adjusted revenue. Thus, this is the maximum loss the plan could sustain on a subgroup assuming it must enroll persons for the entire four-year period (i.e., the calculation does not exclude the profitable years among persons who are on average unprofitable over the entire four-year period.) There were 13,027 people, or just over a quarter of the entire sample, on whom a plan would have sustained a loss by enrolling them over these four years.

The next four rows are formed from those with a loss in 1989 (i.e., spending in excess of age-sex-adjusted means). Finally, the last four rows are formed from excluding those with expenses in the lowest fifth of the 1989 expense distribution. This last group should be thought of as a plan that was not appealing to a group that spent nothing in 1989, but had a representative group of those who spent something.

The third column shows two possible methods for handling high-cost cases. The first is reinsurance (labeled "reins"), which is an outlier system. Using this method all spending in excess of a certain threshold is fully insured by an actuarially fair system whose premium is deducted proportionately from all payments.[38] The thresholds used here are spending above the 1st and 5th percentiles, which are twelve and three times the mean spending, respectively. The second method is ceding high risks (mandatory high-risk pooling or MHRP). Each year the plan can cede one or five percent of its risks. It chooses this group as the highest 1 or 5 percent of spenders in the prior year.[39] This is, of course, a different group of persons each year. The actuarily fair premium for the excluded group is averaged over the remaining persons and deducted from revenue.[40]

The fourth column shows two risk adjustment methods, demographic (age and sex) ("demog") and HCCs (used in a prospective fashion). The final three columns show the loss rates, first with no reinsurance or pooling, and then with reinsurance and pooling, respectively.

The first row shows that with age-sex-adjusted payment the loss rate would be 179 percent among the group that had perfect unfavorable selection; in other words, this is the maximum loss that could be averted through selection methods. Fully reinsuring all dollars above the 1st percentile (5th percentile) would drop that loss rate to 140 percent (87 percent).

The last two columns of the second row show that ex ante ceding the entire spending of the top 1 percent (5 percent) of spenders in the prior year would have a smaller effect than reinsurance; it would only drop the loss rate from 179 percent to 169 percent (155 percent). This smaller effect reflects the lack of perfect correlation in who is in the top 1 percent from year to year. Recall that the plan ceded to the pool those in the top 1 percent (5 percent) the prior year, but relative to reinsurance it fully bears the spending of those who newly appear in the top 1 or 5 percent. Some portion of this new spending, of course, may be random.

The third and fourth rows show how adding HCCs as risk adjusters (in addition to age and sex) alters the loss rate. The maximum
loss rate even with no reinsurance or pooling falls 59 percentage
points to 120 percent and with reinsurance for the top 5 percent it
drops all the way to 33 percent. The combined effects of HCCs and
reinsurance emphasize that the two strategies are complements and
not substitutes.

The next four rows show the effect of including everyone who had
above-average costs in 1989 for their age-sex group. With no reinsurance or pooling, loss rates among this group for the following
four years are substantial: 78 percent with demographic adjusters
and 25 percent with HCCs. But reinsuring all spending above the
95th percentile actually converts this group to a gain of 6 percent
if HCCs are used as adjusters. This further emphasizes the com-
plementarity of risk adjustment and special treatment of high-cost
cases.

The final four rows show effects in a more representative group,
the top 80 percent of spenders in 1989. This group generates losses
under any method, but the losses are small, especially with HCCs as
risk adjusters. These last results show that (1) a plan needs enrollees
in the lowest quintile of prior expenses to break even in the future
(these will be mainly people who spent nothing in the prior year);
and (2) reinsurance and pooling do not much affect profits and losses
in this group.[41]

Partial Capitation, Supply-Side Cost Sharing, or Mixed Schemes

The theoretical literature reviewed in chapters 3 and 5 made substantial use of mixed capitation and fee-for-service reimbursement
methods. The empirical risk adjustment literature, however, has
confined itself to analyzing the effect on selection of covariates such
as diagnosis within fully prospective (high-powered) schemes, but
mixed schemes clearly blunt selection incentives by lowering the
weight on the capitated payment. In addition, they provide some
revenue at the margin to reduce stinting.

On the other hand, they raise the likelihood of pricing errors because many more prices must be set for any given size administrative budget, and the likelihood of a sizable error should increase as
the amount of resources invested in setting a price decreases. Moreover, full capitation, assuming the entity that accepts the capitation

makes resource allocation decisions and keeps any residual, has the greatest incentive to produce efficiently. In order to make further headway on the question of partial capitation and other risk adjustment methods, I turn to a simulation of insurance market equilibrium.

Simulating Market Equilibrium under Different Risk Adjustment Regimes

Because it is difficult to experiment with risk adjustment schemes in the real world, Keeler, Carter, and Newhouse (1998) used a simulation of the results of health plan competition under various risk adjustment methods to shed light on which method might be preferred. The results suggested that a mixed, or not fully prospective, method is better. I give considerable attention to this evidence, because it is the only evidence of its kind that I know; nonetheless, the results are clearly dependent on the assumptions of the simulation.

In the Keeler, Carter, and Newhouse (1998) model, three plans with fixed characteristics compete for the business of 10,000 hypothetical individuals, with a "payer" managing the competition among the three health plans. Typically the payer would be an employer, a coalition of employers, or the government.[42] Each of the three competing plans may choose a different generosity of benefits. Their choice of generosity in turn serves as a selection mechanism, because sicker people are assumed to differentially prefer more generous plans.[43] The model, however, is incomplete, both because it arbitrarily fixes the number of competing plans at three and because it does not attempt to explain why the plans choose the treatment levels or benefit generosity that they do. In work I discuss further in this chapter, Frank, Glazer, and McGuire (2000) describe a model in which plans choose benefit generosity to maximize profit.

In the Keeler, Carter, and Newhouse (1998) model, the plan chooses its benefit generosity by choosing a level on the average person's marginal valuation curve and providing all services whose value exceeds that level (figure 6.1). Plans offering more generous benefits pick a lower point on the curve and provide more services; the chosen point, however, is the same for all enrollees in the plan. Thus, the rationing in each plan is analogous to providing all services that result in a certain level of Quality Adjusted Life Years (QALYs) per dollar or more, where the valuation on the QALY is that of the average person.[44] This is, of course, optimal for those

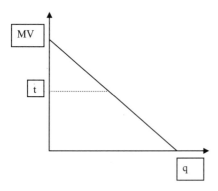

Figure 6.1
Marginal valuation and the choice of t.

enrollees who have the chosen level of generosity as their preferred level and pay an actuarily fair premium. For most simulation runs plans are not allowed to change their initial choice of generosity. An example might be that once plans choose the composition of their network, they do not change it.

As is generally the case in employment-based health insurance plans that offer choice, plans must accept all enrollees who wish to join and must charge them the same premium. Plans either cannot or do not actively select specific enrollees. In that sense the model is like the Cutler-Reber model (1998) discussed in chapter 4. The limitation to three plans in the market is important, but seems to characterize roughly the evolution of many U.S. local markets, as well as the behavior of a number of employers.[45] As a benchmark, Keeler, Carter and Newhouse (1998) also include a single hybrid plan with a large deductible of $2,000. (Average spending is assumed to be $1,600.) The hybrid nature is that people receive care according to their individual preferences up to the level of the deductible (they spend their own money in accordance with their preferences for care); after the level of the deductible, however, the plan is like a managed care plan that is geared to those with middle-income tastes for care—that is, plans do not honor individual preferences but rather provide treatment up to the middle-income threshold.

Because plans must accept all who join, the key issue is who wishes to join which plan. In making their choices, the simulation assumes consumers are fully informed about both the generosity of the plan and their own disease state. Moreover, the simulation assumes consumers choose so as to maximize their own utility, which varies not only according to their disease state (how sick they are) but also how much they value health care services in a given disease state.

The model's purpose is to test different risk adjustment schemes for payments to plans. The payer or sponsor, in designing the risk adjustment scheme, wants those choosing more generous plans to pay more but wants to minimize differences in enrollee payment due to sickness; that is, the payer's principle is that the enrollee should not bear the risk of sickness.

The principal normative outputs of the simulation model are the differences in consumer surplus that are associated with the various risk adjustment schemes, which are measured as the difference from the first best outcome. Other outcomes of the model include the distribution of enrollees among plans, as well as the distribution of spending and out-of-pocket payment among different people with different disease types along with associated risk premiums.

A Summary of the Model's Results

Flat (i.e., unadjusted) capitation leads to poor performance of the market. Not surprisingly, those who are sicker and those who value health care more highly choose more generous plans, but without any subsidies from the payer (i.e., no risk adjustment) premiums rise at this plan and the relatively healthy move to less generous plans; in other words, there is a premium spiral analogous to that in the Cutler-Reber model.

Two nonfeasible options are included as benchmarks. Fully adjusting premiums for the sickness of those enrolled in each plan ("full severity adjustment") reduces the premium spiral problem substantially, but is not feasible because each person's risk is not precisely known. Cross-subsidization of plans—or having the payer pay the difference in the cost of the average risk who actually enrolls in each plan—similarly reduces selection problems substantially, but is also not feasible since each person's risk is unknown.

The feasible options that were simulated include partial severity adjustment, outlier payments, and blends of capitation and fee-for-service payment.[46] These are, of course, less successful in addressing selection than the nonfeasible options, although they improve over no risk adjustment. The results suggest that a blend of capitation and fee-for-service is preferable to fully prospective capitation.

The Details of the Model

The model characterizes people by disease (expected expense), luck, and tastes for health care versus other goods. Specifically, all people have one of four types of (chronic) disease of increasing severity, which for concreteness Keeler, Carter, and Newhouse (1998) term mild, moderate, diabetic, and cancer. A person's actual demand or use in any period is the product of disease type and luck; those with more severe disease and bad luck spend more. Because luck is not known ex ante to either the plan or the enrollee, it does not affect plan choice and is mostly suppressed in the operation of the model.

Premiums are set to just cover health plan costs, net of any payer payments to the plan (cross subsidies from risk adjustment) or co-payments received by the plan. Hence, plan premiums reflect both the generosity of the plan and the mix of enrollees it attracts. For simplicity, Keeler, Carter, and Newhouse (1998) assume plans have no loading charges, so that

Premiums = (Medical care spending – Revenues)/Enrollees.

People choose plans individually based on the expected value of care to them, which varies according to the plan's generosity, the person's taste for health, and the cost of the plan (the size of copayments and premiums). Enrollment is conducted in a series of periods, similar to the discrete time of the Cutler-Reber model. People are locked into their plan choice for one period but can change plans at the beginning of each new period in response to changes in premiums. This reflects the annual open enrollment period of most employer plans that offer choice.

More specifically, the value of services is given by a quadratic utility function, as in Eggleston's model. Letting q be the quantity of services scaled in efficiency units, each with a cost of one, the utility function can be written as:

$$V(q) = aq - 0.5bq^2, \tag{6.2}$$

for a person with average tastes for health and a mild disease. Differentiating, the marginal value of services for this person is

$$v = a - bq, \tag{6.3}$$

which is the function shown in figure 6.1.

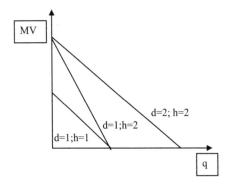

Figure 6.2
Marginal valuations of different individuals.

As noted previously, four diseases or states of health exist. Disease is denoted by a function $D(d)$, $d = 1 - 4$, and is parameterized as multiplying the quantity of services required or demanded by a person with mild disease. In particular $D(1) = $ mild disease $= 1$, $D(2) = 2$, $D(3) = 7$, and $D(4) = 17$. In what follows I term $D(4)$ "cancer." The marginal valuation function (figure 6.2) thus equals

$$v = a - (b/D(d))q. \tag{6.4}$$

The four disease states have population prevalences of 0.6, 0.3, 0.09, and 0.01, respectively (i.e., 60 percent of the population has mild disease). This distribution of disease-state multiples and prevalences reflects the skewed nature of medical spending. In addition, a "luck" factor, which is not shown in figures 6.1 and 6.2, multiplies each individual's demands for care.[47] Although luck does not affect plan choice, it does affect short-run risk premiums, especially in the large deductible plan, because it affects actual out-of-pocket spending.

In addition to differing by disease states, enrollees divide into three groups according to the dollar value they place on health, where the dollar value multiplies demand vertically. (Recall that disease multiplies demand horizontally.) For concreteness refer to these three groups as poor, middle, and rich, and denote them by $h(i)$, with average $h(i) = 1$. Specifically, $h(1) = 0.6$, $h(2) = 1$, and $h(3) = 1.8$, with probabilities of 0.4, 0.4, and 0.2, respectively. To keep the model more transparent, the dollar value placed on health is assumed to be independent of disease.[48] Although the designation of poor, middle, and rich identifies these groups with income, those with low multiples also include those who distrust medical providers, and those with a high value include hypochondriacs and those who are willing to treat aggressively in exchange for small chances of success.

Health plans are characterized by treatment thresholds t. In particular, a plan provides care until the marginal value for a person with given tastes for health (i.e., a middle income person) equals t. That is, each plan picks a quantity of services q such that

$$v = a - bq = t, \quad \text{or} \quad q = (a - t)/b. \tag{6.5}$$

This implies that within plans the marginal value of additional treatment is the same across each disease type. Such an allocation of services maximizes value for a fixed budget if everyone has the same tastes for health (the same $h(i)$) and is equally weighted.

Marginal cost (MC), which is one by assumption, must equal marginal value (MV) at an optimum. Marginal value is hv, so at an optimum $v = 1/h$. Because of the plan's policy, $v = t$, so at an optimum, $t = 1/h$ for persons with health value h. Because health plans offer the same threshold for all, independent of income or taste for health, a plan that sets its threshold for middle income people will have $h = 1$ and will overtreat poor people (relative to their willingness to pay) and undertreat rich people.

To deal with moral hazard but provide some risk protection, plans have a 10 percent coinsurance rate, with a $2000 annual cap on out-of-pocket spending. Their remaining revenue comes from premiums and from risk adjustment payments by the payer.

Risk adjustment means that for a person of disease type d the payer transfers $G(d)$ to the plan. The payer may also make payments of a proportion r times spending on services. This latter payment method is a blend of FFS and capitation payments. With a blend at rate r, informed patients would prefer that the treatment level shift to $v = (1 - r)/h$, because the marginal cost of provision of a unit of care to the plan falls from 1 to $1 - r$.[49] In some scenarios Keeler, Carter, and Newhouse (1998) assume plans respond to these preferences and shift the treatment threshold; in other cases, plans do not shift the threshold. If plans shift the threshold, one can show that a deadweight loss of $0.5r^2 \eta q$ results, where η is the elasticity of demand.[50]

Outlier payments are an alternative to blended payments. They are characterized by a loss threshold and an insurance rate above the threshold. The simulations allow outlier payments to equal 10 percent of the payer's budget. The outlier threshold, scaled in units of q, is the loss on a case plus the capitation payment plus episode payments, if any. Episode payments are lump sums provided by payer for specified combinations for disease and luck. They equal 90 percent of the cost of very large episodes (over \$30,000 of cost) at an HMO with $t = 1$ minus the capitation payment. Total payer payments are held constant across all risk adjustment strategies, reflecting a fixed payer health care budget.

An important point is that half the enrollees are movers and half are stayers with respect to choice of plan. In particular, within each disease type d and health status type h half the population is movers. Each period the movers pick the plan that maximizes their utility in that period, where the utility function U is

$$U = U(q, p, c) = V(q) - p - c^*(c), \tag{6.6}$$

where q is the quantity of services, p is the premium, c is the cost sharing amount, and c^* is certainty equivalent of the cost sharing. (Recall that actual cost sharing is influenced by luck, which is not known ex ante.)

The stayers initially choose the plan whose t is closest to where their Marginal Value = Marginal Cost and never move thereafter. Alternatively, stayers can be thought of as people with a very long lock-in period. Without stayers in the model, the simulations do not converge; namely, there is no equilibrium.

Although the device of stayers may appear to be ad hoc to bring about stability, it has an economic rationale. If, as is sometimes the case, changing plans entails changing physicians, there can be a fixed cost to change plans because of the time required by both the new physician and the patient to learn about each other.

Moreover, empirically there appears to be substantial inertia in changing health plans (Neipp and Zeckhauser 1985; Samuelson and Zeckhauser 1988; Marquis, Kanouse, and Brodsley 1985). Thaler (1980) calls this the "endowment effect." For example, Samuelson and Zeckhauser examined health plan choices of the roughly 9,000 employees of Harvard University. In 1980 two plans dominated the choices of the group; one plan had a 62 percent market share, and the other a 31 percent share. In the next few years several new plans entered, and by 1986 the dominant plan's market share had fallen to 30 percent. Samuelson and Zeckhauser, as a test of what they termed "status quo bias," examined the annual health plan choices of old and new employees. Controlling for age, they found that new employees were significantly more likely to opt for the new plan entrants than the existing employees.

The notion of inertia is also supported by absolutely low rates of plan switching over time. In the Neipp-Zeckhauser (1985) study, only about 3 percent of Harvard University employees changed plans annually, and in the Medicare program only about 6 percent of HMO enrollees change plans annually (Physician Payment Review Commission 1996b).

The Keeler, Carter, and Newhouse (1998) simulations sort through the group of 10,000 hypothetical people in random order, assigning the stayers to the plan that is initially optimal for them according to their utility function and assigning the movers initially to the cheapest plan. It then calculates premiums conditional on this assignment of people to plans and re-sorts the people, changing the movers to the optimal plan for them, updating the premiums at the sending and receiving plan at each change. This repeats until no one changes plans or there is a regular cycle (such a cycle almost never occurred).

Keeler, Carter, and Newhouse (1998) compute several different types of outcomes in equilibrium for each risk adjustment scheme:

1. *Enrollment* in each plan that is offered.

2. *Premium differences* among the plans that are offered, as well as *spending* in each plan and average spending over all plans (enrollment weighted).

3. *Payment fairness.* This is the ratio of the payer's total payment to the cost of providing plan members' care at a plan where the enrollees have the average taste for health ($t = 1$). (Cost for these purposes is net of any other plan revenues such as cost sharing.) If the fairness ratio is 1.0, the payer's risk adjustment payments (together with other plan revenue) exactly cover the cost of the sickness mix of enrollees in the plan. If the ratio is less than 1.0, the plan suffers from adverse selection and conversely; in other words, if the ratio is less than 1.0, payer payments do not offset the average sickness of the plan's enrollees.

4. *Risk premiums*, both short-term and long-term, that arise from random variation in cost sharing. Short-term risk is the usual notion of risk in the literature; it is the random variation that an individual may be exposed to during a single contract period, typically a year. Long-term risk, in contrast, reflects the notion that disease status may change over time, and that if it does the person may wish to change insurance plans. Typically health status will worsen, and the person will then want more generous insurance. Keeler, Carter, and Newhouse (1998) do not actually compute this risk over time, but instead compute it as the variance of the sum of annual premiums and cost sharing across persons with a similar value of health h. These persons, of course, are in different disease states and have enrolled in the plan that maximizes their utility. Such a computation reflects the idea that full lifetime insurance would have this variance be zero. Keeler, Carter, and Newhouse, in calculating risk premiums, assume constant risk aversion with a risk aversion parameter equal to 0.0005.

5. *Welfare loss*. Welfare losses arise from people being induced to choose plans that do not match their taste for medical services because of the structure of premiums across plans. The welfare loss shown is equal to the consumer surplus at the first-best outcome minus the actual consumer surplus. Even at the first best there is some loss of potential consumer surplus because with only three plans everyone's tastes cannot be perfectly matched.[51] Specifically, consumer surplus is $V_{dh}(q_{dt}) - q_{dt}$, where d as earlier indexes disease type, t indexes treatment level, and h is the value placed on health. (Recall that price is normalized to 1 and hence drops out of the second term which represents spending on medical care.)

In addition to this conventional notion of welfare loss, Keeler, Carter, and Newhouse (1998) compute the welfare loss if one assumes the value of health for each person is the average value. This egalitarian assumption would represent one-tier medicine.

Results of the Simulations

The results that Keeler, Carter, and Newhouse (1998) obtain under various adjustment schemes are shown in tables 6.10 and 6.11. The first column of table 6.10 shows the results if everyone is in one plan whose treatment cutoff t is set at the preferences of the middle-income

Table 6.10
Simulation Results

	Single HMO with t = 1	Each person enrolled at HMO with t closest to 1/h	Only FFS plan, $2000 deductible, t = 1 beyond cap	Flat capitation	Blended payment, r = 0.25, no moral hazard	Blended payment, r = 0.25, 25% moral hazard
Enrollment: Stingy HMO	0	4,000	0	6,320	6,200	6,550
Enrollment: Middle HMO	10,000	4,000	10,000	2,500	2,570	2,310
Enrollment: Generous HMO	0	2,000	0	1,180	1,230	1,140
Premium difference: Middle-stingy		494		1,166	800	784
Premium difference: Generous-middle		329		984	886	609
Average spending: Stingy		1,067		822	815	1,138
Average spending: Middle	1,600	1,600	1,528	2,080	1,998	2,287
Average spending: Generous		1,956		3,116	3,267	3,154
Average spending: Total	1,600	1,458	1,528	1,407	1,421	1,633
Fairness: Stingy		1		1.30	1.17	1.12
Fairness: Middle	1	1	1	0.77	0.88	0.88
Fairness: Generous		1		0.63	0.79	0.83
Short-run risk premium	20	19	89	17	117	71
Long-run risk premium*	25	25	116	140		

Welfare losses for various subgroups:

Per Person (all)	91	21	61	87		
Per potential poor mover	131	24	84	76	79	110
Per potential middle mover	15	15	13	120	122	43
Per potential rich mover	133	11	109	362	315	193
Per potential mover $d = 1$ (healthy)	47	10	25	131	127	58
Per potential mover $d = 2$	83	17	54	145	115	88
Per potential mover $d = 7$	289	62	252	196	237	251
Per potential mover $d = 17$ (cancer)	570	80	700	1,124	1,124	1,586
Egalitarian perspective (all)	0	87	56	101	100	44

Source: Keeler, Carter, and Newhouse 1998.

Note: Each column is a particular configuration of plans and payment methods. All values except enrollment and fairness ratios are in dollars.

*For movers with h = 1.

Table 6.11
Simulation Results: Alternative Risk Adjustment Schemes

	Flat capitation (repeated from above)	10% outlier, no moral hazard[a]	100% severity adjustment[b]	50% severity adjustment[b]	Episode (90% of any episode > $30,000)[c]	Cross-subsidy: Premium = Avg Diff
Enrollment: Stingy HMO	6,320	6,230	4,480	5,960	5,680	5,060
Enrollment: Middle HMO	2,500	2,490	4,190	2,820	3,080	3,150
Enrollment: Generous HMO	1,180	1,280	1,330	1,220	1,240	1,790
Premium difference: Middle – Stingy	1,166	869	337	725	633	494
Premium difference: Generous – Middle	984	839	668	905	757	329
Average spending: Stingy	822	814	810	812	810	811
Average spending: Middle	2,080	1,937	1,602	1,955	1,868	1,473
Average spending: Generous	3,116	3,407	2,893	3,238	3,296	3,556
Average spending: Total	1,407	1,426	1,504	1,430	1,444	1,511
Fairness: Stingy	1.30	1.19	1	1.16	1.11	0.99
Fairness: Middle	0.77	0.85	1	0.91	0.93	0.91
Fairness: Generous	0.63	0.81	1	0.80	0.89	1.09
Long-run risk premium[d]	140	144	111	116	83	71
Welfare loss per person (potential movers only)	151	150	82	125	109	101
Per potential poor mover	76	79	93	79	79	140
Per potential middle mover	120	130	63	100	85	87
Per potential rich mover	362	330	97	267	215	54

Per potential mover $d = 1$ (healthy)	131	131	41	113	96	56
Per potential mover $d = 2$	145	117	50	84	60	12
Per potential mover $d = 7$	196	274	345	231	244	587
Per potential mover $d = 17$ (cancer)	1,124	1,124	1,124	1,124	1,124	1,124
Egalitarian perspective (all)	101	102	97	111	93	70

Source: Keeler, Carter, and Newhouse 1998.

Notes: All values except enrollment and fairness ratios in dollars. The average welfare losses for potential movers for the two blended cases shown in this table are $143 and $100, respectively.

[a] In this plan, 10 percent of the payments are set aside to cover the highest cost cases.

[b] In the 100 percent severity adjustment plan, perfect adjustment for the mix of the four diseases in each plan is possible; in the 50 percent plan the adjustment is half of the 100 percent adjustment.

[c] In this plan the plan pays 90 percent of the cost of all episodes costing more than $30,000.

[d] For movers with $h = 1$.

group. The average cost by assumption equals $1,600. Also by assumption any risk adjustment payments are correct on average, so in this one-plan world the fairness ratio is one. The deadweight loss is $91 per person. Because the plan is geared for the middle-income group, the deadweight loss is concentrated among the poor, who would like less care (this calculation assumes consumer sovereignty and no externalities) and among the rich, who would like more. The welfare losses are proportional to the parameterization of expected disease, because any deviation from the ideal cost/effectiveness criterion at the individual level is multiplied by the scale factor for the disease (e.g., for cancer $(D(4))$ the multiple is 17). The short-term risk premium is small and so is the long-term premium, because people pay the same premium irrespective of their disease or health status, and out-of-pocket spending is low.

The second column of table 6.10 is the optimum using standard welfare economics. Each person is assigned to the plan closest to his or her preferences. Poor persons, who are all assigned to the stingy plan, spend $533 less than the average income person ($1,600–$1,067), and rich persons, who are in the generous plan, spend $356 more than the average person ($1,956–1,600).[52] The premium differences represent purely the differences in the threshold t because of the assumption that disease state is independent of taste for health. Payer payments are fair for the same reason. The deadweight loss is only $21, the minimum possible with only three plans.[53] From an egalitarian viewpoint, this three-tier system is unattractive because the poor receive less care than the average person, and the rich receive more.

The third column shows the results if everyone is in a large deductible FFS plan with managed care beyond the deductible. The deadweight loss is less than if everyone is in a single plan at the average taste level because the deductible permits some tailoring of the quantity of care to tastes (income). This gain in welfare, of course, assumes there are no externalities of the form that others are willing to pay for an individual's health care consumption. Because of the large deductible, the short-run risk premium increases to $89 (luck plays more of a role in determining out-of-pocket payment in this plan), and the long-term risk premium of $116 reflects the variation in cost sharing from sickness. (Sick people also have higher out-of-pocket spending because of the deductible.) From an egalitarian point of view, the poor do not fare well.

The fourth column shows the effect of choice among three plans with no risk adjustment. In this world persons initially choose a plan and then the half of the group that are "movers" may choose a different plan in the next period. The outcome shown in the table is the equilibrium outcome to which the model converges.[54] The results are very different from the economically efficient case of the second column. Sicker people naturally prefer the more generous plans, because they pay directly for only 10 percent of their use. To break even, the premiums at the more generous plans have to rise, which makes the stingier plans more attractive. Without the assumption that half of the 2,000 rich people stay with the generous plan no matter what, the generous plan would disappear in a premium spiral. (Stayers of other income groups do not prefer this plan initially and hence are not assigned to it.) With a total enrollment of 1,180, 1,000 of whom are stayers, only 180 of the initial 5,000 movers prefer this plan in equilibrium. Comparing spending in the stingy plan in the first-best case and this one, one observes that spending has fallen by almost a quarter, due entirely to an enrollment in the stingier plan that is on average healthier than in the first-best case. Correspondingly, the enrollees in the middle and generous plans are sicker. These differences in average sickness result in premium differences among the plans that are double and triple the first-best case.

The fairness ratios, or what the payer pays each plan relative to its risk mix, exactly reflect the risk mix differences among the plans, because the payer payment is by assumption uniform in this case. The welfare loss in this case, $87, is about the same as in the single-plan case. Thus, one of the gains from having multiple plans, that tastes can be better matched, is approximately offset by the welfare losses from selection. The model, however, does not account for another possible gain, that competition may induce greater efficiency in the production of services. The largest welfare losses from selection are among rich, healthy people who move to stingy plans and among poor, sick people, who move to generous plans to get care of low, but positive value to them. The long-term risk premium is $140, reflecting the preference of the sick for the generous plan, and that if one becomes sick the premium increase to join the generous plan is substantial.

The various risk adjustment schemes have different effects (tables 6.10 and 6.11). A blend or partial capitation at a 25 percent rate with no moral hazard (i.e., no plan response to the provision of partial payment and thus no change in plans' treatment thresholds) has modest benefit. But with moral hazard the effect of the blend is larger; the stingiest plan in effect becomes 25 percent more generous and thus becomes more attractive to the middle-income group.

The blend with moral hazard, in fact, is one of the most attractive feasible options among those considered. The fairness ratios are relatively close to 1.0, and the welfare losses are favorable in comparison with many of the other feasible options. The blend looks favorable in spite of assuming away two possible behavioral responses that should make the blend even more attractive relative to an unadjusted capitation. First, Keeler, Carter, and Newhouse (1998) assume no active selection efforts on the part of the plans; any such efforts, however, would surely be less with a blend than with unadjusted capitation. Second, they assume that plans actually do deliver the services they say they will—thus, they assume away stinting. Any stinting, however, should also be less under a blend. On the other hand, Keeler, Carter, and Newhouse ignore any change in efficiency of production, which should be less with a blend.

Outlier payments also have modest effects if plans do not respond by altering their treatment thresholds (table 6.11). If they do respond, the deadweight loss increases substantially for the sickest group (not shown in the tables).

Complete severity adjustment for disease, the intent of risk adjustment, would have a large effect; the welfare loss is about halfway between the first best and the loss with uniform capitation (table 6.11). There is still some welfare loss because the generous plan is still a bargain for the sick, who pay the same premiums as the healthy.

Halfway adjustment, which is about what the best of today's risk adjusters can do, has a less-than-proportionate effect on welfare loss. Event payments, which in this model are 90 percent of the costs of episodes costing more than $30,000, are more successful than halfway adjustment, but not as successful as full adjustment.[55] These event payments, however, clearly differ from those observed in the real world, in that existing event payments are both limited and tend to be in a context of non-discretionary care. For example, the New York state small group risk pool, as well as the Israeli risk adjustment system, makes extra payments to health plans for enrolling a person with AIDS and a handful of other specific and not common diseases, whereas the payments in the simulation model are for *all* cases whose cost is above $30,000.

The rightmost column in table 6.11 shows the substantial effect if the payer cross-subsidizes the plans such that the premium difference facing consumers equals the difference in what would be spent in each plan if that plan enrolled the average risk mix rather than its actual mix. Because this difference is not known in actual situations, this is not a feasible option.

Among the methods considered here, the risk adjustment methods that can be implemented in practice are blended payments, outlier payments, and partial severity adjustments. (Event payments could be introduced, but the applicability of the foregoing results to event payments is limited to those situations where care is relatively nondiscretionary and any remaining variance within the event is random. There may well not be enough such cases to be quantitatively important.)

These results support the theoretical work favoring blended payments, although for somewhat different reasons than the theoretical work. With selection, most people choose plans that are too stingy for them relative to a first-best allocation, so the moral hazard from the blend can actually increase welfare.[56] The theoretical work on blended payments, in contrast, focuses on the reduction of stinting and active efforts to select, behaviors that are assumed away here, as well as the loss of production efficiency, which is also assumed away. Outlier payments are similar to blended payments for outlier cases and to fully prospective payments for other cases.

There remains the question of what the proper blend is. As the models in chapters 4 and 5 indicate, an answer to that question in principle requires knowing the costs and benefits of selection, the costs and degree of stinting (i.e., the degree of agency), and the degree of inefficiency induced by moving away from capitation. In practice, these parameters will not be known. Moreover, the optimum depends upon contractual arrangements at varying levels in the delivery system (e.g., plan with medical group, medical group with individual physician). Progress will almost certainly require experimentation with various arrangements.

Carveouts: Another Instrument to Combat Selection

Carveouts represent an alternative way for purchasers or health plans to contract with selected providers for certain services. In the sense I use the term, however, they are devices by which purchasers remove consumer choice for certain services and are therefore an additional instrument to reduce selection. The most common services that are subject to being carved out are mental health and substance abuse services (Newhouse, Buchanan, Bailit et al. 2001). About a third of those who have private group health insurance are part of a mental health carveout arrangement.[57]

If a service such as mental health is carved out from other services, a purchaser will typically hold a competition among suppliers of the carved-out service and will select one such supplier for a defined period of time. The competing health plans that provide medical services are then notified that they are not to include the carved-out service in their premium structure. In the case of carved-out mental health services, for example, beneficiaries seeking such care are told to call a toll-free number. They will typically reach a nurse, clinical psychologist, or social worker who works for a managed behavioral health care plan. This person will attempt to screen the patient's needs on the telephone. He or she may then refer the patient for a limited number of visits to a provider that is part of the managed behavioral health plan's network.

Carveouts eliminate selection for the carved-out service by definition; because there is no choice of plan from which to receive that service, there can be no selection among plans that a single employer offers.[58] At the same time, the use of carveouts imposes its own costs. Foremost among them are coordination and cost shifting between the carveout and the medical plan.

Even without a carveout, if a patient is seeing both a primary care physician and a specialist, coordination between the two can often be a problem. The primary care physician, for example, may not be aware of how the specialist is treating the patient—for instance, what drugs the specialist has prescribed. But coordination will almost always be a greater problem in a carveout situation. In the traditional situation, the primary care physician will often have made the referral to the specialist; in a carveout situation this will not be the case. Even if the primary care physician has not made the referral, the primary care physician and the specialist may work for the same organization or have a contractual relationship, which should facilitate communication.

A related problem is cost shifting, especially for visits or medications that may be related to either the carved-out service such as mental health or the non-carved-out service. That is, both organizations may attempt to shift costs to the other. For these reasons the welfare effects of carveouts are ambiguous. For additional material on carveouts, see Frank, McGuire, and Newhouse (1995); Frank, Glazer, and McGuire (2000); and Frank and McGuire (2000).

New Directions for Risk Adjustment: The Optimal Risk Adjustment Literature

The risk adjustment methods described in this chapter have been primarily statistical. They simply sought to estimate the expected cost of a subgroup of individuals—for example, males between 65 and 70—relative to other subgroups. This was a natural starting place given a criterion of paying the expected cost of an individual. And these statistical methods, such as the variation explained by the risk adjusters, are not without an economic rationale; they provide a measure of the difference between the information embodied in the risk adjustment method and the information that might be available to an economic agent engaged in selection, usually taken to be a health plan. The greater this difference, of course, the greater is the agent's potential gain from selection.

Recently a literature has developed that looks at the issue more explicitly as an economic problem. This literature terms the type of risk adjustment described in this chapter conventional risk adjustment. The newer literature's main result is that conventional risk adjustment is better than no risk adjustment, but it can generally be improved upon by paying more than expected cost for some subgroups and less for others, a method that it terms optimal risk adjustment. The newer literature is at present theoretical, and whether it has any practical implications is still unclear. In this section I discuss three papers from this literature.

The seminal paper in this literature is Glazer and McGuire (2000a), which uses the standard Rothschild-Stiglitz (R-S) framework of two risk types distinguished by a differing probability of illness.[59] Following the R-S model, plans must accept anyone who enrolls, but they can choose the characteristics or the dimensions of their product. Unlike the R-S model, however, there is a regulator (a payer or a sponsor) who attempts to risk-adjust premiums among plans. Because the regulator does not observe the true risk type of plan enrollees, risk adjustment cannot be perfect. The regulator, however, does observe a "signal" or a proxy variable that is correlated with the true risk type. To fix ideas, think of the signal as age, which is correlated with some unobserved health status variable that defines the true risk type. That is, old persons are more likely to be high risk, but there are high-risk persons at each age.

Glazer and McGuire's principal result, which they formally prove in the context of the model, is that the regulator should pay more than expected cost for signals indicating higher-risk types (e.g., old persons) and pay less than expected cost for signals indicating low-risk types. Their emphatic conclusion is: "We fundamentally disagree that [conventional risk adjustment] is the right way to think about and do risk adjustment" (Glazer and McGuire 2000a, 1055).

The intuition for Glazer and McGuire's result is as follows. Suppose for simplicity that there are only two values of the signal, for example, old and young. Within the group of old persons are healthy and unhealthy persons, and similarly for the group of young. The higher proportion of unhealthy persons among the old, however, gives age value as a signal of expected cost. Hence, conventional risk adjustment pays more for old persons.

Equilibrium in the R-S model, if it exists, is a separating equilibrium with all high-risk (unhealthy) persons in one plan and all low-risk persons in another. Because high-risk persons are disproportionately old, the plan with all the high risks will have disproportionately more old persons and under conventional risk adjustment will receive more money than the plan with low risks. But the plan with all high risks will receive too little money relative to an optimum because the additional money is simply based on the expected cost of an old person, which is less than the expected cost of a high-risk person given that the category of old contains both high- and low-risk persons. Conversely, the plan with low risks receives too much money. The remedy is to have the regulator overpay relative to expected cost for old persons and underpay for young persons.

As the signal's ability to distinguish high- and low-risk persons improves, the difference between conventional and optimal risk adjustment narrows. In the limit, if the signal or combination of signals perfectly distinguishes high- and low risk persons, conventional and optimal risk adjustment are equivalent.

The remedy of over- and underpaying on imperfect or noisy signals poses several problems. First, to achieve the appropriate degree of amplification, or over- and underpayment, the regulator must estimate not only the expected cost of those with a given risk adjustment signal, as in conventional risk adjustment, but also the correlation of that expected cost with the true risk. This means the expected cost of each risk type must itself be estimated. How this is to be done empirically is not clear. Moreover, if the correlation could be estimated, it would seem that the true risk must be known, so conventional adjustment based on true risk could be implemented. At a minimum, there are more demands on the data in this framework. It is for this reason that I have described this literature as a glimmer in theoreticians' eyes. Further, all the previous comments about difficulties of determining appropriate weights and updating apply in this context.

Second, the basic setup assumes that plans only compete on, or that consumers only sort themselves on, the basis of the consumer's unobserved (to the regulator) risk type (healthy or unhealthy) rather than on the basis of the signal itself (old or young). In other words, following R-S, plans are assumed to configure themselves so that high and low risks sort themselves into the two plans but not so that old and young sort themselves into plans, other than as a by-product of sorting on risk type. Yet inducing separation on the signal itself would not seem difficult; for example, plans, if they chose to, could have many geriatricians and few pediatricians in their networks. If risk adjustment overpaid for the elderly and underpaid for children, it would pay all plans to specialize in the care of the old persons, and there would be a market failure in the provision of care to the young.

Glazer and McGuire (2000a) have considered this possibility. They say that "if overpayment on some signal were in place, one could assume that plans would try to provide services attractive to the 'old,' say, in order to attract these people.... We have carried out some preliminary analysis of [this] case ... a risk adjustment policy that implements the first best may not exist [in this case]. Conventional risk adjustment will not, however, generally be second best" (Glazer and McGuire 2000a, 1066). Although they do not go into detail, they hint at an envelope theorem argument that the loss from a little over- and underpayment is small relative to the gains. Even accepting the correctness of this qualitative argument, this would seem to complicate even further the issue of how much to overpay.

Third, following the standard R-S assumption, Glazer and Mc-Guire assume that selection is costless and hence sorting by risk type is complete. If sorting is not complete, as is the case in reality, the degree of incompleteness must also be measured because it will determine the optimal degree of amplification.

Fourth, and related to the preceding two points, the costs of selection are themselves endogenous and will respond to the risk adjustment methods. Overpayment on a given signal increases not only the average profit for the favored group but also increases the difference in profit from enrolling a good risk rather than a bad risk within the favored group, for example, enrolling a healthy old person rather than a sick one (and conversely in the underpaid group). This could spur efforts by plans to find new ways to have risk types sort themselves within each group or pursue old methods more intensively. For example, not only might marketing directed at the elderly be stepped up, but there might be increased efforts to attract the healthy elderly, for example, having few oncologists but offering exercise classes and health clubs. Yet such efforts are socially unproductive.

Furthermore, the spur to new or more intensive marketing efforts is stronger if the signal is not very strong, because the amount of overpayment is *inversely* related to the strength of the signal. The intuition of the inverse relation follows from the observation that the strongest possible signal, one that is perfectly correlated with risk type, implies the optimality of conventional risk adjustment. For signals that are almost perfectly correlated, there is only a modest move away from conventional risk adjustment. As the strength of the signal goes to zero, however, the degree of amplification to achieve an optimal result (i.e., the amount of the over- and underpayment) goes to infinity.

This raises the issue of the choice of adjusters. In the model one would use all signals with any information. Suppose, however, one uses or has available only a weak signal, so the increment in explained variation from including using that signal as a risk adjuster is small. If such a signal is the only adjuster used, the degree of over- and underpayment is substantial.[60] Suppose, for example, left-handed people have a tiny increment in their probability of disease and that whether a person was left- or right-handed was the only risk adjuster. Then optimal risk adjustment would greatly overpay for left-handers and underpay for right-handers, whereas not including any risk adjuster would pay the same irrespective of handedness. Intuition suggests that one may not want to incorporate the weak signal as a risk adjuster at all.

Finally, the political economy of this method is problematic. Medicare's transition to conventional diagnostic risk adjusters is a lengthy one (at least five years), in part to protect plans from rather modest gains and losses. The average plan, for example, is projected to lose only 7 percent of its revenues when PIP-DCGs are fully implemented, and the plan at the 90th percentile of the loss distribution will only lose between 11 and 12 percent. These values could potentially be much greater with amplification of signals, which would most likely stymie attempts to improve the formula or at best lead to even longer transitions.

I conclude by briefly mentioning two other recent efforts in this line of work. The first, also by Glazer and McGuire (2000b), is directed at the problem of selection through service distortion. Here Glazer and McGuire build on the effort by Frank, Glazer, and McGuire (2000) that I have already mentioned. Frank, Glazer, and McGuire considered the problem of selection behavior through distorting provision of specific services. Using a Medicaid data set, they found that it was especially profitable to stint on mental health services because of the positive covariance between spending on mental health services and spending on physical health services. In other words, if a health plan can persuade high users of mental health services to enroll elsewhere, it will save more than the cost of the mental health services.

To remedy this incentive Glazer and McGuire propose a risk adjuster that varies the payment to health plans in proportion to the covariance of the spending on that service with total medical care spending. Glazer and McGuire (2000b) stop short of empirical application. Based on Frank, Glazer, and McGuire's (2000) results, however, the Glazer-McGuire approach would pay more than the expected cost of mental health services in order to offset the loss on other services that plans would suffer by attracting patients who used many mental health services.

Of the ideas considered in this section, this one seems closest to application. That said, in my judgment it is not yet ready for prime time. It requires that costs be allocated to services, but this requires some arbitrariness when a person has multiple health problems; if, for example, a person recovering from a heart attack is also depressed, is the cost of the physician visit allocated to cardiovascular services or mental health services? And how narrowly are services defined? Are a cholecystectomy (gall bladder operation) and a laminectomy (removal of a disk) all part of one surgical service, or is the cholecystectomy part of a general surgical service and the laminectomy part of a specialty surgical service? Are specialty services further disaggregated into, for example, neurosurgery and orthopedic surgery? If so, and if neurosurgeons and orthopedic surgeons both do laminectomies, as in fact is the case, where does that spending go? Moreover, one should account for the behavioral consequences of any change in enrollment patterns that over- or underpayment by service induces. Implicitly, the method assumes that changes in enrollment leave the covariances of spending across services unchanged, but there is no obvious reason this should be the case.

Moreover, there could be implications that will strike many noneconomists as odd and that could pose a political problem to adoption. For example, if some services are to be paid above cost, others must be paid below cost to satisfy the budget constraint. A likely candidate for underpayment is primary preventive services, because they probably attract healthy persons, but many noneconomists, citing data on suboptimal prevention levels, will find it difficult to accept that preventive services should be reimbursed at less than cost.[61] And there is the issue, as with all risk adjustment methods, that the observed mix of services is not necessarily the efficient mix of services, so that, for example, the observed covariance of spending on mental health services with other services is not necessarily the same covariance that would be observed if service delivery were efficient.

Finally, as emphasized in the prior section, risk adjustment is not the only tool to address plan incentives to distort provision of specific services in order to attract good risks. To the degree the incentives are concentrated in a small number of services, the issue may be better addressed by carving out those services.

Shen and Ellis (2002) have also contributed to this literature, constructing a model geared to the American Medicare program. They assume plans can perfectly select individuals on the basis of their expected cost and that, given a risk-adjusted payment, which is the same for all persons enrolled in health plans, all unprofitable patients are cared for in the fee-for-service system (traditional Medicare). Health plans, however, provide care at lower cost, both to society and to the government, than the fee-for-service system. Specifically, cost in health plans is simply a linear function of cost in fee-for-service plans. Consumers are indifferent about their source of care.

In contrast to the earlier emphasis on selection, stinting, and social welfare, the payer's (or the government's) objective is purely to minimize its cost. Selection occurs, but the government cares about it only insofar as it influences its cost. Similarly, less care or at least less spending occurs in health plans, but the government also cares about this only insofar as it influences cost. Under these assumptions social cost minimization would require that everyone be enrolled in health plans, but this would not minimize the government's cost since it would have to pay for everyone at the cost of the most expensive person; otherwise by assumption the plan would dump expensive persons to the fee-for-service sector.

Shen and Ellis (2002) proceed to derive a set of cost-minimizing risk adjustment weights, which depends upon the distribution of spending in the population, the plan's expected spending (which may be a function of variables it observes but are not used in the risk adjustment formula), and the degree of cost reduction health plans achieve. Their new insight is that, at least in this context, conventional risk adjustment will generally not minimize the government's cost (subject to the constraints that all are cared for and plans cover their costs).

In the Shen-Ellis (2002) model the government wants to increase the rate it pays plans to induce a plan to accept the marginal person when the saving from doing so (because the government pays less for that person in a health plan) outweighs the increased payments that must be paid for all persons already in health plans who are in the same subgroup of patients defined by the risk adjustment scheme. This depends on the distribution of spending in the population, the degree of cost savings in a health plan relative to fee-for-service, and the power of the risk adjusters (or the subgroups into which the risk adjusters classify persons). The greater the cost savings, of course, the more the government should pay health plans and the higher should be plan enrollment. Similarly, the better the risk adjusters, the greater should be plan enrollment since the cost of increasing the payment to induce the HMO to accept the marginal person only has to be paid within the subgroup.

In my view this model as it stands has no immediate applicability, even in the context of Medicare. It is clear that plans cannot perfectly select, but the degree of imperfection is not clear, nor is the degree of cost savings that health plans can achieve. More important, optimal treatment is not necessarily that observed in the fee-for-service system nor that given by health plans. Furthermore, consumers, or at least Medicare beneficiaries, do not appear indifferent about where they get their care. Related to these points is the fact that the government has objectives other than cost minimization.

A Different Direction: The Business Case for Quality

I alluded in chapter 2 to some of the evidence showing that the quality of medical care is often suspect, or more generally that medical care appears to produce well within its production possibility frontier. Several factors may be responsible for this including the difficulty consumers have in distinguishing poor quality from the effect of the disease, a rapid rate of technical change that makes it difficult for physicians and others to keep up, distortions induced by administered pricing methods, and the political economy of health care, meaning there are objectives other than efficiency.

One conceptual response would tie payment to various process measures of quality or outcome. For example, primary care physicians may be paid partially on the basis of their patients' ratings of satisfaction, and health plans and hospitals may be paid more for reducing medical errors or for exhibiting greater compliance with process measures of care, such as prescribing beta-blockers after a heart attack. Efforts to improve information about provider performance, such as the publication of hospital cardiac surgery mortality rates discussed in chapter 3, could potentially shift demand among providers and hence change the rewards for producing quality. Although British general practitioners are principally paid by capitation, they receive additional monies for certain preventive measures; this also can be seen as a payment for a process measure of quality.

A movement to change payment in this fashion, sometimes termed strengthening the business case for quality, is sufficiently new that little is known about it. I am skeptical about the prospects from moving in this direction, but before detailing my reservations I made some general comments. First, the movement clearly presumes that consumer information is now not sufficient and cannot be made sufficient to move the production of medical care tolerably close to the production-possibility frontier, similar to the assumption I have made in this book. Second, quality improvement may in many cases require substantial fixed costs, for example, a computerized order entry system. Hence, the effect on any given provider of some payers' basing payment on quality measures will be a function of the market share of those payers adopting such measures; experiments by only a few payers to pay on quality measures may not accomplish much. Third, the current mix of payment incentives varies among providers and hence the response to changed initiatives will vary among providers. Capitation, for example, provides an incentive to minimize readmissions to hospitals; payment on the basis of the stay or the day does not.

My reasons for skepticism are several. First, payment on specific process measures of quality, such as beta-blockers after a heart attack, can distort resource allocation to the measured areas and away from unmeasured areas (the multitasking problem or "teaching to the test"). It is therefore hard to know whether on balance patients are better off, though in many cases they will likely be. Second, payment on outcomes or on process measures that depend on patient behavior can introduce selection. Additional payment for better blood pressure or blood-sugar control, for example, may induce selection against noncompliant patients. And there is a variant of the problem that arises with optimal risk adjustment lurking here. Certain groups of patients—for example, poorly educated patient—may on average be less compliant, but attempting to address this issue by paying a differential for poorly educated patients will increase the reward for employing screening methods to detect the compliant, but poorly educated patient. Third, any data used for payment must be audited or otherwise verified. Not only the outcome and process measures, but also any risk adjustment measures must be verified, at least on a sample of patients. This is likely to be costly. Fourth, where relevant, paying on the basis of process measures must account for contraindications; depending on the measure and number of contraindications, this could be cumbersome and lead to gaming. Fifth, process measures used for payment must be kept current as medical knowledge grows. This is feasible but adds to the cost and potentially introduces distortion between updates. Sixth, payments on some measures, such as patient satisfaction, may not be readily actionable by the provider. Seventh, one important source of quality problems is the lack of coordination across providers (Institute of Medicine 2001). For example, when patients are discharged from a hospital to a nursing home or to their own homes, followup may be poor. If a patient is referred from one physician to another, tests are sometimes rerun because the results of the original tests are not available. To some degree these coordination problems stem from the lack of a reward in a fee-for-service system for coordination. The reward may not be there because of the difficulty in verifying the provider's effort. Insofar as better coordination reduces cost, capitation introduces such a reward, as does payment on outcomes, but both bring with them selection problems, another example of the trade-off between selection and efficiency-in-production.

The Conundrum of Health Care Financing

In chapter 1, I emphasized the information difficulties a traditional indemnity insurer faced in determining an optimal lump-sum payment for medical care. I used those difficulties to explain why traditional indemnity medical insurance did not operate like automobile insurance, which typically pays the insured a lump sum conditional on some observed variable—for example, a certain amount for a damaged fender. Rather than paying a lump sum, perhaps conditional on some observed variables such as age or diagnosis, traditional indemnity insurance reimbursed the insured as a function of observed spending, for example, 80 percent of spending above a deductible. But doing so led to problems of moral hazard, which in the context of indemnity insurance could only be addressed by placing greater risk on the insured. Reimbursing observed spending, when combined with free choice of physician, also required rules about limiting unit prices the insurer would pay; that is, the use of administered prices.

In an effort to improve the trade-off between risk bearing and moral hazard, and possibly to improve the efficiency of health care delivery, indemnity insurance has now been largely abandoned in most developed countries. Features of managed care, including risk bearing by suppliers and new forms of administered prices, have arisen. The information difficulties, however, are still present. Many of the features and incentives of the payment systems discussed in this book flow from these difficulties. The inability of reimbursement to approximate future expected cost, for example, led the DRG system to include outlier payments and tie payments to procedures as well as to diagnosis. The inability to predict spending also causes incentives to select under pure capitation, a principal rationale for mixed capitation and fee-for-service methods.

Furthermore, the inability to predict spending means some party or parties must bear risk. There are three possible candidates. Individual consumers can bear risk through demand-side cost sharing such as deductibles, but they have less ability to bear risk than providers or groups of consumers. Providers can bear risk through supply-side cost sharing or partial or full capitation methods, but that induces problems of selection and stinting. Finally consumers as a group, that is, taxpayers or premium payers, can bear risk through insurance that pays on a fee-for-service basis with no ceiling on total spending.

In chapter 1, I emphasized the problems of an administered fee-for-service price system for medical services. In much of the remainder of the book I emphasized the issues that price competition in medical services market—with some elements of administered prices—raises. One possible response to the difficulties in competitive arrangements is that there should be a socialized or single-payer system. Socialized in this context could mean several things. It could mean, as in Canada, one insurer and providers that do not compete on price because the government sets fees. Such an arrangement, of course, raises precisely the set of administered pricing difficulties discussed in chapter 1 in the context of Medicare.[62] Although elements of those difficulties remain in many competitive arrangements (e.g., risk adjustment methods), competitive arrangements tend to minimize reliance on administratively set prices.

Alternatively, socialized could mean, as in Israel (and to a limited degree in Britain), a tax-financed single payer with some price competition on the provider side. The HMO part of the American Medicare program is also a single payer with price competition. Competition on the provider side, however, raises the issues of selection and stinting described in the last four chapters of this book.

In addition to its greater use of administratively set prices, a single fee-for-service plan for the population or a national health service has other drawbacks. It cannot reflect as well the heterogeneity in tastes for medical care services, which may arise for many reasons other than differences in income.[63] Some people may, for example, want to use alternative providers and ask why they should subsidize the (presumptively) higher costs for those who wish to use conventional (allopathic) providers if they are all part of the same plan.[64]

Eliminating poorly performing providers is more difficult in a single system than in a more competitive arrangement. For example, it is virtually impossible not to have every physician and hospital participate in the traditional Medicare plan. Although providers must accept traditional Medicare's prices (or not provide services to Medicare patients), only consumers' ability to steer away from poor providers promotes efficient production. Consumer monitoring is certainly helpful but hardly seems sufficient in this context. For example, the variations in care for a similar problem across regions are large (Phelps 2000), suggesting poor consumer ability to monitor.[65]

If, on the other hand, multiple plans are allowed to compete on the basis of price, two problems emerge:

1. Efficiency requires matching tastes to plan, but sicker people are differentially attracted to more generous plans. Because premiums are a function of the average mix of risks in the plan, rich healthy people pay a surcharge (relative to their expected costs) if they prefer a generous plan and poor sick people who want the generous plan because of their illness receive more care than they wish to pay for (based on their own willingness-to-pay). This, of course, assumes that the amount of care should reflect an individual's tastes for care and willingness to pay, an assumption that is standard in welfare economics, but is often not accepted in health policy circles (Rice 1998). It is for this reason that Keeler, Carter, and Newhouse (1998) include the calculations that assume egalitarian tastes.

2. Employer or sponsor prices to employees that do not fully reflect the mix of risks in the plan give positive windfalls to stingy plans and negative windfalls to generous plans. The extreme is a lump sum payment by the employer at some fraction of the lowest price plan, a not uncommon American arrangement. Relative to the employer's paying a set percentage of the premium, this increases the price of the generous plan to the employee and exacerbates the selection.

This is the conundrum of medical pricing; all arrangements that can be implemented have important drawbacks. Although variation in ideology plays a role in the payment methods that different countries use, the wide variation in institutional arrangements around the world as well as the ongoing efforts at attempting to reform and improve those arrangements in almost every country are consistent with that conundrum.

Notes

Introduction

1. This statement oversimplifies, since the National Health Service pays additional fees for certain services, especially preventive services.

2. In the economics literature, Kessel 1958 is an early and somewhat polemical discussion that the code of ethics was a device to suppress price competition.

3. In the usual case in the literature the person demanding insurance is assumed to know more than the insurer; in fact, however, the asymmetry may work in either direction. That is, the insurer may know that a person is an above-average risk, but the person may not know this. In that case if, for reasons of law or custom, the insurer cannot raise prices, one can observe the dumping phenomenon described in the text.

4. Supplementary private insurance frequently exists both in countries with a national health service and in those with social insurance, however.

5. In the United States this is beginning to change with the advent of "hospitalists" or "intensivists," who limit their practices to hospital care.

Chapter 1   Fee-for-Service Medicine and Its Discontents

1. On the potential inapplicability of the competitive model even in a world with little insurance, see Kessel (1958), who made the case that the American Medical Association acted to cartelize the industry. Later literature, however, has used a monopolistically competitive model; McGuire 2000 has an excellent discussion of this literature. In my view, however, some of this literature overly abstracts from the role of insurance in price determination. A large literature has also devoted much attention to whether consumer demands are exogenous or stable.

2. Several early and now classic papers in health economics, for example, Pauly 1968, ignore this institutional reality, and simply assume the price received by the physician is set as in any competitive market. Indeed, the well-known comment on Pauly's paper by Crew (1969)—that Pauly should have considered the possibility that the actual price comes from a simple monopoly model and thus that insurance or any subsidy to consumption could be welfare improving—is subject to the same criticism; that it ignores the institutions of how price is set in this industry.

3. A classic work in health economics in which how price is set is unimportant is Grossman 1972.

4. Indeed, this is how Arrow's 1963 paper characterized health insurance. In later papers (Arrow 1973, 1976) he relaxed this assumption.

5. A loading is an amount above the actuarial value that compensates the insurer for expenses and includes profit, if any. The explanation for the purchase of insurance in the case of nonrepair, a phenomenon that is certainly observed, is presumably that insurance is bundled such that many states of the world are insured in one policy and that because of transaction costs the consumer cannot choose exactly which states of the world to insure. Thus, some consumers may not have wanted insurance for some states but were unable to find their preferred insurance policy from the menu of policies available. For example, the damage to the fender may be substantial or slight, but either way a repair would be the cost of a new fender. If the damage is slight, the consumer may decide to keep the lump sum and not repair the fender. Moral hazard, however, precludes writing a contract under which the consumer received nothing if the consumer decided the damage was slight, and the scope for error (and heterogeneous consumer tastes) precludes writing a contract under which the insurer decides if the damage was slight. Thus, it is not possible to buy insurance only against larger fender dents. There are some analogies with pooling of heterogeneous risks in health insurance policies.

6. The most common type of policy with a quasi lump-sum benefit of which I am aware is a so-called dread disease policy, which pays a fixed amount per day in the hospital for patients with certain diagnoses, usually cancer. Even these policies, which are not common, are conditional upon utilization (e.g., hospitalization) rather than being a pure lump-sum conditional upon a diagnosis. Moreover, they are typically supplement some underlying basic coverage.

7. The ability of the physician to bill the patient amounts above the price called for in the insurance contract is termed "balance billing." Not surprisingly, physicians generally favor it because it allows them the ability to recover additional monies from those with a relatively high willingness-to-pay, while obtaining the insurance amount from those with relatively low willingness to pay. Insurers, however, typically disallow it; in the limit if physicians were able to price-discriminate perfectly, it would be disadvantageous for wealthier individuals to purchase insurance; they would pay the premium but when sick would still face the prices that they would have faced with no insurance (ignoring any income effects that would reduce their willingness to pay). Balance billing, however, can be more than a device to extract inframarginal surplus from patients with a high willingness to pay. If prices in part affect quality by changing the effort physicians put into their work, and if consumers value quality differently, balance billing can be welfare improving. See Glazer and McGuire 1993.

8. Recently, as the physician market has become more concentrated, the transactions costs have presumptively fallen.

9. This was, however, not the case in the Medicaid program, which covers certain poor women and children, certain disabled individuals, and poor elderly. Each state could set fees in its Medicaid program, and many, though not all, states paid fees that were low relative to Medicare and private insurance. As a result, many physicians were unwilling to treat Medicaid patients, and economists produced models of physician pricing with physicians facing a downward-sloping demand curve until price reached the Medicaid price level, where demand became perfectly elastic, similar to

models of a domestic monopolist who also sold on the world market (e.g., Sloan, Mitchell, and Cromwell 1978).

10. An analogous assumption was also made in some quarters (not among insurers, however!) that medical treatment was independent of the price facing the consumer. Because being sick is unpleasant and going to the doctor is unpleasant, the argument was that consumers went when and only when they were sick and "needed" care. That care seeking is independent of the price facing the consumer is also known to be false (Newhouse and the Insurance Experiment Group 1993, chap. 4).

11. Many argue on moral grounds that the services delivered should be independent of the patient's income (e.g., Evans 1984; Hurley 2000). Although sometimes confused in the public debate, this is a different claim than that the services delivered should be independent of price. Failure to consider price in the context of a budget constraint, of course, will generally lead to a suboptimal—perhaps a very suboptimal—outcome.

12. Not only has the number of American physicians grown, the number of applicants to medical school exceeds the number of places by a factor of more than two (and typically has done so in each of the past 25 years). See Barzansky, Jonas, and Etzel 1999.

13. See also the comment by Schnabel (1972). A PPO is typically an indemnity insurance plan (the plan reimburses incurred costs, subject to a deductible and a coinsurance rate) with the proviso that any cost sharing (deductible or coinsurance rate) will be lower for certain preferred providers. The preferred providers may be, and often are, those providers who have agreed to bill the insurer at a discount, although in principle they could also be physicians with conservative practice styles (meaning they tend to treat diseases less intensively than other physicians). A point-of-service plan is an addition to an HMO plan; subject to a deductible, coinsurance rate, and stop-loss feature, the plan will pay something if the consumer seeks care from a provider outside the HMO (not "in-network"). The cost sharing for the point-of-service plan is usually substantial, say, a $500 or a $750 deductible, with 20 percent coinsurance above that to a maximum of $2,500 to $5,000. Under these circumstances there is relatively little out-of-network use; typically 85–95 percent of all use would be in the HMO or in-network. See also table 2.2.

14. A classic early source on variation across providers is Wennberg and Gittelsohn 1973. There are numerous subsequent articles by Wennberg and his colleagues documenting the variation. Chassin, Brooks, Park et al. (1986) show that variation persists even if large groups of physicians across different areas are compared. Although there are many articles describing the variation, there are many fewer that attempt much analysis of its causes, but see Phelps 1992 and 2000.

15. Moreover, even if such physicians were named, actual insurer spending would depend on the distribution of illness among consumers, and therefore it would not be straightforward for an insurer to name a weighted price to each consumer ex ante and have the budget constraint satisfied ex post, though this could be construed as the risk being borne by the insurer.

16. The issue is the degree to which monopoly rents would be present.

17. Similar to the usual life table assumption, these values use physician earnings at various ages at a point in time.

18. One might, for example, argue that many physicians value direct patient contact. Radiologists and pathologists tend to have little patient contact, whereas pediatricians and (as of 1985 at least) psychiatrists have a lot.

19. The additional training for the medical subspecialties would justify some income differences, but the training is typically only one or two years, which could hardly justify the size of differentials shown in table 1.1.

20. One test of this hypothesis would be whether similar differentials existed in other countries with different financing institutions (e.g., the United Kingdom). Unfortunately, I have been unable to find data on this point.

21. Entry was controlled by the number of medical school places and to a controversial degree by the number of residency slots in the specialty. In later years immigration substantially increased entry, which I cover in what follows.

22. In the long run, if there were no control over entry, excess capacity would develop in the hospital-based specialties. Whether specialties controlled entry was arguable. Even if the specialties could not control entry, however, one may have observed substantial rents for two reasons: (1) Insurance for out-of-hospital physician services spread rapidly in the 1950s and 1960s. One indication is that in 1950 17 percent of payments for physician services were covered by insurance. These would have been almost entirely inpatient services. By 1970 56 percent of payments were covered, and by 1974 65 percent (Newhouse 1981, appendix B). Much of this new coverage was for outpatient services, since only about a third of physician services at that time were inpatient (Newhouse, Phelps, and Schwartz 1974). There may have been rents from this new outpatient coverage because the stock of physicians would likely not shift specialties (because of sunk training costs) and the flow of new physicians was modest (in 1960 the annual flow of new U.S. medical graduates was about 3 percent of the stock). (2) As described in the text, rents tended to be higher for new procedures, but the flow of new procedures varied by specialty in ways that probably would have been difficult to foresee and again would have mainly been adjusted for through the flow of new entrants. Tom McGuire has pointed out to me that one test of differential rents across specialties is the degree to which managed care has changed the relative income of various specialties; to implement this test properly, however, would require that one control for any differential in the demand of managed care plans for various specialties, since many managed care plans have incentives for primary care physicians to care for a problem themselves rather than refer a patient to a specialist (St. Peter, Reed, Kemper et al. 1999).

23. Implicitly, productivity increases faster than inflation.

24. In 1998 the median cardiovascular surgeon earned $454,000 (net of expenses), more than any other specialist; invasive and interventional cardiologists earned $387,000. By contrast, the median internist earned $141,000, the median general pediatrician $135,000, and the median psychiatrist $141,000 (Medical Group Management Association 1999).

25. For example, coronary artery bypass grafting, angioplasty, and catheterization.

26. Necessary conditions for induced demand are that average cost exceeds marginal cost and that income effects are not so large that physicians substitute leisure. Although physician hours have trended down over time, in American Medical Association surveys they rose 1.5 percent from 1988 to 1991 and fell 4.2 percent from 1991 to 1998 (Zhang and Thran 1999). A closer look, however, shows that hours are reasonably stable except for the years 1995 and 1998 (e.g., the fall from 1991 to 1997 is only 2 percent) and that the change in hours from 1988 to 1997 was only 0.5 percent. Thus, there is little evidence that physicians substitute leisure. Rents in the sense used in the text are that price exceeds average cost.

27. Gruber (2000) discusses the latter type of inefficiency.

28. For a view that much of the increase in medical costs over time was welfare enhancing, see Newhouse 1992.

29. For an early proposal, using after-tax dollars to finance the deductible, see Feldstein 1971. Feldstein and Gruber 1995 is a more recent contribution along similar lines. If the deductibles are financed with before-tax dollars, they are termed Medical Savings Accounts in the United States (Pauly et al. 1991).

30. David Cutler and Richard Zeckhauser (1997) show that the optimal structure of demand-side cost sharing depends on the source of asymmetric information between the insured and the insurer; if the asymmetric information is purely on the probability of an insured event occurring, then a deductible is optimal. If, however, the asymmetric information is purely on the extent of the loss, if an event occurs, then a corridor deductible is optimal. (A corridor deductible is one that comes into play after the insurer has covered a certain amount of initial expenses. Such deductibles were moderately common in the early days of American indemnity insurance, but are now rarely seen in health insurance.) All the evidence discussed in the text applies to standard deductibles, in which the consumer is responsible for (self-insures) the initial expenses. To the degree the consumer anticipates exceeding the deductible, he or she will act more like an insured consumer (Keeler, Newhouse, and Phelps 1977).

31. This view oversimplifies. In the RAND experiment the deductible appeared to reduce both beneficial and harmful (iatrogenic) services, such that on balance there was no net effect on health care outcomes; see Newhouse and the Insurance Experiment Group 1993, chap. 11.

32. A comparable deductible would be much more today. From 1980 to 1998, the GDP deflator rose by a factor of approximately 2.5 and medical spending per person rose by more than a factor of 5.

33. Calculated from data in Manning, Newhouse, Duan et al. 1988, tables A.10 and B.1. That services over the deductible may contain rents is supported by the differential in earnings between inpatient- and outpatient-based specialists referred to previously in the text.

34. To the degree that these families anticipated spending more than the deductible, their demand in the time before they exceeded the deductible would be higher than with no insurance (Keeler, Newhouse, and Phelps 1977).

35. Some may argue that this is because of the tax subsidy to health insurance in the U.S. tax code, but it seems unlikely that families would want such a policy even absent any tax subsidy. Moreover, until recently tax subsidies for individuals, including the self-employed, were much less than those for group insurance. To my knowledge, one does not observe policies with such large deductibles being bought in the individual market on any kind of widespread scale anywhere in the developed world.

36. And there was a nontrivial amount of variation in unit price across physicians. Within two different sites the coefficients of variation in fees for a standard office visit for an adult ranged from 0.15 to 0.25, depending on specialty and site.

37. Interested readers should consult Newhouse and the Insurance Experiment Group, especially chap. 11.

38. Pauly and Ramsey (1999) have persuasively argued that demand-side cost sharing has a role to play in managed care, even beyond its role in controlling the initiation of episodes.

39. A similar result was found by Weissman and Epstein (1994) in comparing Medicaid and privately insured patients. Gruber, Kim, and Mayzlin attribute the difference between their finding and the Medicare literature to a lower income effect in Medicaid (because of the lower share of physician income that Medicaid represents).

40. Newhouse (1992) argues that the common perception of a large welfare loss may be misplaced. For example, the rate of increase in real health care costs is not so different among developed countries, despite their having very different financing arrangements. This is consistent with a high average product of the new technology in every developed country but a low marginal product in the United States.

41. The reader may wonder why those who valued the device did not simply purchase it out of pocket. The answer is that cochlear implants are an inpatient procedure, and Medicare regulations prohibit hospitals from charging additional amounts to inpatients beyond what Medicare pays. Thus, hospitals could not sell the device. And, as a matter of medical protocol, hospitals and their medical staffs would not have allowed physicians to implant devices that a patient brought in off the street.

42. The 12 percent figure includes Part B premium payments. Data from Congressional Budget Office web site Current Budget Projections, May 2000 (http://www.cbo.gov/showdoc.cfm?index=1944&sequence=0&from=7).

43. Congressional Budget Office 2000 and the testimony of Dan Crippen, Director, Congressional Budget Office, before the Committee on Finance, United States Senate, March 18, 1999. For a more optimistic long-term view see Board of Trustees of the Federal Hospital Insurance and Supplementary Medical Insurance Trust Funds 2000.

44. The Prospective Payment Assessment Commission (ProPAC) was established in 1984 to advise the Congress on the implementation of the PPS for hospitals. The Physician Payment Review Commission (PPRC) was established in 1987 to advise the Congress on physician payment reform. The Balanced Budget Act of 1997 combined these two commissions into the Medicare Payment Advisory Commission. From 1993 to 1996 I served as a commissioner on the PPRC, in 1996 and 1997 I chaired ProPAC, from 1997 to 2001 I was the vice-chair of MedPAC, and I continue to serve as a commissioner of MedPAC for a term that will end in 2004.

45. The Balanced Budget Act of 1997 also authorized medical savings accounts and a private fee-for-service plan. No supplier of medical savings accounts, however, has come forward, and the private fee-for-service option is in its infancy. For further discussion of these options, see Newhouse 2002.

46. By decade the real growth rates in Medicare were 10.0 percent in the 1970s, 6.9 percent in the 1980s, and 5.4 percent from 1990 to 1999. The data from 1970 to 1994 are calculated from Medicare program payments (Health Care Financing Administration 1996, 206) and the GDP deflator. The post-1994 data are from the Congressional Budget Office, Historical Budget Data (http://www.cbo.gov/showdoc.cfm?index=1821&sequence=0&from=7#top) and the Bureau of Economic Analysis, National Income and Product Accounts (http://www.bea.doc.gov/bea/dn/gdplev.htm) and from Levit, Cowen, Lazenby et al. 2000.

47. The nominal rate of growth was projected to be 6.9 percent and inflation was projected to be 3.2 percent. See ⟨http://www.cbo.gov/showdoc.cfm?inde2241&sequence=2⟩.

48. The CBO projects real federal revenue growth of 1.7 percent over the next decade.

49. Medicare had 38.4 million beneficiaries in 1998 or 14 percent of the population. The adult children of Medicare beneficiaries, of course, are also vitally interested in the program.

50. The preceding Medicare cost projections do not include a drug benefit.

51. For more information on issues with Medicare, see the various March and June reports of the Medicare Payment Advisory Commission (since 1999 these reports are available on the Web at ⟨http://www.medpac.gov⟩). For a discussion of how Medicare might procure prescription drugs, see Huskamp et al. 2000.

52. And especially after Blue Cross and Blue Shield insurance.

53. Allowable costs included costs legitimately related to patient care.

54. I have used the GDP deflator to convert nominal dollars to real dollars.

55. The Tax Equity and Fiscal Responsibility Act (TEFRA) enacted one year earlier than PPS actually moved away from full cost reimbursement.

56. Before 1997 the Prospective Payment Assessment Commission had the responsibility for recommending an update factor for hospital services.

57. The DRG weights in this paragraph are taken from Prospective Payment Assessment Commission (1997b, appendix E). The weights typically only change slightly from year to year unless there is a substantial change in how the diseases in the group are treated clinically.

58. In addition to the wage adjuster, slightly higher payments are made to hospitals in metropolitan areas.

59. In fiscal year 2000 this amount is $14,050. More specifically, outlier payments begin when accounting costs for the case exceed $14,050 above the DRG payment amount plus any Indirect Medical Education and Disproportionate Share payments, adjusted by the following factor: .711(Hospital Wage Index) +.289. 0.711 is the average share of hospital costs assumed to vary with the wage index.

60. Ellis and McGuire (1988) showed that case-based outliers are relatively inefficient if the object is insurance at the hospital rather than the case level.

61. As currently structured, the payment for poor patients is really a subsidy to hospitals that treat large numbers of Medicaid patients that is paid through the Medicare program. Ironically, given the current structure of these payments, they offer an incentive not to serve the uninsured. See Nicholson 1997.

62. Nonmetropolitan areas were the omitted category.

63. Except for β_6, which had a t-statistic over 3, all other t-statistics were over 10.

64. The payment formula also collapsed the three city-size dummies into one variable. Because teaching hospitals tended to be in larger cities, which had higher costs, this change also served to reduce the regression coefficient relative to a regression that mimicked the payment formula.

65. Admissions fell 26 percent from 1980 to 1995 and length of stay fell 14 percent, so patient-days fell 37 percent (U.S. Bureau of the Census 1997, 129).

66. In addition to a regression that did not mimic the payment formula, several other technical mistakes were made: (1) The logarithm of the arithmetic mean of the case mix index and cost per case was used, rather than the geometric mean, which is the appropriate mean if the relationship at the patient level is multiplicative, as the log-log specification was implicitly assuming. (2) Reimbursement linearized a nonlinear formula. (3) Adding 1.0 to the resident/bed ratio before taking logs to eliminate zero values was a poor approximation, since the mean resident/bed ratio was around 0.14. (4) The formula implicitly assumed that (the logarithm of) cost per case was linearly related to (the logarithm) of the case-mix index, but this assumption was not tested. (5) The formula implicitly assumed variance was everywhere constant. See Rogowski and Newhouse 1992 and Dalton and Norton 2000 for an analysis of some of these issues.

67. One piece of evidence that the additional costs were not for training was that as the number of residents expanded over time, the empirical level (β_1 estimated on later years of data) fell. Between 1989 and 1997 the number of residents rose 21 percent while the empirical level fell 33 percent. (The source of these numbers is unpublished data from the Medicare Payment Advisory Commission.) If the relationship between residents and hospital costs were causal, the empirical level should have remained constant. If training costs, however, were passed on to resident salaries, the fall should have been proportional to the increase in residents. That it is more than proportional is consistent with the omission of resident salaries and other "direct" costs from the estimation of the empirical level. Undoubtedly real direct medical education costs as defined by Medicare move roughly proportionately with numbers of residents, because a large part of the costs are resident salaries. Thus, if they were added in to the left-hand-side variable of the regression, the fall in the empirical level would not have been as large.

68. Patients with a psychiatric diagnosis who were hospitalized in general medical and surgical beds, however, were reimbursed under the PPS. Other excluded hospitals included children's hospitals, certain cancer hospitals, and so-called long-term hospitals, which were defined as having an average length of stay of more than twenty-five days.

69. Some of the fall in patient-days was attributable to a fall in admissions, which decreased 6 percent from 1983 to 1984 and another 9 percent from 1984 to 1985. The financial incentives of the PPS seemingly favored increased admissions (and decreased length of stay), so the fall surprised many analysts. It is usually attributed to increased monitoring of the necessity for inpatient admissions at the time of the PPS, although this has never (to my knowledge) been rigorously shown; some portion of the fall is also probably attributable to developments in technology permitting more use of outpatient surgery; in particular, many cataract operations, which are common in the Medicare population, started to shift to an outpatient site at about this time, a shift encouraged by the monitors.

70. The claim of no health effects is controversial; for some differing evidence, see Cutler 1995.

71. These figures applied to the under 65, but there is no reason to think the situation was substantially different for the over 65, as the subsequent decline indicated.

72. Because marginal cost is less than average cost, paying marginal cost would require additional lump-sum payments to cover total cost; determining lump sums independent of observed hospital-specific costs would pose an additional complexity.

73. The response of hospitals to the exclusion of capital costs, as well as to other incentives of the PPS, was mitigated to the degree that Medicare accounted for only about a third of hospital revenue on average, although there was substantial variation in this value across hospitals.

74. The exceptions include: Sole community hospitals (597 hospitals as of July 2000), which are hospitals located more than 35 miles from another hospital or satisfying certain other conditions. Sole community hospitals are paid the higher of their costs in certain years or the PPS rate. Critical access hospitals (204 hospitals as of July 2000) are also defined as located more than 35 miles from another hospital or 15 miles in mountain terrain and are smaller than fifteen beds (25 beds in limited cases) and have an average length of stay less than four days. They are reimbursed their reasonable costs. Medicare Dependent Small Rural hospitals (around 300 hospitals) are under 100 beds, not a sole community hospital, and have at least 60 percent of their patient days paid by Medicare. They are reimbursed in the same way as sole community hospitals. Additionally, if their admissions drop by 5 percent for reasons outside their control, Medicare will make additional payments to compensate for fixed costs. Rural health clinics (around 3,500 clinics) are located in areas with relatively few health care providers, furnish primarily outpatient services, and are reimbursed on the basis of their costs. See Medicare Payment Advisory Commission 2001 for further discussion.

75. But see Newhouse 1989 for some early evidence.

76. The constraint of clinical coherence also increased within-group variance.

77. When the weights in the PPS were initially set, data were much sparser, not only because historical data were not generally available but also because those data that were available were only a 20 percent sample. Now, however, 100 percent samples of many years are available.

78. The rule the HCFA follows is that the standard error of the weight (calculated from the charges for cases in the DRG) should be less than 5 percent of the mean.

79. See Glazer and McGuire 1994 and Ma 1994.

80. Section 1886(e)2 of the Social Security Act, enacted in 1983. This language was removed in the Balanced Budget Act of 1997, leaving the commission discretion about how to assess rates. Nonetheless, the commission continued to use this framework until 2002. Words in brackets are mine; words in parentheses are in the original.

81. Also, and particularly relevant to a program for the elderly, a nontrivial amount of advance lies in perfecting existing procedures such that they can be performed on patients who would otherwise have been considered too risky, but such advance is particularly difficult to measure because the procedures or techniques are not new. The increase in invasive procedures among those over 85 is an example (Fuchs 1999). On the difficulties in measuring productivity, see Cutler et al. 1998; Cutler, McClellan, and Newhouse 2000: and Berndt, Cutler, Frank et al. 2000.

82. Between 1984 and 1988, the HCFA attempted to hold down the use of post-acute care by administrative methods. In 1988 two different court cases held that these methods were illegal; thereafter, until the payment reforms of the 1997 Balanced Budget Act, post-acute care showed very rapid growth. The payment cuts in the Balanced Budget Act, as well as a large effort directed at fraud and abuse, caused a dramatic change; between 1997 and 1999 spending on home health care fell 45 percent.

83. As a result of the unbundling and resulting increase in hospital margins, the Prospective Payment Assessment Commission in 1997 recommended a zero update for hospitals in 1998, which the Congress enacted and which formed around a third of all estimated savings in Medicare achieved by the Balanced Budget Act of 1997.

84. For three of the ten DRGs the hospital was paid a blend of the DRG payment and the per diem. These DRGs were surgical DRGs, where a substantial portion of the total cost was incurred on the first day. For the remaining seven DRGs, the per diem payment was doubled for the first day.

85. Rehabiliation hospitals and units as well as long-term hospitals were allowed to keep some of any subsequent cost reductions.

86. The 58 percent figure comes from General Accounting Office (1999).

87. Two-thirds of SNFs are now for-profit, although I do not know how this figure has changed over time (Health Care Financing Administration 1998).

88. The previous example that a hospital PPS with 1,420 rather than 500 DRGs will redistribute monies away from rural hospitals shows that even the hospital system, which has been in place for seventeen years, and has many more categories into which to classify patients, does not fully adjust for case mix differences across hospitals.

89. Probably as a result of this incentive, hospital-based SNFs and rehabiliatation units when compared with freestanding SNFs and rehabilitation hospitals grew disproportionately rapidly after 1988 (Newhouse 2002).

90. Home health agencies, for example, argue that patients should have a choice of home health agency.

91. Payment to the outpatient department is for the use of the facility and supplies only; physician fees are reimbursed separately.

92. Residents, however, have recently won the right to bargain collectively with their hospital.

93. Nicholson and Song (2001) estimate that the teaching adjustment accounted for 43 percent of the expansion in residents. Kathleen Dalton, in an unpublished doctoral dissertation at the University of North Carolina, found no relationship between the post-PPS variation in Direct and Indirect Medical Education payments and number of residents. But it is the change in payments and change in residents that is relevant to this issue.

94. McClellan does not deal with exempt hospitals, or with the outpatient department.

95. I show in chapter 3 and 5 that the optimal cost-sharing fraction, and in some cases the nature of the contract itself, varies with the degree of agency. For example, Chalkley and Malcolmson (1998) show that a block contract is optimal if the hospital is benevolent, whereas a cost and volume contract is optimal if the hospital is self-interested. Rogerson (1994) also points out that if demand at a hospital responds to treatment intensity and the hospital's provision of intensity responds to reimbursement, that the markup of an administered price over marginal cost should be greater where the intensity response is less.

96. The correlation coefficient across individual physicians within specialty ranged from 0.52 for dermatology and psychiatry to 0.80 and 0.81 for orthopedics and rheumatology, respectively. The reliability of the specialty mean (the degree to which the

mean of two groups of roughly 100 physicians would agree) was over 0.99 for all specialties.

97. I thus ignore any market power the physician may have in a monopolistically competitive model; see McGuire 2000.

98. McGuire and Pauly (1991) later showed that if income effects were sufficiently important, physicians would respond to fee increases by reducing demand.

99. Prior to 1997 the Physician Payment Review Commission had this responsibility.

100. See Physician Payment Review Commission 1996a, chap. 10, for more detail on the Volume Performance System, and see Medicare Payment Advisory Commission 1998, II, chap. 8, for more detail on the Sustainable Growth Rate System.

101. All figures are deflated by the GDP chain type price index from 1970 to 1990 from the Economic Report of the President (1999), table B.3. Real GDP growth is taken from the same table. Federal tax revenue is taken from the same source (table B.78, Total Receipts), and its growth is adjusted to account for the transition quarter in 1977. Tax revenues are from fiscal years and the deflator is from calendar years. Medicare spending on physicians is from the Physicians and Suppliers row of table 55 in the Medicare and Medicaid Statistical Supplement (Health Care Financing Administration 1996). (Physicians are the dominant component in this total.) Medicare spending growth is slightly understated since the figures exclude payments to physicians and suppliers serving patients in HMOs, which grew as a share of the program over the twenty years, although not by enough to cause a serious understatement.

102. Unlike the hospital coverage, Medicare physician coverage was voluntary. But because of the subsidy, around 95 percent of those eligible purchase it.

103. The two larger domestic programs, Social Security (pensions) and the Medicare hospital insurance program, were both financed from payroll taxes.

104. On the excessive volume from rents, see the first annual report of the Physician Payment Review Commission (1987): "The [then prevailing] payment methodology has come under increasing criticism because of the poor incentives it provides for cost-effective service delivery. In particular, it has been criticized for: encouraging increases in physician charges and the volume of services" (ix). In its third annual report (Physician Payment Review Commission 1989), the commission linked its recommendation for an expenditure target to the rapid increase in spending but then went on to say: "But unlike other cost containment mechanisms, expenditure targets would provide an opportunity for physicians to help the program achieve the goal of cost containment through changes in practice style. If physicians were able to reduce the magnitude of increases in utilization of services, Medicare could meet its budget goals while physicians avoided diminished fee updates.... Expenditure targets would provide a collective financial incentive to the medical profession to slow expenditure growth by reducing services of little or no benefit to beneficiaries" (207–208).

105. The quantity of services is usually called "volume" in this literature.

106. As described in the text that follows, rents in fees for surgical procedures were widely perceived to be greater than rents in fees for so-called evaluation and management services. This was implicitly a principal rationale for the reform of the fee schedule that the RBRVS represented.

107. See the various annual reports of the Physician Payment Review Commission for additional details.

108. As described earlier, the update factor in the hospital PPS system is not explicitly tied to GDP growth. Although the PPS update factor was by law to depend upon a factor price index, the change in productivity, coding change, and technical change, the method for calculating these items has a considerable element of judgment. See the various annual reports of the Prospective Payment Assessment Commission and the Medicare Payment Advisory Commission, especially chap. 4 of the March 2000 report of the Medicare Payment Advisory Commission.

109. Nonetheless, and perhaps surprisingly, the distribution of physician group size does not differ between nonmetropolitan, small metropolitan, and large metropolitan areas (Emmons and Kletke 1997).

110. Some physicians will not accept new Medicaid patients but will continue to treat an existing patient who loses eligibility for private insurance and becomes eligible for Medicaid.

111. Although Medicare has not (to my knowledge) used this principle in setting physician prices, it has used it in setting prices for health plans; as described in the text, certain "nondiscretionary" admissions lead to higher reimbursement than certain "discretionary" admissions in its new risk adjustment system. Furthermore, the presence of private payers in the market complicates Medicare price setting, because it principle Medicare should account for how private payers will react.

112. In June 2001 the Health Care Financing Administration was renamed the Centers for Medicare and Medicaid Services, but for convenience I will use the old name.

113. The original version of the RBRVS as proposed by Hsiao, Braun, Dunn et al. (1988) contained differentials for variation in the number of years spent in training. Those differentials were designed to equate the rate of return across specialties to training. Congress dropped this provision when it adopted the RBRVS. At first blush it appears that had this provision remained as part of the payment system, the problem discussed in the text would have been addressed. Some reflection, however, will show that this is not the case, because the issue is the amount of training time devoted to the particular problem for which the fee is paid (e.g., 1 week). That need bear no relationship to the total amount of time in training (e.g., 5 years). As a separate point, a competitive market would not equalize monetary rates of return across specialties if there are nonpecuniary differentials, as there surely are. Radiologists and pathologists, for example, have little patient contact; many patients of oncologists die rather soon after seeing the oncologist, and pediatricians see mostly well children. Perhaps physicians have to be paid more to enter a specialty where they will not have much personal contact with patients or where many of their patients have terminal conditions.

114. More precisely, the procedures that account for most of their income are unique to the specialty.

115. Thus, assume that marginal cost equals or exceeds average cost. This is a simpler case than if marginal cost is less than average cost.

116. One can gather patient reports of their experiences, for example, with reasonable validity and reliability (Cleary, Edgman-Levitan, Roberts et al. 1991; Cleary 1999). So-called process measures of care (e.g., given a diagnosis, was a certain test performed) are gathered from the medical record; these data are as valid as the medical record is valid (validity is thought to be better in institutional settings). Outcome data need to

be adjusted for differences in the underlying disease mix of patients across providers; the ability to measure that disease mix is frequently poor and, at the physician level, must be measured on a small sample (Hofer et al. 1999). With good reason the various proxies for quality used in the economics literature would not pass muster with most clinicians as adequate measures of quality. Worse, as I come to in what follows, if a price were placed on certain measured dimensions of quality, resources may be shifted from unmeasured dimensions. The RBRVS does not attempt to adjust for different quality of service across providers.

117. The early history is given in Langwell and Hadley 1986.

118. The five-year moving average was lagged three years (i.e., was from years t-3 to t-8) because of data availability.

119. The disabled were not disaggregated by age group.

120. Refinements have also been made in the payments for those disabled who are eligible for Medicare. See ⟨http://www.hcfa.gov/stats/hmorates/cover00/enclose3. htm⟩.

121. The HCFA Web site referred to in the previous note gives a detailed example of how the additional payment operates.

122. Except the service may be disallowed as not medically necessary if it does not appear appropriate to the diagnosis. This, however, is clearly not sufficient to generate accurate diagnosis data.

123. The government, for example, assessed large civil and criminal penalties against Columbia-HCA for such upcoding.

124. In practice, it is hard to imagine how any recoupment of such payments could be made hospital-specific. The estimates of upcoding are made nationally on a small sample of bills and hospital charts; it would be extremely expensive to make hospital-specific upcoding estimates. The result, however, is to reward hospitals that code aggressively. The situation is analogous to the potential reward to taxpayers who are aggressive in taking itemized deductions.

125. Although coding practices generally change as financial incentives change, admissions of enrollees in Medicare HMOs are only about 5 percent of all hospital admissions (and less than a sixth of all Medicare hospital admissions) and hospital coding tends to follow the same process for all payers.

126. In 2002 the beneficiary can disenroll at any time in the first six months of enrollment; in 2003 and after, disenrollment is permitted at any time in the first three months of enrollment.

127. For more detail on the ACR, see Medicare Payment Advisory Commission 1998.

128. There are few plans in rural areas; hence, the potential lack of competition there is moot.

129. The variation in rents to plans across areas may stem from variation in unit prices or amount of overservicing.

130. Arguably the "site-of-service" adjustment for unbundling might be treated as rebasing.

Chapter 2   The Integration of Medical Insurance and Medical Care

1. One might say separate industries since hospitals, skilled nursing facilities, and so forth can be considered separate industries.

2. Some local markets are dominated by a few managed care plans, which weakens price competition in the plan market.

3. See, for example, Woolhandler and Himmelstein 1997. On shifting rents, see Reinhardt 1996.

4. The rhetoric of price competition, however, tended to run ahead of reality, and in practice these efforts were limited. See Propper and Söderlund 1998.

5. In addition to Propper and Söderlund 1998, see Smith 1998 for material on the British experience. On the Dutch attempts, see van de Ven et al. 1994, 1998; on the Israeli experience, see Shmueli et al. 1998; and on Switzerland, see Beck 2000. For a general overview, see van de Ven and Ellis (2000).

6. The exceptions were those individuals who belonged to an HMO.

7. As described in chapter 1, an indemnity policy did not pay a set amount conditional upon an exogenous event but rather a specified portion of medical spending. In that sense, it did serve to indemnify the insured against the financial loss from medical treatment.

8. After the mid-1970s most large and medium-size employers were self-insured and only hired an insurer to process paperwork associated with claims.

9. Blue Cross and Blue Shield plans had a market share about equal to the commercial insurers for most of this period.

10. The physician group and not the HMO technically employed physicians at group model HMOs such as Kaiser Permanente, but this distinction is economically unimportant.

11. As explained earlier, it was common in Blue Cross and Blue Shield plans for providers to agree to be bound by such a fee, but in other cases they retained the right to balance bill the patient. The fee schedule or maximum fees, however, were high enough that balance billing of privately insured patients was virtually nonexistent.

12. By far the largest such organization was the Kaiser Permanente Health Plan, which for many years had over half the enrollees in such organizations.

13. The legislation was enacted in 1973 and implemented in 1976. Prior to the 1970s HMOs were usually called prepaid group practices.

14. See especially Rice 1998, but also Hurley 2000.

15. The first individual practice associations were sponsored by county medical societies in California in an effort to keep the Kaiser Health Plan from entering the market or to compete with the Kaiser plan.

16. As others have pointed out, the "new" arrangements have made HMOs in this respect similar to the traditional Blue Shield plans of the 1940s–1980s.

17. This was in the spirit of Variable Cost Insurance that Taylor and I proposed in the early 1970s. See chapter. 1.

18. Note that the high rate of in-network use occurs even though there is surely selection; that is, only those who want an option to use out-of-network physicians will opt to pay the (often substantially) higher premiums of the POS plan rather than simply remain in the HMO. Despite there being little out-of-network use, POS premiums are sometimes substantially above pure HMO premiums because of selection. For example, one HMO offered at Harvard University provides both a pure HMO and a POS option, but quoted a 30 percent surcharge for the POS plan. In fact, the actuarily fair premium for a given individual in a POS plan might be less than in an HMO, because some use that would otherwise be in-network and financed through the premium is now out-of-network and financed outside the premium. This difference could in principle more than offset any additional premium attributable to the use of out-of-network providers.

19. Nonetheless, the HMO had to compete in the labor market for physicians; since physician earnings in the private market contained rents, HMO compensation presumably included most of those rents as well.

20. I ignore the effect of any deductible, as well as income effects from both the price change and the premium. Ignoring income effects is reasonable if the price of the service in question is small relative to income (e.g., the price of an office visit) and if the premium is largely subsidized by the employer or by government, as it generally is.

21. This is analogous to the tort liability principle of placing liability with the party who can most affect the outcome and/or is best informed, one rationale for having the physician liable at tort for negligence. See Danzon 1985.

22. Formularies are in effect a "network" for drugs that increase the degree of price competition in the pharmaceutical market, just as networks of other providers do in other markets. The financial incentives to physicians and patients to use the on-formulary drug give the drug company an incentive to lower unit price. Because the marginal revenue of a drug typically greatly exceeds the marginal production cost, a drug company can trade lower unit prices for increased volume and keep its recovery of fixed costs constant. The drug company has an incentive to lower price because the committee making up the formulary will take price into account to a greater degree than the individual physician did in the era before formularies; at that time the physician might or might not know the cost of the drug to the patient (and the patient was typically uninsured for drugs). In other words, formularies substantially increase the price elasticity of demand to the pharmaceutical manufacturer. The price can be lowered further because the drug manufacturer who markets to a formulary committee can also save on marketing costs. Earlier drug company marketing efforts were mainly directed at individual physicians; individual salesmen or "detail men," for example, visited physicians in their offices to persuade them of the merits of their company's drugs. This was much more labor intensive than marketing to the committee of a health plan that is choosing a formulary, and there are now fewer detail men than earlier.

23. James Baumgardner (1991) has shown how command-and-control methods of a specific type may be formally modeled, and how their ability to reduce moral hazard becomes more valuable as the capabilities of medicine increase. His model thus makes the type of insurance contract endogenous.

24. The investigators defined inappropriate to mean that the clinical risks to the patient outweighed the expected benefit. Cost of the procedure was not explicitly considered in the definition. Assuming that some of the procedures had benefits that outweighed the risks but did not outweigh the costs, this definition is more restrictive than a standard of economic efficiency. See also the discussion in chapter 3. British physicians, who are under a tighter budget constraint, created more expansive definitions of inappropriate than American physicians; see Brook 1993.

25. From 1980 to 1998 the percentage of the population over 65 grew from 11.3 to 12.7 percent (a 12 percent increase) and the median age rose from 30.0 to 35.2 years (U.S. Bureau of the Census 1999, 15).

26. The reduction in hospital use with no change in outpatient use is an example of supply-side incentives affecting provider decisions on intensity of treatment rather than patients' seeking care in the first place.

27. See also Institute of Medicine 2000.

28. See Weiler, Hiatt, Newhouse et al. 1991 for more details.

Chapter 3   The Management of Moral Hazard and Stinting

1. The omission of cost from the Chassin, Brook, Park et al. (1986) definition of appropriateness, described in chapter 2, reflects the difficulties physicians have with cost. Another example that explicitly brings out the tension clinicians have about cost is the following quotation from a physician: "It is professionally unethical and politically insensitive to suggest that we cannot afford to institute measures that increase the safety of our patients. But it is shortsighted to overlook the fact that hospitals and medical groups will quietly decide whether they can afford to invest in new safety measures" (Brennan 2000, in the context of explaining why relatively few hospitals have adopted computer systems to reduce medical injury).

2. This is generally the case even under perfect information and even if the insurer does not regulate prices.

3. One also requires that the price net of insurance not be above a hypothetical competitive price; see Crew 1969.

4. If fees are less than marginal cost, there is presumably a lump-sum payment to keep the physician in business.

5. Although a traditional fee-for-service system offers financial incentives to overserve with respect to the quantity of reimbursed services, some aspects of quality, such as physician concentration on the task at hand, may not be reimbursed. To the degree the patient is unable to monitor those dimensions, physicians have a financial incentive to underserve. Professional ethics can play a role in alleviating this market failure.

6. As already pointed out, the following discussion is in the context of models that assume a competitive supply side. McGuire (2000), using a monopolistic competition model, emphasizes that even patients' ability to observe of quality or quantity does not necessarily prevent stinting on dimensions of care that are not reimbursed. In effect, the physician can exploit any market power he or she has to underserve.

7. I will not take up here issues around imperfections in competition because of few suppliers. On that topic see, for example, Encinosa and Sappington 1997.

8. Hospital-specific mortality rates were published in 1990, and surgeon-specific rates in December 1991. There also appear to have been positive results from publicity about obstetrical services in the state of Missouri (Longo et al. 1997).

9. Although some of this increase may have resulted from coding changes, the disproportionate increase in high-risk patients was also seen nationally, in that bypass surgery rates increased 15 and 11 percent in men and women over 85 years of age respectively, compared with 4 percent among those ages 65–69 between 1987 and 1995 (Fuchs 1999). Performing major surgery on older patients is riskier.

10. Among the reasons that care for acute myocardial infarction is easier to measure is that it is easier to control for the beginning of and the severity of the event than for many chronic diseases such as lower back pain.

11. Other factors contribute to the noisy signal. Claims are relatively rare events; the average physician experiences less than one claim per year. And time to disposition is several years, by which time the physician may be behaving differently. Nonetheless, physicians substantially overestimate the likelihood of a claim (Weiler, Hiatt, Newhouse et al. 1991, table 6.1).

12. Sloan et al. (1989) show that five years of past claims experience is predictive of claims experience in the next three years, so there is some signal in the fact of a claim. Given the lack of association between the fact of a claim and negligence, however, this result is not compelling.

13. There could still be an effect of cost sharing on episode size if the additional episodes being treated with less cost sharing were less severe; in that case the lack of an observed effect would reflect two offsetting effects, the on average less severe episode with less cost sharing combined with more intensive treatment of each given episode. The data, however, give little evidence to suggest this was the case.

14. Thus, this third piece of evidence is less compelling in that it is also consistent with much less responsiveness of informed patients to variation in quality than in their decisions to seek any care. I do not find that explanation of the results plausible, however.

15. Compliance rates in filling prescriptions are far from 100 percent (Newhouse and the Insurance Experiment Group 1993, chap. 5). See Prosser 2000 for an example where patients appear to rationally discontinue prescribed therapy for multiple sclerosis, because they prefer to live with the disease than the side effects of the not very effective treatment.

16. In a later paper, Ellis and McGuire (1990) modify the model to include demand-side cost sharing with a bargaining model solution without any important changes in their conclusions for my purposes here.

17. The model's assumption that physicians make the resource decisions for a hospital follows the precedent of an earlier model of the hospital as a physicians' cooperative (Pauly and Redisch 1973).

18. The first-order condition for the physician deciding on the quantity of services is

$$U_\pi \pi_q + U_B B_q = 0. \tag{3.2}$$

Define the physician's marginal rate of substitution between profits and quantity or services as

$\mathrm{MRS}_{\pi, q} = (\partial U/\partial q)/(\partial U/\partial \pi) = U_B b/U_\pi = \mathrm{MRS}_{\pi, B} b = \alpha b,$ \hfill (3.3)

since $b = B_q$ and defining $\alpha = \mathrm{MRS}_{\pi, B}$.

19. For a review of the literature on differences between for-profit and not-for-profit hospitals, see Sloan 2000. See also Cutler 2000.

20. Differentiating (3.4) with respect to q and letting marginal cost be c(q), we have using (3.2) and (3.3):

$\alpha b(q) = c(q)$, since from (3.2) $d\pi/dq = -U_B b/U_\pi = $ (using 3.3) $- \alpha b$.

21. With full insurance the patient will want all services with positive marginal (expected) benefit.

22. $\alpha = U_B/U_\pi$, so if $\alpha < 1$ another dollar of benefit to the patient generates less utility for the doctor than another dollar of profit to the hospital.

23. Because profit $\pi = R(q) - C(q)$, with a linear reimbursement system the physician acts to maximize:

$U(\pi, B) = U(a + rC - C, B) = U(a + (r - 1)C, B).$ \hfill (3.7)

Assume for simplicity the cost function is linear (i.e., constant marginal cost), differentiate (3.7) with respect to q, and set the result equal to 0:

$U_\pi(r - 1)C_q + U_B B_q = U_\pi(r - 1)c + U_B b = 0.$ \hfill (3.8)

Since $\alpha = U_B/U_\pi$, we have after dividing through by U_π

$(r - 1)c = -\alpha b,$ \quad or \quad $(1 - r)c = \alpha b.$

Efficiency requires that marginal benefit equals marginal cost or that $b = c$, so the optimal α is defined by

$(1 - r) = \alpha,$ \quad or \quad $r = 1 - \alpha.$

This result does not hold if the patient is not passive, but it will still be true that only in a special case is full prospective payment optimal. See Ellis and McGuire 1990.

24. This objective function in turn has analogies with a variety of assumed objective functions for nonprofit institutions; Newhouse (1970), for example, assumed the hospitals attempted to maximize the quantity and quality of services subject to a break-even constraint.

25. Contractible in this context means the quantity of services can be independently verified, so the payer can vary payment according to the quantity of services as part of a contract that would be enforceable in court.

26. Some aspects of what would generally be considered quality—for example, immunization rates or the percentage of heart attack patients receiving beta-blocking drugs—can be observed and indeed are part of the American HEDIS measures of the quality of health plans. Thus, the model refers to those aspects of quality that cannot be observed or can only be observed at a cost sufficiently large that it does not pay to observe them.

27. Usual estimates of the deadweight loss from taxation are around 30 percent (Ballard et al. 1985).

28. More precisely, it may explain why it was the method used by the Blue Cross Association to reimburse hospitals, a method that the Medicare program chose to emulate.

29. Health Care Financing Administration 1998, 78.

30. This formulation goes back at least to Shleifer 1985.

31. If, at the extreme, the hospital is perfectly benevolent (is a perfect agent for the purchaser), the optimal contract is simply to give the hospital a fixed sum; it will do the right thing; that is, what the purchaser wants done. Chalkley and Malcolmson call this a block contract.

32. The cardiac procedures are thought to have particularly high rents, so some reduction from the quantity levels observed in private insurance may represent reductions in overservicing. Medicaid levels, of course, could induce underservicing.

33. Effects may vary widely, however, depending upon the disease. Cutler, McClellan, and Newhouse (2000) find that heart attacks among Massachusetts HMO subscribers are treated the same way as among those with an indemnity insurance plan despite 40 percent lower reimbursement rates.

34. Frank and McGuire (1998) have proposed a definition of parity that requires not only the same demand-side cost sharing but also the same shadow supply price for mental health as for other medical services, where shadow supply price is used in the sense that I use it in chapter 6 of this book. Although I agree with this definition, I do not elaborate here because of doubts about whether one can make it operational. Other formulations use Quality Adjusted Life Years, but these assume the same variation across persons. I touch on this concept again in chapter 6.

35. Even at the level of the physician group, capitation tends to be for only the services of the primary care physician (Newhouse, Buchanan, Bailit et al. 2001).

36. Or, even if observable, may be exploited by a physician with market power.

37. Arbitration clauses in labor-management agreements provide one example of an alternative mechanism, although a neutral party (i.e., not solely the health plan) should oversee the appointment of the panel of arbitrators (Newhouse 1996a). The high cost of using the courts is exemplified by medical malpractice, where transaction costs exceed damages paid to injured patients (Danzon 1985; Weiler 1991).

38. See also the discussion in Gold et al. 1996 of whether cost-benefit or cost-effectiveness analysis should be used to evaluate health care interventions, a debate that largely turns on whether willingness-to-pay is relevant.

39. For a moving account of what a dying patient called "the rationing of empathy," see Schwartz 1995.

Chapter 4   Selection and the Demand Side

1. I have not analyzed the sponsor's decisions about which plans to offer, or even the decision to offer multiple plans. Other than the descriptive fact that in the United States multiple plans are more commonly available at larger employers (and the speculation that more heterogeneous tastes among employees lead to an employer to offer more plans), little analytical work has been undertaken on employer choices. Long and Marquis (1999) provide valuable descriptive data. Keenan, Beeuwkes Buntin, McGuire et al. (2001) document almost no use of risk adjustment by American employers. In addition to the menu of plans employers choose to offer, it would be

useful to have some investigation of what premium "tiers" employers choose to have, for example, individual and family only (two tiers); individual, employee and spouse, employee, spouse and children (three tiers); or four or more tiers (e.g., adding single employee and children).

2. See, for example, Pauly 1985.

3. Although there is no variance in rates within plan, there is variation between plans, and there is variation between individual and family rates.

4. Although Harvard does request bids from plans in a per enrollee format, to my knowledge there has never been a request from the health plans to price in any other fashion.

5. Most American employers with 100 or more employees self-insure and for the past quarter century such employers have been exempt from state insurance regulation.

6. If in fact the insurer was protecting against a bad risk's demanding the policy, this is the indemnity insurance equivalent of stinting in the managed care context. I thank Tom McGuire for pointing out this connection.

7. The lifetime reserve days do not renew, whereas a new episode of illness can begin after sixty days outside the hospital.

8. And all but 8 percent of the remaining beneficiaries have such coverage through employers or the Medicaid program or are among the 16 percent of the Medicare population who have enrolled in HMOs (computed from Exhibit 1 in Poisal and Chulis 2000).

9. One may ask about the basis for the actuarial values in the table. They are actuaries' estimates and their source is unknown. The analogous values in the economics literature tend to be based on elasticity estimates from the RAND Health Insurance Experiment.

10. Feldman and Dowd 1982 is an earlier example of such a model. Both models are in the spirit of Akerlof 1970.

11. Because Medicare HMOs have discretion over what supplementary benefits to offer, it is not fully accurate to say that plan characteristics are given exogenously, but for practical purposes the flexibility is not much greater than if the employer specifies plan characteristics. Even in the private employer case, plans retain flexibility over which providers are in their network, so in practice plan characteristics are never fully specified from outside. But the assumption of passive plans with exogenous characteristics simplifies the exposition in this chapter.

12. In fact the first term does not equal the efficient price because it is the savings for the average HMO enrollee, and the efficient price would equal the savings for the marginal HMO enrollee (h_C), which will be greater than the average savings. In practice, however, the second term is likely to dominate.

13. This assumes the employer subsidy rule is of the linear form described in the text, $a_k + \beta P_k$, and does not vary by employee.

14. Very few switched from the HMO to the PPO, but those who did also had an average age of 46.

15. But the insurer with the PPO did react by eliminating that option at Harvard and offering an HMO instead.

Chapter 5   Selection and the Supply Side

1. Randall Ellis (1998) has put forth a model treating the same phenomena. Ellis' assumptions differ in three ways from Eggleston: dumping is costless; dumping is based on ex post realized patient severity; and the total profitability constraint determines the equilibrium level of dumping. Ellis's model implies that an increase in physician agency (the weight attached to patient benefit) results in more, not less dumping. This comes about because physicians make the treatment decisions and hospital administrators make the dumping decisions. As physician agency increases, moral hazard increases, which exacerbates selection. See also McClellan 1997 and Frank, Glazer, and McGuire 2000.

2. Unless the insurer offers the employees multiple options.

3. See also Cave 1985 and Crocker and Snow 1985.

4. In the subsidy schedule referred to in chapter 4, β is greater than zero.

5. Medical underwriting refers to the small group insurance market, in which an insurer may refuse to offer insurance to all members of the group. This may be the only equilibrium, if for example, one of a small number of individuals is very sick, because the others may be able to obtain insurance more cheaply in the individual market. Preexisting condition clauses mean that an insurer need not provide services for conditions that existed at the time the insurance contract was sold. Sometimes these clauses are for a limited period of time; for example, after six months of coverage, services for the condition are covered. Sometimes, however, they are never covered. Both medical underwriting and preexisting condition clauses emphasize that insurance markets tend to not quote premiums on a spot basis at the individual or family level.

6. The costlier is selection, the greater the degree of pooling that emerges.

7. See also Beeuwkes Buntin 2000.

8. Ethics do not always trump financial considerations, however; many American physicians do not accept Medicaid patients into their practices because Medicaid fees are too low.

9. Of course, competition in the insurance market serves to keep rents out of the cost of insurance. The key is to keep the competition over the price of a given risk.

10. Medicare and some employers have some regulatory control over information going to beneficiaries.

11. Although much of this spending may not be predictable in advance of the hospitalization, it seems clear that some of it is; that is, some patients are known to be sicker and to require a longer stay than others.

12. In Eggleston's model the health plan replaces the hospital of the Ellis-McGuire model, and the physician is an agent for the plan as well as the patient.

13. An issue in all models of selection is what happens to those selected against. In Eggleston's description of her model they are not insured. In the context of the Medi-

care at-risk program, however, those selected against will not be uninsured but will probably enroll in the traditional Medicare program. In the case of selection by physicians and private competing physician groups, those the group selects against may use other physicians who may not necessarily be paid on a capitation basis. Eggleston's model may apply in individual insurance markets, but it is less obviously applicable to behavior within an employer group where all will typically be enrolled in some plan. In the case in which all persons in the group are enrolled in one of a set of risk-bearing health plans, in a symmetric equilibrium physicians may try to reduce average enrollee risk, but some must fail. In the Medicare context, however, equilibrium is not symmetric because of traditional Medicare. Not all employer arrangements are symmetric either; some employers contract with plans that bear risk but also self-insure other plans on their menu. Furthermore, the effort to select, even if unsuccessful, could have adverse consequences; patients may be treated poorly if the physician is trying to persuade them to enroll elsewhere. At a minimum, if patients continually find that physicians do not want to treat them, there is no usual physician-patient relationship.

14. Formally this means each patient costs the same amount per unit of service. The assumption does not rule out costless activities, such as being brusque to undesirable patients.

15. Note this does not correspond to the Rothschild-Stiglitz model, where health plans have the ability to introduce any contract.

16. This description is analytically the same as Eggleston's own description but varies in the narrative. Eggleston says that if the physician exerts effort t, the enrollee's risk type is discovered with probability t, and that if the person is high risk, the person is then denied access to the plan. Although direct denial seems implausible, the physician may counsel the patient to join a different plan such as traditional Medicare with a similar effect.

17. In Eggleston's model the actual proportion that finds it utility maximizing not to enroll is actually a random variable with a mean of $t\mu$. For simplicity I simply work with expectations and assume that plans are risk neutral.

18. Agency in this sense is slightly different than common agency (an agent's serving two principals) (Holmstrom and Milgrom 1991). Here patients do not impose an incentive scheme; patients affect physician demand through reputational effects, and physicians internalize patient effects as part of physician's utility function (medical ethics). If the health plan, which contracts with or employs the physician, were the perfect agent for patients, of course, there would be no divergence between the two principals.

19. The model also could be applied to certain transactions between physicians and hospitals, with physicians interested in hospital profits or margins.

20. McGuire and Pauly (1991) use a similar formulation.

21. If there is no capitation and the physician is paid entirely fee-for-service, s is negative and the physician earns a profit on each service delivered.

22. See the appendix for the derivation.

23. An injunction reinforced in some jurisdictions by so-called Good Samaritan laws.

24. The regulator also sets the capitation amount R, but in this model R only affects the physician's ability to remain in business, so the assumption is that R is set sufficiently high to achieve this objective and no higher. This makes R a function of s.

25. This is a different justification for positive patient cost sharing than that of Pauly and Ramsey (1999), who have a model with a provider-determined maximum on services rather than cost sharing. Pauly and Ramsey's model applies more naturally in the context of a hospital, which may set capacity. See also McClellan 1997.

26. This puts Neipp and Zeckhauser's (1985) discussion of inertia in health plan choice in a new light.

27. An earlier study by the Physician Payment Review Commission (1996a) of those enrolling and disenrolling between 1989 and 1994 found similar results for those enrolling; if the methods were the same, those enrolling used 28 percent fewer services in the prior twelve months, close to the 23 percent value of the later study. In the earlier study, however, those disenrolling used markedly more services in the six months after disenrolling.

28. The earlier Physician Payment Review Commission Study (1996a) carried out a similar analysis of health plan enrollees in the 1989–1994 period and found a 25 percent reduction in mortality in the year following enrollment after adjusting for age and sex. This compares with the 21 percent difference in the year following enrollment found in the later study shown in figure 5.2.

29. The administrative method for updating physician payments in the traditional plan, however, does not allow for an increase in the sickness level of those in the traditional plan. This is because of the Volume Performance Standard and Sustainable Growth Rate features, which reduce unit fees or price if quantity or volume of services rises. As a result, there was a selection-induced fall in physician payment in the traditional plan.

30. The ten types were recommended by the National Association of Insurance Commissioners, whose task is to administer regulation of insurance markets including solvency regulations.

31. Negative accounting profits arose because of regulatory lag; DRG weights were set on 1981 data, and technology had changed three years later when the Prospective Payment System was introduced.

32. At these hospitals the per case payment was a function of the hospital's historical per case costs updated for inflation. Not all cases could be cared for at such hospitals; 75 percent of those in rehabilitation hospitals, for example, had to have one of ten DRG groups and receive three hours or more of therapy per day. Average length of stay in long-term hospitals had to average 25 days or more.

33. Notice that in Eggleston's model, unlike in Ellis and McGuire's, the provider and the patients value the benefits of treatment X similarly.

34. This expression can be derived by adding the terms for expected utility when ill and well and substituting from the normalization of the marginal utility of income $\eta = (1 - \delta\lambda)/(1 - \delta)$.

35. To derive the expression for X^*_D, substitute $(aX - 0.5bX^2)$ for B(X) in the expression for E(U) and differentiate with respect to X.

36. To derive the expression for X^*_S, substitute $(aX - 0.5bX^2$ for $B(X)$ in the expression for $E(V)$ and differentiate with respect to X.

37. One can normalize the utility of being not in the health plan to zero by setting utility loss from illness $K = Y/\delta_H$, where one assumes for convenience that there is no premium P for the alternative plan. This does not fit the facts of the Medicare situation, where traditional Medicare is generally costlier to the beneficiary than the managed care health plan. Eggleston refers to the alternative as being uninsured; this could be interpreted as insurers not quoting any price to insure a high-risk individual. In fact, some individuals report that insurers will not sell them insurance; this could be a result of limited pooling in the context of the Rothschild-Stiglitz model (Newhouse 1996b).

38. It is not realistic that an employer considers provider welfare; in the private context, therefore, the results that follow would have to be modified to remove the term in provider welfare. Also, to avoid double counting of patient benefits from agency, set the agency parameter a to zero for provider welfare when computing social welfare. (The assumption is the regulator wants to account for patient benefits from agency, but does not want to count them again as provider benefits.)

39. Adding together the disutility from e and t in this particular fashion has no justification other than mathematical simplicity.

40. I continue to normalize the population so that $N = 1$.

41. The optimal X is found by maximizing: Total benefit − Total cost $= aX - 0.5bX^2 - (1 - e)c_0X$. Differentiating with respect to X and setting the result equal to zero gives

$$a - bX - (1 - e)c_0 = 0,$$

which yields the previous expression.

42. See the derivation that follows.

43. Formally Eggleston introduces prevention into her model by adding a parameter p, which reduces the probability of illness from δ to $(1 - p)\delta$ and adds to effort cost such that γ is now a function of $p : \gamma = \gamma(t + p)$. Thus, a provider can get a good risk mix either through selection or prevention. To account for prevention, she also modifies the provider's agency utility to $a(B(X) - K)$, so that provider loses aK if consumer becomes sick (that is, prevention fails). She then derives the result that is stated in the text, that better risk adjustment decreases prevention.

44. Randomized designs to assess the effect of counseling for exercise are unusual (Simons-Morton, Calfas, Oldenburg et al. 1998; Wee, McCarthy, Davis et al. 1999). Norris, Grothaus, Buchner et al. (2000), in a randomized trial of 812 patients, found no effect of a counseling intervention at six months. Another randomized trial comparing two interventions found both groups improved, but had no control group that did not receive the intervention (Dunn, Marcus, Kampert et al. 1999). Only about a quarter of smokers report that physicians counsel them to stop, perhaps because physicians think such counseling is ineffective and therefore a poor use of their time (Newhouse and the Insurance Experiment Group 1993, 208). The Tobacco Use and Dependence Clinical Practice Guideline Panel, Staff, and Consortium Representatives (2000), however, report that brief counseling is an effective intervention.

45. Decreased cost sharing did, however, increase the use of certain preventive services such as eye examinations.

Chapter 6   Risk Adjustment, Market Equilibrium, and Carveouts

1. Although Chapman obtained all the numerical results described in the text, I have drawn some additional conclusions from them; thus, he is not responsible for any errors in the inferences.

2. The sample enrolled for five consecutive years has more children, more older adults, and more women than the population of the IPA at a point in time, but the distribution of health spending appears little affected. Chapman examined those not continuously enrolled for the entire period but who were enrolled for entire calendar years; their distribution of spending is similar to that of the sample he analyzes. He does not report the number of deaths (they would have been excluded by the limitation to those enrolled for five years), but this was an under 65 population that primarily had employment-based insurance; thus, one would expect few deaths (the annual death rate for the under 65 population, including those not employed, was only about 2.6 per thousand in 1996). In the over 65 group, however, results are sensitive to the treatment of those who die during the year because of the many more decedents, who account for about a quarter of total annual acute care spending in this age group. See Beeuwkes Buntin, Garber, McClellan et al. 2001 for the importance of decedents to risk adjustment methods in the Medicare population.

3. Thus, "inflation" is measured as $\Delta(pq)$ rather than Δp.

4. In Chapman's sample average spending among the top 5 percent of spenders was eleven times the mean.

5. The negative numbers for the lowest 80 percent of spenders mean that on average they spent less than the mean.

6. Though the earlier data are also consistent with selection arising entirely from the actions of consumers.

7. Users will gain more information about the plan through experience than nonusers. Thus, the nonusers may have a greater tendency to remain with their initial choice.

8. This decomposition is from Newhouse et al. 1989. See also Newhouse et al. 1994.

9. Almost all the studies in the literature are of annual spending; if one tried to explain variation in spending over a shorter period, more of the variation would be random and conversely. This is because random events that can cause high spending in a month, say, such as an auto accident or a heart attack do not generally repeat each month.

10. The optimal risk adjustment literature, which I take up at the end of this chapter, criticizes this criterion as lacking an economic foundation (Glazer and McGuire 2000b). I find this criticism overstated. The conventional criterion simply tries to provide a measure of the financial incentive of an economic agent to engage in selection. See the discussion of optimal risk adjustment that follows.

11. This figure comes from squaring ρ and adding the result to the 15 percent value. For a similar finding in the Dutch context, see van Vliet 1992.

12. An ideal adjuster would also account for the variance in the v term, but analysts have not tried to estimate the variance of v. Terming an adjuster that incorporates variance in v ideal assumes the cost of incorporating information on v is ignorable.

13. The 13 percent value is the 8 percent overspending rate estimated by the Congressional Budget Office plus the 5 percent that Medicare takes off the top by paying 95 percent of the AAPCC.

14. In particular, the proportion of enrollees with short periods of enrollment may be disproportionately high.

15. Profit rates fall by more than 50 percent when the high spenders are underrepresented by half rather than fully excluded because the denominator of the profit rate (cost) increases, in addition to the fall in the numerator.

16. Additional detail is as follows: Reflecting the skewness of spending, the top 5 percent of spenders spent at a rate 10.6 times greater than the mean in 1989. But that group remained well above the mean in subsequent years; it was 3.4 times as much as the mean in 1990 and 2.8 times in 1993. At the other extreme, the 15 percent of individuals with no expense in 1989 on average spent less than 60 percent of the mean in 1993. The bottom 50 percent in 1989 had had a spending rate that was only 9 percent of the 1989 mean. By 1993 they had still only risen to a rate two-thirds of the mean.

17. The t, $t + 3$ and t, $t + 4$ values are substantially more imprecise in these calculations than the t, $t + 1$ and t, $t + 2$ values. They are not only based on averaging fewer periods, but each individual R^2 in the t, $t + 3$ and t, $t + 4$ calculations is based on fewer observations because the majority of participants in the RAND Experiment were only enrolled for three years.

18. Beebe was able to study six years worth of data, one more year than Chapman or Newhouse et al. (1989).

19. Because of costs of selection, van Barneveld et al. (2000) suggest that health plans may not select individuals with small gains and losses. Using a criterion of plus or minus 33 percent of the mean profit as small, they go on to argue that conventional measures of selection overstate the problem of selection. Although it is clear that selection will be less severe if plans ignore small gains and losses, ignoring them in the context of profit maximization would seem to require the assumptions that the costs of selection are mostly fixed per person costs and that a plan can tailor its selection efforts toward highly profitable or unprofitable persons. Yet neither altering its product nor its mass marketing efforts seems to fit these assumptions. And there is the obvious issue of what constitutes a small gain and loss.

20. If a physician orders more services, the dollar value of a unit of services will fall, all else equal.

21. Interestingly, this is *not* true of Spearman rank correlations (not shown), suggesting the greater correlation among the very high spenders is attributable to the amount spent.

22. In addition to reducing the incentive to select against the chronically ill, outlier schemes insure against random fluctuations in overall plan profit, if the plan enrollment is sufficiently small that the law of large numbers does not render such random fluctuations minimal.

23. Adding diagnostic adjusters does not change Chapman's results presented in the prior section on the persistence of health care spending. The values in the correlogram in table 6.3 change by less than 0.01 if they are based on residual expenditure after accounting for ACGs rather than on raw spending data.

24. Profit rates were defined as follows: (reimbursement − cost of claims)/cost of claims.

25. Chapman used the spring 1995 version of Ambulatory Care Groups and the fall 1996 version of Hierarchical Co-existing Conditions.

26. The group prospective method, however, does offer some advantages when dealing with what Chapman terms post-adjustment bias; see the text.

27. The age adjustment uses dummy variables for each five-year age-sex group, except those under 5 years of age are subdivided into under 1 year of age and 1–4 years of age, and those over 65 years of age are collapsed into one age group.

28. The group prospective method behaves more like the retrospective method than the individual prospective method. One can infer that it is picking up some of the random year-to-year variation and not just the change in the permanent component.

29. Although the retrospective method does worse than prospective adjustment with respect to post-adjustment incentives, Chapman (1997) finds that the compromise of group prospective adjustment does not.

30. For the group in the third row the retrospective adjuster does slightly worse.

31. A third study by van Barneveld (2000) is also relevant to this discussion. He compares three risk adjustment models, one with only demographics, one with demographics plus prior cost, and a mixed model of demographics and current cost that places the same weight on current cost as the coefficient of prior cost in the prior cost regression (0.41). He purports to find (his table 8.1) that the prior cost model (a prospective model) has a substantially lower absolute error than use of current cost in the mixed model and therefore has better incentives for selection than current cost (see his figure 8.3). There are several problems with van Barneveld's result, starting with the possibility of an error. With squared error as a criterion, van Barneveld's result is impossible; 0.41 times current cost must explain more variance in current cost than 0.41 times prior cost, provided the demographic variables he uses have been optimized. Because he used absolute error rather than squared error as a criterion, his result is mathematically possible, although it seems improbable. More important, he bases his measure of incentives to select on the measure of absolute error in the current period, but from the plan's point of view, reimbursing a portion of prior cost differs only from reimbursing current cost by a discount factor (which should be modest for a one year difference) and the possibility that the enrollee dies or disenrolls in the next period. In short, van Barneveld needs to consider a period longer than one year when measuring the plan's incentive to select.

32. See Dunn, Rosenblatt, Taira et al.'s note 31, page 3-47.

33. Chapman finds some evidence that this advantage of retrospective risk adjustment does not survive when new (nonrandom) groups are formed from risk-adjusted data. The advantage of the group prospective method, however, does survive.

34. These were as follows: (1) The prospective method was used, so a diagnosis in year t only affected payment in year t + 1 and then only by the increment of expected spending in the year after the diagnosis; (2) discretionary admissions are in the lowest weight category; and (3) one-day stays did not count.

35. In cases in which the HMO passes down a capitation to a physician group, the HMO could in principle risk-adjust that capitation to match the capitation in the risk adjustment formula and so keep its risk down.

36. Wholey, Feldman, Christianson et al. had around 1,700 observations from all HMOs in the 1988 to 1991 time period; thus, there are around 400–500 unique HMOs in their sample. They report the mean annual expense per HMO as $86 million, the mean number of non-Medicare enrollee-years as 75,800, and the mean marginal cost per member-year at HMOs not offering Medicare as $810. There were 9,600 Medicare enrollee-years, but no marginal cost figure for Medicare enrollees is given (the average AAPCC in these years was around $3,600 per year). Not counting the variable costs of treating the Medicare enrollees, which substantially biases the estimate of the percentage of total costs that are variable down, an estimate of the variable costs from the non-Medicare enrollees at the mean non-Medicare enrollment is $61 million (75,800 × $810), or more than 70 percent of the mean total costs of $86 million.

37. The possibility of gaming is suggested by an incident that happened to me several years ago when I bought a new automobile. The manufacturer had the dealer distribute a questionnaire to buyers on satisfaction with the dealer. I was to mail the questionnaire back to the manufacturer. I infer the results had some consequences for the dealer because the salesman at the dealership offered me a free lubrication for my car if I would return the questionnaire to him instead of mailing it directly to the manufacturer. I have no way of knowing how many customers took advantage of the free lubrication, nor what the dealer did with the returned questionnaires.

38. This is how the PPS for hospitals operates (see chapter 1), although it would be a technical improvement to change the financing of outliers to be DRG-specific (Medicare Payment Advisory Commission 2000b). Thus, DRGs with disproportionately high outlier spending would have their base reimbursement reduced more than 5 percent. Under the current system, reimbursement for nonoutlier cases is on average too high in DRGs with disproportionately high outlier spending and conversely.

39. Plans can obviously do better than this if they can predict spending that will not recur or new spending in a future period.

40. Because pooling is implemented with an equal percentage of persons coming from each plan, it will result in a different pattern of risks than reinsurance with a given spending threshold across plans (assuming the distribution of risks across plans is not identical). Plans that have a worse distribution of risks will on average be ceding worse risks to the pool and conversely. Under the high-risk pooling method, the loss rates across all plans will be greater than under reinsurance because a common threshold across plans (reinsurance) minimizes the aggregate losses to plans. If each plan can cede a given percentage of its risks and if some plans have worse risks than others, the pool will contain some persons whose expected spending is below the threshold and exclude some whose spending is above it.

41. Indeed, reinsurance increases the losses with HCCs as adjusters. The intuition for this result is that some of those in the lowest 20 percent in 1989 have spending in the top 1 or 5 percent in future years and that spending is reflected in the premium charged for the reinsurance. The premium is netted out from revenue with reinsurance, but it is not netted out in the base case.

42. In other literature the payer is sometimes called a sponsor.

43. They are more likely to avail themselves of the benefit.

44. A QALY accounts for any reduction in the quality of life from illness or infirmity. If there is no reduction (i.e., if the person is in perfect health), expected remaining QALYs in a lifetime equal life expectancy.

45. In 1995 62 percent of insured workers had a choice of two or more health plans (Jensen et al. 1997).

46. Keeler, Carter, and Newhouse (1998) refer to the blend as "first dollar reinsurance," but I have not used that term here to avoid confusion. The blended payment applies to all expenditure, whereas reinsurance is conventionally assumed to apply to costs at or above the mean.

47. Luck factors are independent of disease and multiply demand by 0.2, 0.8, and 6.4 with probabilities 0.6, 0.3, and 0.1 respectively.

48. In a well-known paper, McNeil, Weichselbaum, and Pauker (1981) interviewed twenty-five middle and high executives of three management-consulting firms and twelve firefighters to ascertain their preferences for treatment of laryngeal cancer. There was no systematic difference between these two groups in how they traded off the loss of normal voice function (from surgical treatment) against increased life expectancy, supporting the assumption of independence.

49. I assume the number of premium payers or taxpayers is large and so ignore the effect on the individual's premium or tax rate.

50. This result normalizes p to be 1.

51. Keeler, Carter, and Newhouse (1998) add a small random number to each person's h in order to break ties in choosing plans. Zero welfare loss would require a plan for each person that matched that person's level of h, including the random element. The random element differences out in comparing plans.

52. The premium differences are 90 percent of the spending differences because of the 10 percent coinsurance payments.

53. As mentioned in note 51, Keeler, Carter, and Newhouse (1998) add a small random number to h to avoid ties in choice of plan by the simulated population. These numbers generate a small welfare loss; to avoid such a loss, there would have to be a plan for each person.

54. Equilibrium here means that no one changes plan after the model iterates.

55. Under this scheme the plan pays 90 percent of the entire cost, not just the portion above $30,000.

56. This is somewhat analogous to the case analyzed by Crew (1969), in which the moral hazard from insurance could potentially increase welfare by reducing the loss from any monopoly pricing.

57. The one-third figure is calculated as follows. Frank and McGuire (2000) quote a figure from Oss that 53 million people were enrolled in mental health carveouts as of about 1995. Carveouts would be highly unusual in individual insurance, so it is likely that virtually all of the 53 million had group health insurance. At that time there were about 160 million persons insured with private group health insurance. Some Medicare HMO enrollees may have been part of carveout arrangements, but they are few enough in number that they would not materially affect this calculation.

58. I ignore selection of the place of employment on the basis of health care benefits.

59. Glazer and McGuire distinguish acute and chronic illness; both risk types have the same probability of acute illness and differ in their probability of chronic illness. The

assumption of acute illness with similar probabilities is unimportant for the ensuing discussion.

60. Payment does not differ much if one adds an unimportant risk adjuster to a set of existing risk adjusters, however.

61. An unrelated factor that cuts in the other direction for preventive services is the plan's inability to reap a later return if the individual changes health plans and if the market is not perfectly competitive.

62. Except that Medicare must meet prices paid by private insurers or risk access problems. With only one public plan if payment is kept below a hypothetical competitive level, access problems may develop in the long run from lack of entry or under-the-table payments may develop, as happened in Eastern Europe (Kornai and Eggleston 2001).

63. Even ardent egalitarians would presumably honor many of the differences in tastes that did not arise from income differences.

64. One example would be Christian Scientists.

65. I implicitly assume that variation in taste across individuals mainly averages out at the regional level, and that therefore it is not a prime candidate for explaining systematic variation across regions.

References

Academy of Actuaries. 1993. "Health Risk Assessment and Health Risk Adjustment—Crucial Elements in Health Care Reform." Mimeo., Risk Adjustment Work Group, May.

Akerlof, George. 1970. "The Market for Lemons." *Quarterly Journal of Economics* 84: 488–500.

Allen, Robin, and Paul Gertler. 1991. "Regulation and the Provision of Quality to Heterogeneous Consumers: The Case of Prospective Pricing of Medical Services." *Journal of Regulatory Economics* 3: 361–375.

Anderson, Gerard F., and Judith R. Lave. 1986. "Financing Graduate Medical Education Using Multiple Regression to Set Payment Rates." *Inquiry* 23: 191–199.

Anderson, Gerard F., and Jean-Pierre Poullier. 1999. "Health Spending, Access, and Outcomes: Trends in Industrialized Countries." *Health Affairs* 18(3): 178–192.

Arrow, Kenneth J. 1963. "Uncertainty and the Economics of Medical Care." *American Economic Review* 53: 941–973.

Arrow, Kenneth J. 1973. "Optimal Insurance and Generalized Deductibles." Publication No. R-1108-OEO. Santa Monica, CA: RAND.

Arrow, Kenneth J. 1976. "Welfare Analysis of Changes in Health Coinsurance Rates." In *The Role of Health Insurance in the Health Services Sector*, ed. Richard N. Rosett. New York: National Bureau of Economic Research. Reprinted in *Collected Papers of Kenneth J. Arrow*, Vol. 6: *Applied Economics*, 235–254. Cambridge: Harvard University Press, 1985.

Averch, Harvey, and Leland L. Johnson. 1962. "Behavior of the Firm under Regulatory Constraint." *American Economic Review* 52: 1053–1069.

Baker, George. 1992. "Incentive Contracts and Performance Measurement." *Journal of Political Economy* 100: 598–614.

Ballard, Charles L., Don Fullerton, John B. Shoven, and John Whalley. 1985. *A General Equilibrium Model for Tax Policy Evaluation*. Chicago: University of Chicago Press.

Barzansky, Barbara, Harry S. Jonas, and Sylvia I. Etzel. 1999. "Educational Programs in US Medical Schools, 1998–1999." *Journal of the American Medical Association* 282: 840–846.

Bates, David W. 2000. "Using Information Technology to Reduce Rates of Medication Errors in Hospitals." *British Medical Journal* 320: 788–791.

Bates, David W., Lucian L. Leape, D. J. Cullen et al. 1998. "Effect of Computerized Order Entry and a Team Intervention on Prevention of Serious Medication Errors." *Journal of the American Medical Association* 280: 1311–1316.

Baumgardner, James. 1991. "The Interaction between Forms of Insurance Contract and Types of Technical Change in Medical Care." *RAND Journal of Economics* 22: 36–53.

Bazzoli, Gloria. 1985. "Does Educational Indebtedness Affect Physician Specialty Choice?" *Journal of Health Economics* 4: 1–19.

Beaulieu, Nancy D. 1998. "Quality Information and Quality Competition in the Managed Health Care Insurance Market." Unpublished Ph.D. diss., Harvard University.

Beck, Konstantin. 2000. "Growing Importance of Capitation in Switzerland." *Health Care Management Science* 3: 111–119.

Becker, Edmund R., Daniel Dunn, and William C. Hsiao. 1988. "Relative Cost Differences among Physicians' Specialty Practices." *Journal of the American Medical Association* 260: 2397–2402.

Beebe, James C. 1985. "Medicare Reimbursement Regression to the Mean." Baltimore: Health Care Financing Administration.

Beeuwkes Buntin, Melinda J. 2000. "Competition and Payment Systems under Medicare." Unpublished Ph.D. diss., Harvard University.

Beeuwkes Buntin, Melinda J., Alan M. Garber, Mark McClellan et al. 2001. "The Costs of Death in the Medicare Program: Implications for Payments to Medicare + Choice Plans." Mimeo.

Berk, Marc, and Alan C. Monheit. 1992. "The Concentration of Health Expenditures: An Update." *Health Affairs* 11(4): 145–149.

Berndt, Ernst R., Susan Busch, and Richard G. Frank. 2000. "Treatment Price Indices for Acute Phase Major Depression." In *Medical Care Output and Productivity*, ed. Ernst R. Berndt and David M. Cutler, 463–505. Chicago: University of Chicago Press.

Berndt, Ernst R., David M. Cutler, and Richard G. Frank et al. 2000. "Medical Care Prices and Output." In *Handbook of Health Economics*, ed. Anthony J. Culyer and Joseph P. Newhouse, 119–180. Amsterdam: North-Holland.

Blendon, Robert J., Drew E. Altman, John Benson et al. 1995. "The Public's View of the Future of Medicare." *Journal of the American Medical Association* 274: 1645–1648.

Board of Trustees of the Federal Hospital Insurance and Supplementary Medical Insurance Trust Funds. 2000. "Annual Reports." Washington, DC: Government Printing Office (http://www.hcfa.gov/pubforms/tr/).

Braun, Peter, Douwe Yntema, Daniel Dunn et al. 1988. "Cross-Specialty Linkage of Resource Based Relative Value Scales." *Journal of the American Medical Association* 260: 2390–2396.

Brennan, Troyen A. 2000. "The Institute of Medicine Report on Medical Errors—Could It Do Harm?" *New England Journal of Medicine* 342: 1123–1125.

Brennan, Troyen A., Carol M. Sox, and Helen R. Burstin. 1996. "Relation between Negligent Adverse Events and the Outcomes of Medical-Malpractice Litigation." *New England Journal of Medicine* 335: 1963–1967.

Brook, Robert. 1993. "Maintaining Hospital Quality: The Need for International Co-operation." *Journal of the American Medical Association* 270: 985–987.

Brook, Robert, and Elizabeth McGlynn. 1991. "Quality of Care." In *Health Services Research*, ed. Eli Ginzberg, 284–314. Cambridge: Harvard University Press.

Carter, Grace M., Joseph P. Newhouse, and Daniel Relles. 1990. "How Much Change in the Case Mix Index is DRG Creep?" *Journal of Health Economics* 9: 411–428.

Cave, Jonathan. 1985. "Subsidy Equilibrium and Multiple-Option Insurance Markets." In *Advances in Health Economics and Health Services Research: Biased Selection in Health Care Markets*, ed. Richard Scheffler and Louis F. Rossiter, 6, 27–45. Greenwich, CT: JAI Press.

Center for Research in Ambulatory Health Care Administration. 1993. *"Physician Compensation and Production Survey: 1993 Report Based on 1992 Data."* Englewood, CO: The Center. September.

Chalkley, Martin and James M. Malcolmson. 1998. "Contracting for Health Services When Patient Demand Does Not Reflect Quality." *Journal of Health Economics* 17: 1–19.

Chalkley, Martin and James M. Malcolmson. 2000. "Government Purchasing of Health Services." In *Handbook of Health Economics*, ed. Anthony J. Culyer and Joseph P. Newhouse, 847–890. Amsterdam: North-Holland.

Chapman, John David. 1997. "Biased Enrollment and Risk Adjustment for Health Plans." Unpublished Ph.D. diss., Harvard University.

Chassin, Mark R., Robert H. Brook, Rolla E. Park et al. 1986. "Variations in the Use of Services by the Medicare Population." *New England Journal of Medicine* 314: 285–290.

Chassin, Mark R., Edward L. Hannan, and Barbara A. DeBuono. 1996. "Benefits and Hazards of Reporting Medical Information Publicly." *New England Journal of Medicine* 334: 394–398.

Chassin, Mark R., Jacqueline Kosecoff, Rolla E. Park et al. 1987. "Does Inappropriate Use Explain Geographic Variations in the Use of Health Care Services? A Study of Three Procedures." *Journal of the American Medical Association* 258: 2533–2537.

Cleary, Paul D. 1999. "The Increasing Importance of Patient Surveys." *British Medical Journal* 319: 720–721.

Cleary, Paul D., Susan Edgman-Levitan, Marc Roberts et al. 1991. "Patients Evaluate Their Hospital Care: A National Survey." *Health Affairs* 10(4): 254–267.

Cochrane, John. 1995. "Time Consistent Health Insurance." *Journal of Political Economy* 103: 445–473.

Congressional Budget Office. 1997. "Predicting How Changes in Medicare's Payment Rates Would Affect Risk-Sector Enrollments and Costs." Washington, DC: Congressional Budget Office. March.

Congressional Budget Office. 2000. "The Budget and Economic Outlook: Fiscal Years 2001–2010." Washington, DC: Congressional Budget Office. January.

Crew, Michael. 1969. "Coinsurance and the Welfare Economics of Medical Care." *American Economic Review*, 59: 906–908.

Crocker, Keith J., and Arthur Snow. 1985. "The Efficiency of Competitive Equilibria in Insurance Markets with Asymmetric Information." *Journal of Public Economics* 26: 207–219.

Culyer, Anthony J., and Heather Simpson. 1980. "Externality Models and Health: A Rückblick over the Last Twenty Years." *Economic Record* 56: 222–230.

Cutler, David M. 1994. "A Guide to Health Care Reform." *Journal of Economic Perspectives* 8(3): 13–29.

Cutler, David M. 1995. "The Incidence of Adverse Medical Outcomes Under Prospective Payment." *Econometrica* 63: 29–50.

Cutler, David M., ed. 2000. *The Changing Hospital Industry: Comparing Not-for-Profit and For-Profit Institutions*. Chicago: University of Chicago Press.

Cutler, David M., Mark McClellan, and Joseph P. Newhouse. 2000. "How Does Managed Care Do It?" *RAND Journal of Economics* 31: 526–548.

Cutler, David M., Mark McClellan, Joseph P. Newhouse, and Dahlia K. Remler. 1998. "Are Medical Prices Declining?" *Quarterly Journal of Economics* 113: 991–1024.

Cutler, David M., and Sarah Reber. 1998. "Paying for Health Insurance: The Tradeoff between Competition and Adverse Selection." *Quarterly Journal of Economics* 113: 433–466.

Cutler, David M., and Richard J. Zeckhauser. 1997. "Reinsurance for Catastrophes and Cataclysms." Working Paper 5913. Cambridge: National Bureau of Economic Research.

Dalton, Kathleen, and Edward C. Norton. 2000. "Revisiting Rogowski and Newhouse on the Indirect Costs of Teaching: A Note on Functional Form and Retransformation in Medicare's Payment Formula." *Journal of Health Economics* 19: 1027–1046.

Danzon, Patricia. 1985. *Medical Malpractice*. Cambridge: Harvard University Press.

Darby, Michael, and Edi Karni. 1973. "The Optimal Extent of Fraud." *Journal of Law and Economics* 16(1): 67–88.

Decker, Sandra. 1993 . "The Effect of Medicaid on Access to Health Care and Welfare Participation." Unpublished Ph.D. diss., Harvard University.

de Meza, David. 1983. "Health Insurance and the Demand for Medical Care." *Journal of Health Economics* 2: 47–54.

Department of Health and Human Services. 1983. "Report to Congress: Hospital Prospective Payment System for Medicare, December 1982." Publication No. 381-858:170. Washington, DC: Government Printing Office.

Dranove, David. 1987. "Rate Setting by Diagnosis Related Groups and Hospital Specialization." *RAND Journal of Economics* 18: 415–427.

Dranove, David, Daniel Kessler, Mark McClellan, and Mark Satterthwaite. 2000. "More Information Is Good Except When It Isn't." Mimeo.

Dranove, David, and Mark Satterthwaite. 1992. "Monopolistic Competition when Price and Quality Are Imperfectly Observable." *RAND Journal of Economics* 23: 518–534.

Dranove, David, Michael Shanley, and William D. White. 1993. "Price and Concentration in Hospital Markets: The Switch from Patient to Payer Driven Competition." *Journal of Law and Economics* 36: 179–204.

Dranove, David, and William D. White. 1987. "Agency Costs and the Organization of Health Care Delivery." *Inquiry* 24: 405–415.

Dunn, Andrea L., Bess H. Marcus, James B. Kampert et al. 1999. "Comparison of Lifestyle and Structured Interventions to Increase Physical Activity and Cardiorespiratory Fitness: A Randomized Trial." *Journal of the American Medical Association* 281: 327–334.

Dunn, Daniel L., Alice Rosenblatt, Deborah A. Taira et al. 1995. "A Comparative Analysis of Methods of Health Risk Assessment: Final Report." Mimeo., October 12.

Economic Report of the President, 1999. 1999. Washington: Government Printing Office. February.

Eddy, David M. 1998. "Performance Measurement: Problems and Solutions." *Health Affairs* 17(4): 7–25.

Eggers, Paul. 1980. "Risk Differential Between Medicare Beneficiaries Enrolled and Not Enrolled in an HMO." *Health Care Financing Review* 1(3): 91–99.

Eggleston, Karen. 1999. "Selection, Production Efficiency, Risk Adjustment, and Agency: Optimal Payment Systems for Health Services." Unpublished Ph.D. diss., Harvard University.

Eggleston, Karen. 2000. "Risk Selection and Optimal Health Insurance-Provider Payment Systems." *Journal of Risk and Insurance* 67: 175–198.

Ehrlich, Issac, and Gary S. Becker. 1972. "Market Insurance, Self-Insurance, and Self-Production." *Journal of Political Economy* 80: 623–648.

Ellis, Randall P. 1998. "Creaming, Skimming, and Dumping: Provider Competition on the Intensive and Extensive Margins." *Journal of Health Economics* 17: 537–555.

Ellis, Randall P., Gregory C. Pope, Lisa Iezzoni et al. 1996. "Diagnosis-Based Risk Adjustment for Medicare Capitation Payments." *Health Care Financing Review* 17(3): 101–128.

Ellis, Randall P., and Thomas G. McGuire. 1986. "Provider Behavior under Prospective Reimbursement: Cost Sharing and Supply." *Journal of Health Economics* 5: 129–152.

Ellis, Randall P., and Thomas G. McGuire. 1988. "Insurance Principles and the Design of Prospective Payment Systems." *Journal of Health Economics* 7: 215–237.

Ellis, Randall P., and Thomas G. McGuire. 1990. "Optimal Payment Systems for Health Services." *Journal of Health Economics* 9: 375–396.

Ellis, Randall P., and Thomas G. McGuire. 1993. "Supply-Side and Demand-Side Cost Sharing in Health Care." *Journal of Economic Perspectives* 7(4): 135–151.

Emmons, David W., and Phillip R. Kletke. 1997. "An Examination of Practice Size." In *Socioeconomic Characteristics of Medical Practice, 1997*, ed. Martin L. Gonzalez, 21–30. Chicago: American Medical Association.

Encinosa, William E., and David E. M. Sappington. 1997. "Competition Among Health Maintenance Organizations." *Journal of Economics and Management Strategy* 6: 129–150.

Enthoven, Alain C. 1988. *The Theory and Practice of Managed Competition*. Amsterdam: North-Holland.

Epstein, Arnold M. 1998. "Rolling Down the Runway: The Challenges Ahead for Quality Report Cards." *Journal of the American Medical Association* 279: 1691–1696.

Evans, Robert G. 1984. *Strained Mercy*. Toronto: Butterworths.

Feldman, Roger, and Bryan Dowd. 1982. "Simulation of a Health Insurance Market with Adverse Selection." *Operations Research* 30: 1027–1042.

Feldstein, Martin S. 1971. "A New Approach to National Health Insurance." *The Public Interest* 23: 93–105.

Feldstein, Martin S., and Jonathan Gruber. 1995. "A Major Risk Approach to Health Insurance Reform." In *Tax Policy and the Economy*, vol. 9, ed. James M. Poterba, 103–130. Cambridge: The MIT Press.

Frank, Richard G., Ernst R. Berndt, and Susan Busch. 1999. "Price Indexes for the Treatment of Depression." In *Measuring the Prices of Medical Treatments*, ed. Jack Triplett, 72–117. Washington, DC: Brookings Institution.

Frank, Richard G., Jacob Glazer, and Thomas G. McGuire. 2000. "Measuring Adverse Selection in Managed Health Care." *Journal of Health Economics* 20: 829–854.

Frank, Richard G., and Thomas G. McGuire. 1998. "Economic Functions of Carve-outs." *American Journal of Managed Care* 4(SP): SP31–SP39.

Frank, Richard G., and Thomas G. McGuire. 2000. "Economics and Mental Health." In *Handbook of Health Economics*, ed. Anthony J. Culyer and Joseph P. Newhouse, 893–954. Amsterdam: North-Holland.

Frank, Richard G., Thomas G. McGuire, and Joseph P. Newhouse. 1995. "Risk Contracts in Managed Mental Health Care." *Health Affairs* 14(3): 50–64.

Frank, Richard G., and David Salkever. 1991. "The Supply of Charity Services by Nonprofit Hospitals: Motives and Market Structure." *Rand Journal of Economics* 22(3): 43–55.

Friedman, Milton. 1991. "Gammon's Law Points to Health Care Solution." *Wall Street Journal*, November 12, A-20.

Friedman, Milton, and Simon Kuznets. 1945. *Income from Independent Professional Practice*. New York: National Bureau of Economic Research.

Fuchs, Victor R. 1974. *Who Shall Live?* New York: Basic Books.

Fuchs, Victor R. 1999. "Health Care for the Elderly: How Much? Who Will Pay for It?" *Health Affairs* 18(1): 11–21.

General Accounting Office. 1999. "Medicare Home Health Agencies: Closures Continue with Little Evidence Beneficiary Access Is Impaired." Publication No. GAO/HEHS-99-120. Washington, DC: Government Printing Office.

Glazer, Jacob, and Thomas G. McGuire. 1993. "Should Physicians Be Permitted to 'Balance Bill' Patients?" *Journal of Health Economics* 12: 239–258.

Glazer, Jacob, and Thomas G. McGuire. 1994. "Payer Competition and Cost Shifting in Health Care." *Journal of Economics and Management Strategy* 3: 71–92.

Glazer, Jacob, and Thomas G. McGuire. 2000a. "Optimal Risk Adjustment in Markets with Adverse Selection." *American Economic Review* 90: 1055–1071.

Glazer, Jacob, and Thomas G. McGuire. 2000b. "Regulating Premium Payments to Managed Care Plans." Mimeo., March 12.

Glied, Sherry A. 2000. "Managed Care." In *Handbook of Health Economics*, ed. Anthony J. Culyer and Joseph P. Newhouse, 707–754. Amsterdam: North-Holland.

Gold, Marthe, Joanna Siegel, Louise B. Russell, and Milton C. Weinstein, eds. 1996. *Cost-Effectiveness in Health and Medicine*. New York: Oxford University Press.

Goldberg, Lawrence G., and Warren Greenberg. 1978. "The Emergence of Physician-Sponsored Health Insurance: A Historical Perspective." In *Competition in the Health Care Sector: Past, Present, and Future*, ed. Warren Greenberg, 231–254. Germantown, MD: Aspen Systems Corporation.

Green, Jesse, and Neil Wintfeld. 1995. "Report Cards on Cardiac Surgeons: Assessing New York State's Approach." *New England Journal of Medicine* 332: 1229–1232.

Grossman, Michael. 1972. "On the Concept of Health Capital and the Demand for Health." *Journal of Political Economy* 80: 223–255.

Gruber, Jonathan. 2000. "Health Insurance and the Labor Market." In *Handbook of Health Economics*, ed. Anthony J. Culyer and Joseph P. Newhouse, 645–706. Amsterdam: North-Holland.

Gruber, Jonathan, J. Kim, and Dina Mayzlin. 1999. "Physician Fees and Procedure Intensity: The Case of Cesarean Delivery." *Journal of Health Economics* 18: 473–490.

Gruenberg, Leonard, E. Kaganova, and Mark C. Hornbrook. 1996. "Improving the AAPCC (Adjusted Average per capita Cost) with Health-Status Measures from the MCBS (Medicare Current Beneficiary Survey)." *Health Care Financing Review* 17(3): 59–75.

Hannan, Edward L., H. Kilburn Jr., J. F. O'Donnell, G. Lukacsik, and E. P. Shields. 1990. "Adult Open Heart Surgery in New York State: An Analysis of Risk Factors and Hospital Mortality Rates." *Journal of the American Medical Association* 264: 2768–2774.

Hannan, Edward L., H. Kilburn Jr., M. Racz, E. Shields, and Mark R. Chassin. 1994. "Improving the Outcomes of Coronary Artery Bypass Surgery in New York State." *Journal of the American Medical Association* 271: 771–776.

Harris, Jeffrey. 1979. "Pricing Rules for Hospitals." *Bell Journal of Economics* 10: 224–243.

Health Care Financing Administration. 1996. "Medicare and Medicaid Statistical Supplement. 1996." *Health Care Financing Review* (Statistical Suppl.), Publication No. 03386.

Health Care Financing Administration. 1998. *1998 Data Compendium*. Baltimore, MD: Health Care Financing Administration, Office of Strategic Planning. Publication No. 030407.

Hickson, Gerald, William A. Altmeier, and James M. Perrin. 1987. "Physician Reimbursement by Salary or Fee-for-Service: Effect on Physician Practice Behavior in a Randomized Prospective Study." *Pediatrics* 80: 344–350.

Hodgkin, Dominic, and Thomas G. McGuire. 1994. "Payment Levels and Hospital Response to Prospective Reimbursement." *Journal of Health Economics* 13: 1–30.

Hofer, Timothy P., Rodney A. Hayward, Sheldon Greenfield, Edward H. Wagner, Sherrie H. Kaplan, and Willard G. Manning. 1999. "The Unreliability of Individual Physician 'Report Cards' for Assessing the Costs and Quality of Care of a Chronic Disease." *Journal of the American Medical Association* 281: 2098–2105.

Holmstrom, Bengt, and Paul Milgrom. 1990. "Regulating Trade Among Agents." *Journal of Institutional and Theoretical Economics* 146: 85–105.

Holmstrom, Bengt, and Paul Milgrom. 1991. "Multi-Task Principal-Agent Analyses: Incentive Contracts, Asset Ownership, and Job Design." *Journal of Law, Economics, and Organization* 7: 24–52.

Hornbrook, Mark C., and M. J. Goodman. 1995. "Assessing Relative Health Plan Risk with the RAND-36 Health Survey." *Inquiry* 32: 56–74.

Hornbrook, Mark C., and M. J. Goodman. 1996. "Chronic Disease, Functional Health Status, and Demographics: A Multi-Dimensional Approach to Risk Adjustment." *Health Services Research* 31: 283–307.

Hsiao, William C., Peter Braun, Daniel Dunn et al. 1988. "Resource Based Relative Values: An Overview." *Journal of the American Medical Association* 260(16): 2347–2353.

Hsiao, William C., Douwe Yntema, Peter Braun et al. 1988. "Measurement and Analysis of Intraservice Work." *Journal of the American Medical Association* 260(16): 2361–2370.

Hurley, Jeremiah. 2000. "An Overview of the Normative Economics of the Health Care Sector." In *Handbook of Health Economics*, ed. Anthony J. Culyer and Joseph P. Newhouse. Amsterdam: North-Holland.

Huskamp, Haiden A. 1999. "Episodes of Mental Health and Substance Abuse Treatment under a Managed Behavioral Health Care Carve-Out." *Inquiry* 36: 147–161.

Huskamp, Haiden A., Meredith B. Rosenthal, Richard G. Frank, and Joseph P. Newhouse. 2000. "The Medicare Prescription Drug Benefit: How Will the Game Be Played?" *Health Affairs* 19(2): 8–23.

Institute of Medicine. 1986. *For-Profit Enterprise in Health Care.* Washington, DC: National Academy Press.

Institute of Medicine. 2000. *To Err Is Human.* Washington, DC: National Academy Press.

Institute of Medicine. 2001. *Crossing the Quality Chasm: A New Health System for the 21st Century.* Washington, DC: National Academy Press.

Jensen, Gail A., Michael A. Morrisey, Shannon Gaffney, and Derek K. Liston. 1997. "The New Dominance of Managed Care." *Health Affairs* 16(1): 125–136.

Kane, Nancy M., and Paul D. Manoukian. 1989. "The Effect of the Medicare Prospective Payment System on the Adoption of New Technology—The Case of Cochlear Implants." *New England Journal of Medicine* 321: 1378–1383.

Kapur, Kanika. 1998. "The Impact of Health on Job Mobility: A Measure of Job Lock." *Industrial and Labor Relations Review* 51: 282–298.

Keeler, Emmett B., Grace M. Carter, and Joseph P. Newhouse. 1998. "A Model of the Impact of Reimbursement Schemes on Health Plan Choice." *Journal of Health Economics* 17: 297–320.

Keeler, Emmett B., Grace M. Carter, and Sally Trude. 1988. "Insurance Aspects of DRG Outlier Payments." *Journal of Health Economics* 7: 193–214.

Keeler, Emmett B., Joseph P. Newhouse, and Charles E. Phelps. 1977. "Deductibles and Demand: A Theory of the Consumer Facing a Variable Price Schedule under Uncertainty." *Econometrica* 45: 641–655.

Keenan, Patricia S., Melinda J. Beeuwkes Buntin, Thomas G. McGuire et al. 2001. "The Prevalence of Formal Risk Adjustment in Health Plan Purchasing." *Inquiry* 38: 245–259.

Kerr, Eve A., Brian S. Mittman, Ron D. Hays et al. 1996. "Quality Assurance in Capitated Physician Groups." *Journal of the American Medical Association* 276: 1236–1239.

Kessel, Reuben. 1958. "Price Discrimination in Medicine." *Journal of Law and Economics* 1: 20–53.

Kornai, János, and Karen Eggleston. 2001. *Welfare, Choice, and Solidarity in Transition: Reforming the Health Sector in Eastern Europe.* New York: Cambridge University Press.

Krasnik, Allan, Peter P. Groenewegen, Poul A. Pedersen et al. 1990. "Changing Remuneration Systems: Effects on Activity in General Practice." *British Medical Journal* 300: 1698–1701.

Kronick, Richard, Todd Gilmer, Tony Dreyfus et al. 1996. "Improving Health-Based Payment for Medicaid Beneficiaries." *Health Care Financing Review* 17(3): 29–64.

Kuttner, Robert. 1996. "Columbia/HCA and the Resurgence of the For-Profit Hospital Business." *New England Journal of Medicine* 335: 362–367, 446–451.

Laffont, Jean-Jacques, and Jean Tirole. 1993. *A Theory of Incentives in Procurement and Regulation.* Cambridge: The MIT Press.

Langwell, Kathryn, and James P. Hadley. 1986. "Capitation and the Medicare Program: History, Issues, and Evidence." *Health Care Financing Review* (Annual Suppl.): 9–20.

Leape, Lucian L. 1994. "Error in Medicine." *Journal of the American Medical Association* 272: 1851–1857.

Leape, Lucian L., David W. Bates, David J. Cullen et al. 1995. "Systems Analysis of Adverse Drug Events." *Journal of the American Medical Association* 274: 35–43.

Levit, Katherine, R., Cathy Cowan, Helen Lazenby et al. 2000. "Health Spending in 1998: Signals of Change." *Health Affairs* 19(1): 124–132.

Long, Stephen H., and M. Susan Marquis. 1999. "Trends in Managed Care and Managed Competition." *Health Affairs* 18(6): 75–88.

Longo, Daniel R., Garland Land, Wayne Schramm, Judy Fraas, Barbara Hoskins, and Vicky Howell. 1997. "Consumer Reports in Health Care: Do They Make a Difference in Patient Care?" *Journal of the American Medical Association* 278: 1579–1584.

Ma, Ching-to Albert. 1994. "Health Care Payment Systems: Cost and Quality Incentives." *Journal of Economics and Management Strategy* 3: 93–112.

Ma, Ching-to Albert, and Thomas G. McGuire. 1999. "Network Effects in Managed Health Care." Mimeo.

Madrian, Brigitte. 1994. "Employment-Based Health Insurance and Job Mobility: Is There Evidence of Job Lock?" *Quarterly Journal of Economics* 108: 27–54.

Manning, Willard G., Joseph P. Newhouse, Naihua Duan et al. 1988. Health Insurance and the Demand for Medical Care: Evidence from a Randomized Experiment. Publication No. R-3476-HHS. Santa Monica, CA: RAND.

Marquis, M. Susan. 1985. "Cost-Sharing and Provider Choice." *Journal of Health Economics* 4: 137–157.

Marquis, M. Susan, David Kanouse, and Laurel Brodsley. 1985. "Informing Consumers about Health Care Costs." Publication No. R-3262-HCFA. Santa Monica, CA: RAND.

McCall, Nelda, and H. S. Wai. 1983. "An Analysis of Use of Medicare Services by the Continuously Enrolled Aged." *Medical Care* 21: 567–585.

McClellan, Mark. 1993. "The Economics of Medical Treatment Intensity." Unpublished Ph.D. diss., Massachusetts Institute of Technology.

McClellan, Mark. 1997. "Hospital Reimbursement Incentives: An Empirical Analysis." *Journal of Economics and Management Strategy* 6: 91–128.

McCormack, L. A., Peter D. Fox, Thomas Rice et al. 1996. "Medigap Reform Legislation of 1990: Have the Objectives Been Met?" *Health Care Financing Review* 18(1): 157–174.

McGuire, Thomas G. 2000. "Physician Agency." In *Handbook of Health Economics*, ed. Anthony J. Culyer and Joseph P. Newhouse, 461–536. Amsterdam: North-Holland.

McGuire, Thomas G., and Mark V. Pauly. 1991. "Physician Response to Fee Changes with Multiple Payers." *Journal of Health Economics* 10: 385–410.

McNeil, Barbara J., R. Weichselbaum, and Stephen G. Pauker. 1981. "Speech and Survival: Tradeoffs Between Quality and Quantity of Life in Laryngeal Cancer." *New England Journal of Medicine* 305: 982–987.

Medical Group Management Association. 1999. *Physician Compensation and Production Survey, 1999.* Englewood, CO: Medical Group Management Association.

Medicare Payment Advisory Commission. 1998. "Report to the Congress: Medicare Payment Policy." Washington, DC: Medicare Payment Advisory Commission. March.

Medicare Payment Advisory Commission. 1999. "Report to the Congress: Selected Medicare Issues." Washington, DC: Medicare Payment Advisory Commission. June.

Medicare Payment Advisory Commission. 2000a. "Report to the Congress: Medicare Payment Policy." Washington, DC: Medicare Payment Advisory Commission. March.

Medicare Payment Advisory Commission. 2000b. "Report to the Congress: Selected Medicare Issues." Washington, DC: Medicare Payment Advisory Commission. June.

Medicare Payment Advisory Commission. 2001. "Report to the Congress: Medicare in Rural America." Washington, DC: Medicare Payment Advisory Commission. June.

Miller, Robert, and Harold S. Luft. 1994. "Managed Care Plan Performance Since 1980." *Journal of the American Medical Association* 271: 1512–1519.

Miller, Robert, and Harold S. Luft. 1997. "Does Managed Care Lead to Better or Worse Quality of Care?" *Health Affairs* 16(3): 7–25.

Neipp, Joachim, and Richard J. Zeckhauser. 1985. "Persistence in the Choice of Health Plans." In *Advances in Health Economics and Health Services Research*, vol. 6, ed. Richard Scheffler and Louis Rossiter, 47–72. Greenwich, CT: JAI Press.

Newhouse, Joseph P. 1970. "Toward a Theory of Nonprofit Institutions: An Economic Model of a Hospital," *American Economic Review* 60: 64–74.

Newhouse, Joseph P. 1981. "The Erosion of the Medical Marketplace," In *Advances in Health Economics and Health Services Research*, vol. 2, ed. Richard Scheffler. Westport, CT, JAI Press.

Newhouse, Joseph P. 1986. "Rate Adjusters for Medicare under Capitation." *Health Care Financing Review* 7 (Suppl.): 45–55.

Newhouse, Joseph P. 1989. "Do Unprofitable Patients Face Access Problems?" *Health Care Financing Review* 11: 33–42.

Newhouse, Joseph P. 1991. "Criteria for Judging the Recommendations: A Commentary by Joseph P. Newhouse." In *Regulating Doctors' Fees: Competition, Benefits and Controls under Medicare*, ed. H. E. Frech, 365–373. Washington, DC: American Enterprise Institute.

Newhouse, Joseph P. 1992. "Medical Care Costs: How Much Welfare Loss?" *Journal of Economic Perspectives* 6(3): 3–21.

Newhouse, Joseph P. 1996a. "Health Reform in the United States." *Economic Journal* 106: 1713–1724.

Newhouse, Joseph P. 1996b. "Reimbursing Health Plans and Health Providers: Efficiency in Production vs. Selection." *Journal of Economic Literature* 34: 1236–1263.

Newhouse, Joseph P. 2002. "Medicare." In *Economic Performance during the 1990s*, ed. Jeffrey Frankel and Peter Orszag. Cambridge: The MIT Press.

Newhouse, Joseph P., Melinda J. Beeuwkes Buntin, and John D. Chapman. 1997. "Risk Adjustment and Medicare," *Health Affairs* 16(3): 26–43.

Newhouse, Joseph P., Joan L. Buchanan, Howard L. Bailit et al. 2001. "Managed Care: an Industry Snapshot." Mimeo.

Newhouse, Joseph P., and Daniel Byrne. 1989. "Did Medicare's Prospective Payment System Cause Lengths of Stay to Fall?" *Journal of Health Economics* 8: 413–416.

Newhouse, Joseph P., and the Insurance Experiment Group. 1993. *Free for All? Lessons from the RAND Health Insurance Experiment*. Cambridge: Harvard University Press.

Newhouse, Joseph P., Willard G. Manning, Emmett B. Keeler, and Elizabeth M. Sloss. 1989. "Adjusting Capitation Rates Using Objective Health Measures and Prior Utilization." *Health Care Financing Revie* 10(3): 41–54.

Newhouse, Joseph P., Willard G. Manning, Emmett B. Keeler, and Elizabeth M. Sloss. 1994. "Risk Adjustment for a Children's Capitation Rate." *Health Care Financing Review* 15(1): 39–54.

Newhouse, Joseph P., Charles E. Phelps, and William B. Schwartz. 1974. "Policy Options and the Impact of National Health Insurance." *New England Journal of Medicine* 290: 1345–1359.

Newhouse, Joseph P., and Vincent D. Taylor. 1970. "The Subsidy Problem in Hospital Insurance." *Journal of Business* 43: 452–456.

Newhouse, Joseph P., and Vincent D. Taylor. 1971a. "How Shall We Pay for Hospital Care?" *The Public Interest* 23: 78–92.

Newhouse, Joseph P., and Vincent D. Taylor. 1971b. "A New Type of Hospital Insurance: A Proposal for an Experiment," *Journal of Risk and Insurance*, 38: 601–612.

Newhouse, Joseph P., and Gail R. Wilensky. 2001. "Paying for Graduate Medical Education: The Debate Goes On." *Health Affairs* 20(2): 136–147.

Nicholson, Sean. 1997. "Three Essays on Government Intervention in Medical Markets. Unpublished Ph.D. diss., University of Wisconsin.

Nicholson, Sean, and David Song. 2001. "The Incentive Effects of the Medicare Indirect Medical Education Policy." *Journal of Health Economics* 20: 909–933.

Norris, S. L., L. C. Grothaus, D. M. Buchner et al. 2000. "Effectiveness of Physician-Based Assessment and Counseling for Exercise in a Staff Model HMO." *Preventive Medicine* 30: 513–523.

Nyman, John. 1999. "The Value of Health Insurance: The Access Motive." *Journal of Health Economics* 18: 141–152.

Pauly, Mark V. 1968. "Comment." *American Economic Review* 58: 531–537.

Pauly, Mark V. 1980. *Doctors and Their Workshops*. Chicago: University of Chicago Press.

Pauly, Mark V. 1985. "What Is Adverse About Adverse Selection?" *Advances in Health Economics and Health Services Research*, vol. 6, ed. Richard Scheffler and Louis Rossiter. Greenwich, CT: JAI Press.

Pauly, Mark V., Patricia Danzon, Paul J. Feldstein, and John Hoff. 1991. "A Plan for 'Responsible National Health Insurance.'" *Health Affairs* 10(1): 5–25.

Pauly, Mark V., and Scott D. Ramsey. 1999. "Would You Like Suspenders to Go with That Belt? An Analysis of Optimal Combinations of Cost Sharing and Managed Care." *Journal of Health Economics* 18: 443–458.

Pauly, Mark V., and Michael Redisch. 1973. "The Not-For-Profit Hospital as a Physicians' Cooperative." *American Economic Review* 63: 87–99.

Pettengill, Julian and James Vertrees. 1982. "Reliability and Validity in Hospital Case Mix Measurement." *Health Care Financing Review* 4(2): 101–128.

Phelps, Charles E. 1978. "Illness Prevention and Medical Insurance." *Journal of Human Resources* 13 (Suppl.): 183–207.

Phelps, Charles E. 1992. "Diffusion of Information in Medical Care." *Journal of Economic Perspectives* 6(3): 23–42.

Phelps, Charles E. 2000. "Information Diffusion and Best Practice Adoption." In *Handbook of Health Economics*, ed. Anthony J. Culyer and Joseph P. Newhouse, 223–264. Amsterdam: North-Holland.

Physician Payment Review Commission. 1987. *Medicare Physician Payment: An Agenda for Reform*. Washington, DC: Physician Payment Review Commission. March.

Physician Payment Review Commission. 1989. *Annual Report to Congress, 1989*. Washington, DC: Physician Payment Review Commission. April.

Physician Payment Review Commission. 1996a. *Annual Report to Congress, 1996*. Washington, DC: Physician Payment Review Commission. April.

Physician Payment Review Commission. 1996b. *Access to Care in Medicare Managed Care: Results from a 1996 Survey of Enrollees and Disenrollees*. Washington: Physician Payment Review Commission. November.

Poisal, John A., and George S. Chulis. 2000. "Medicare Beneficiaries and Drug Coverage." *Health Affairs* 19(2): 248–256.

Pope, Gregory C., Randall P. Ellis, Arlene S. Ash et al. 2000. "Principal Inpatient Diagnostic Cost Group Model for Medicare Risk Adjustment." *Health Care Financing Review* 21(3): 93–118.

Prendergast, Canice. 1999. "The Provision of Incentives within Firms." *Journal of Economic Literature* 37: 7–63.

Propper, Carol, and Neil Söderlund. 1998. "Competition in the NHS Internal Market: An Overview of Its Effects on Hospital Prices and Costs." *Health Economics* 7: 187–197,

Prospective Payment Assessment Commission. 1997a. *Medicare and the American Health Care System*. Washington, DC: Prospective Payment Assessment Commission. June.

Prospective Payment Assessment Commission. 1997b. *Report to the Congress.* Washington, DC: Prospective Payment Assessment Commission. March.

Prosser, Lisa A. 2000. "Patient Preferences and Economic Considerations in Treatment Decisions for Multiple Sclerosis." Unpublished Ph.D. diss., Harvard University.

Reinhardt, Uwe E. 1996. "A Social Contract for 21st Century Health Care," *Health Economics* 5: 479–499.

Rice, Thomas. 1983. "The Impact of Changing Medicare Reimbursement Rates on Physician-Induced Demand." *Medical Care* 21: 803–815.

Rice, Thomas. 1992. "An Alternative Framework for Evaluating Welfare Losses in the Health Care Market." *Journal of Health Economics* 11: 85–92.

Rice, Thomas. 1998. *The Economics of Health Reconsidered*. Ann Arbor, MI: Health Administration Press.

Rice, Thomas, M. L. Graham, and Peter D. Fox. 1997. "The Impact of Policy Standardization on the Medigap Market." *Inquiry* 34: 106–116.

Rogers, William H., David Draper, Katherine L. Kahn et al. 1990. "Quality of Care Before and After Implementation of the DRG-Based Prospective Payment System: A Summary of Effects." *Journal of the American Medical Association* 264: 1989–1997.

Rogerson, William P. 1994. "Choice of Treatment Intensities by a Nonprofit Hospital Under Prospective Pricing." *Journal of Economics and Management Strategy* 3: 7–51.

Rogowski, Jeannette A., and Joseph P. Newhouse. 1992. "Estimating the Indirect Cost of Teaching." *Journal of Health Economics* 11: 153–171.

Rothschild, Michael, and Joseph Stiglitz. 1976. "Equilibrium in Competitive Insurance Markets: An Essay on the Economics of Imperfect Information." *Quarterly Journal of Economics* 90: 629–649.

Samuelson, William, and Richard Zeckhauser. 1988. "Status Quo Bias in Decision Making." *Journal of Risk and Uncertainty* 1: 7–59.

Schnabel, Morton. 1972. "The Subsidy Problem in Hospital Insurance: A Comment." *Journal of Business* 45: 302–304.

Schneider, Eric C., and Arnold M. Epstein. 1996. "Influence of Cardiac-Surgery Performance Reports on Referral Practices and Access to Care—A Survey of Cardiovascular Specialists." *New England Journal of Medicine* 335: 251–256.

Schneider, Eric C., and Arnold M. Epstein. 1998. "Use of Public Performance Reports: A Study of Patients Undergoing Cardiac Surgery." *Journal of the American Medical Association* 279: 1638–1642.

Schwartz, Kenneth. 1995. "A Patient's Story." *The Boston Globe Sunday Magazine*, July 16.

Shen, Yujing, and Randall P. Ellis. 2002. "Cost Minimizing Risk Adjustment." *Journal of Health Economics* 21. In press.

Shleifer, Andrei. 1985. "A Theory of Yardstick Competition." *RAND Journal of Economics* 16: 319–327.

Shmueli, Amir, Nira Shamai, Yoram Levi, and Miri Abraham. 1998. "In Search of a National Capitation Formula." In *Governments and Health System: Implications of Different Involvements*, ed. David Chinitz and Joshua Cohen, 201–208. New York: John Wiley & Sons.

Simons-Morton, D. G., K. J. Calfas, B. Oldenburg et al. 1998. "Effects Of Interventions in Health Care Settings on Physical Activity or Cardiorespiratory Fitness." *American Journal of Preventive Medicine* 15: 413–430.

Sloan, Frank A. 2000. "Non-Profit Ownership and Hospital Behavior." In *Handbook of Health Economics*, ed. Anthony J. Culyer and Joseph P. Newhouse, 1141–1174. Amsterdam: North-Holland.

Sloan, Frank A., Paula M. Mergenhagen, W. Bradley Burfield, Randall R. Bovbjerg, and Mahmud Hassan. 1989. "Medical Malpractice Experience of Physicians: Predictable or Haphazard?" *Journal of the American Medical Association* 262: 3291–3297.

Sloan, Frank A., Janet Mitchell, and Jerry Cromwell. 1978. "Physician Participation in State Medicaid Programs." *Journal of Human Resources* 13 (Suppl.): 211–245.

Smith, Peter C. 1998. "The Estimation, Application, and Experience of the New Capitation Formula in the United Kingdom." In *Governments and Health System: Implications of Different Involvements*, ed. David Chinitz and Joshua Cohen, 209–224. New York: John Wiley & Sons.

St. Peter, Robert F., Marie C. Reed, Peter Kemper et al. 1999. "Changes in the Scope of Care Provided by Primary Care Physicians." *New England Journal of Medicine* 341: 1980–1985.

Studdert, David, and Troyen A. Brennan. 2000. "The Problems with Punitive Damages in Lawsuits Against Managed Care Organizations." *New England Journal of Medicine* 342: 280–284.

Thaler, Richard. 1980. "Toward a Positive Theory of Consumer Choice." *Journal of Economic Behavior and Organization* 1: 39–60.

The Tobacco Use and Dependence Clinical Practice Guideline Panel, Staff, and Consortium Representatives. 2000. "A Clinical Practice Guideline for Treating Tobacco Use and Dependence: A U.S. Public Health Service Report." *Journal of the American Medical Association* 283: 3244–3254.

U.S. Bureau of the Census. 1997. *Statistical Abstract of the United States: 1997*, 117th ed. Washington, DC: Government Printing Office.

U.S. Bureau of the Census. 1999. *Statistical Abstract of the United States: 1999*, 119th ed. Washington, DC: Government Printing Office.

van Barneveld, Erik M. 2000. *Risk Sharing as a Supplement to Imperfect Capitation in Health Insurance: A Tradeoff Between Selection and Efficiency*. Ridderkerk, Netherlands: Ridderprint.

van Barneveld, Erik M., Leida M. Lamers, René C. J. A. van Vliet, and Wynand P. M. van de Ven. 2000. "Ignoring Small Predictable Profits and Losses: A New Approach for Measuring Incentives for Cream Skimming." *Health Care Management Science* 3: 131–140.

van Barneveld, Erik M., René C. J. A. van Vliet, and Wynand P. M. van de Ven. 1996. "Mandatory High-risk Pooling: An Approach to Reducing Incentives for Cream Skimming." *Inquiry* 33: 133–143.

van de Ven, Wynand P. M. M., and Randall P. Ellis, 2000. "Risk Adjustment in Competitive Health Plan Markets." In *Handbook of Health Economics*, ed. Anthony J. Culyer and Joseph P. Newhouse, 755–846. Amsterdam: North-Holland.

van de Ven, W. P. M. M., René C. J. A. van Vliet, Erik M. van Barneveld, and Leida M. Lamers. 1994. "Risk Adjusted Capitation: Recent Experiences in The Netherlands." *Health Affairs* 13: 118–136.

van de Ven, W. P. M. M., René C. J. A. van Vliet, Erik M. van Barneveld, and Leida M. Lamers. 1998. "Toward a Risk Adjustment Mechanism in a Competitive Insurance Market." In *Governments and Health System: Implications of Different Involvements*, ed. David Chinitz and Joshua Cohen, 179–194. New York: John Wiley & Sons.

van Vliet, René C. J. A. 1992. "Predictability of Individual Health Care Expenditures." *Journal of Risk and Insurance* 59: 443–461.

Wagstaff, Adam, and Eddy Van Doorslaer. 2000. "Equity in Health Care Finance and Delivery." In *Handbook of Health Economics*, ed. Anthony J. Culyer and Joseph P. Newhouse, 1803–1862. Amsterdam: North-Holland.

Wedig, Gerard J. 1993. "Ramsey Pricing and Supply-Side Incentives in Physician Markets." *Journal of Health Economics* 12: 365–384.

Wee, Christina C., Ellen P. McCarthy, Roger B. Davis et al. 1999. "Physician Counseling About Exercise." *Journal of the American Medical Association* 282: 1583–1588.

Weiler, Paul C. 1991. *Medical Malpractice on Trial*. Cambridge: Harvard University Press.

Weiler, Paul C., Howard H. Hiatt, Joseph P. Newhouse et al. 1991. *A Measure of Malpractice*. Cambridge: Harvard University Press.

Weiner, Jonathan P., Allen Dobson, Stephanie L. Maxwell et al. 1996. "Risk-Adjusted Medicare Capitation Rates Using Ambulatory and Inpatient Diagnoses." *Health Care Financing Review* 17(3): 77–99.

Weisbrod, Burton. 1988. *The Nonprofit Economy*. Cambridge: Harvard University Press.

Weisbrod, Burton. 1991. "The Health Care Quadrilemma: An Essay on Technological Change, Insurance, Quality of Care, and Cost Containment." *Journal of Economic Literature* 29: 523–552.

Weissman, Joel S., and Arnold M. Epstein. 1989. "Case Mix and Resource Utilization by Uninsured Hospital Patients in the Boston Metropolitan Area." *Journal of the American Medical Association* 261: 3572–3576.

Weissman, Joel S., and Arnold M. Epstein. 1993. "The Insurance Gap: Does It Make a Difference?" *Annual Review of Public Health* 14: 243–270.

Weissman, Joel S., and Arnold M. Epstein. 1994. *Falling Through the Safety Net: Insurance Status and Access to Health Care*. Baltimore: The Johns Hopkins University Press.

Welch, W. Peter. 1985a. "Medicare Capitation Payments to HMOs in Light of Regression to the Mean in Health Care Costs." In *Advances in Health Economics and Health Service Research*, ed. Richard M. Scheffler and Louis F. Rossiter, 75–96. Greenwich, CT: JAI Press.

Welch, W. Peter. 1985b. "Regression Toward the Mean in Medical Care Costs: Implications for Biased Selection in Health Maintenance Organizations." *Medical Care* 23: 1234–1241.

Wennberg, John, and Alan Gittelsohn. 1973. "Small Area Variations in Health Care Delivery." *Science* 182: 1102.

Wholey, Douglas, Roger Feldman, Jon B. Christianson et al. 1996. "Scale and Scope Economies among Health Maintenance Organizations." *Journal of Health Economics* 15: 657–684.

Williams, Alan H., and Richard Cookson. 2000. "Equity in Health." In *Handbook of Health Economics*, ed. Anthony J. Culyer and Joseph P. Newhouse, 1863–1910. Amsterdam: North-Holland.

Woolhandler, Steffie, and David U. Himmelstein. 1997. "Costs of Care and Administration at For-Profit and Other Hospitals in the United States." *New England Journal of Medicine* 336: 769–774.

Zeckhauser, Richard J. 1970. "Medical Insurance: A Case Study of the Tradeoff between Risk Spreading and Appropriate Incentives." *Journal of Economic Theory* 2: 10–26.

Zhang, Puling, and Sara L. Thran, eds. 1999. *Physician Socioeconomic Statistics: 1999–2000 ed*. Chicago: American Medical Association.

Zuckerman, Steven, Stephen A. Norton, and Diana Verrilli. 1998. "Price Controls and Medicare Spending." *Medical Care and Research Review* 55: 457–478.

Index